PEOPLE OF THE FIRST CRUSADE

PEOPLE OF THE FIRST CRUSADE

The Truth About the Christian-Muslim War Revealed

MICHAEL FOSS

ARCADE PUBLISHING • NEW YORK

Arcade Publishing books may be purchased in bulk at special discounts for sales promotion, corporate gifts, fund-raising, or educational purposes. Special editions can also be created to specifications. For details, contact the Special Sales Department, Arcade Publishing, 307 West 36th Street, 11th Floor, New York, NY 10018 or info@skyhorsepublishing.com.

Arcade Publishing® is a registered trademark of Skyhorse Publishing, Inc.®, a Delaware corporation.

Visit our website at www.arcadepub.com.

10 9 8 7 6 5 4 3 2 1

Library of Congress Cataloging-in-Publication Data is available on file.

ISBN: 978-1-61145-329-4

Printed in the United States of America

CONTENTS

LIST OF MAPS

PEOPLE OF THE
FIRST CRUSADE

INTRODUCTION

In the eleventh century, the Christian lands of western Europe were in trouble. Afflicted by repeated invasions from north and south and east, by the collapse of internal order and safety, by the often cynical and always brutal oppression of the weak and the poor, by the laxity and ignorance of the clergy, and by the unrestrained tyranny of feudal war-lords, life in the West was (in the words of a famous philosopher) 'nasty, brutish, and short'. And the problems were compounded, in the mid-century, when a new influx of raw, rough, nomadic soldiers recently converted to Islam – the Seljuk Turks – overran Jerusalem and the Holy Land, began to throw back the borders of the Byzantine Empire, and thus threatened to inflict severe damage on the territory of the West and on the body of Christendom itself.

All this was known and lamented in the West. Thoughtful people, particularly in the Church, for many years had clamoured for reform. But all the prayers, the sermons, the condemnations and the appeals had amounted to little until, in November 1095, Pope Urban II preached the First Crusade in the French town of Clermont. For his largely ignorant and unreflective audience, the pope threw a harsh light of criticism on the failings of western society. But in doing so he also illuminated a way out of this anarchy. He pointed out, for the lawless feudal bandits of the West, a path towards the East where military prowess and grasping ambition might be reconciled with a work of Christian charity. The recapture of Jerusalem and the Holy Land from the 'infidel' Muslims was a redemptive task worthy of men who might then truly call themselves 'soldiers of Christ'.

This, in the simplest terms, was what was meant by a

crusade. At a stroke, Pope Urban intended to divert the reckless and violent men of the West into the path of right-eousness. They could practise warfare to their hearts' content, in a holy cause. They could plunder the rich and cultivated lands of the Middle East as much as they wished, well away from their European homelands. They could strike a blow for Christ and true faith, by taking and holding the Holy City and the Holy Places.

The proposal made by Pope Urban was accepted by the West – by both knights and ordinary pilgrims – with riotous enthusiasm. But it was a delicate and incalculable business to add religious idealism and a symbolic event – the capture of Jerusalem – to a familiar policy of warfare and conquest. Though it powerfully motivated the people, it was a dangerous con-junction leading to unforseen consequences. Where did the rights of Christ end, and the interests of self begin? How much was owed to faith, and how much to one's own posterity? These were puzzling questions for unsophisticated folk.

The first interest of this book is to follow the adventures of these crusaders in all their puzzlement, to see how rogues discovered conscience and how others, who should have shown conscience, became rogues. And in the middle were very many who were sometimes heroes and sometimes villains. For the his-tory of this crusade is as much a study in character as a story of warfare. In hope and ignorance the crusaders met, and often transcended, fear, pain, disease, want and suffering, leading in so many cases to an early death. What pattern of life and thought made them endure? They also met an enemy – the men of Islam – that was as courageous, selfish, suffering and religious as themselves, but even more disorganized. In a word, the Muslims were just as puzzled as the Christians as to their real aims, and the epic meeting of these two religious cultures, so full of surprises and doubts, is the second interest of this book.

This fateful clash between Christianity and Islam still teaches a lesson for our own times. For the attitudes and prej-udices that were expressed in the First Crusade, on both sides, became the basic currency for all later exchanges, even in our own day, between the two great monotheistic faiths of Mohammed and Christ.

NEWS OF
THE WORLD

At the beginning of the tenth century the bishops of Rheims lamented the state of their age in words that echoed, more or less, the sentiment of all western Europe. 'The wrath of the Lord is breaking out before our very eyes,' they wrote. 'Towns are emptied, monasteries razed, holy houses of God burnt, farms and fields desolated. Everywhere the strong oppress the weak. Like the fish of the sea, men devour each other blindly.'

The tale that was told of poor lives seemed a story without end of pain, pillage and death. For ordinary folk, desolation was the lesson of the times. 'The poor and the peasants,' an English chronicler explained, 'have few friends, if any at all. And this is not surprising, for powerful lords, rulers and landowners, are wholly concerned with worldly things, not with spiritual matters. It is hard enough for a strong man to force a way ahead, to secure even a little prosperity in these bad days – who can spare a thought for the common good?' It was a woeful record, but the folk of the West, who could neither write nor read, did not need this book-learning. The history of their suffering was impressed on their lives, not written on parchment.

Silence, isolation, superstition, a profound ignorance put a limit on their understanding of the world beyond their gates, but they knew enough to be afraid. Such is the way with the weak and they began to see – it was a further cause for despair – that their lords and masters, to whom they were so closely bound by ties of land and service and from whom they expected their only protection, were also afraid.

They went on, the peasants, in the familiar round of their day. They cut trees, cleared land, planted and harvested. Long ago, their forefathers had been part of certain large migrations, travelling westward from steppe-land and arid zones. No one could remember exactly what made them set out. Warfare, demographic pressure, a change in climate, grazing rights, curiosity, some unspoken ache of the spirit, all these things seemed to throw them westward, driven forward by the rising sun. They wandered until they found space to settle or were halted by some gross feature of the earth – an impenetrable forest, a mountain-range, a strong broad river, a seacoast. The new life that they started in these places was not necessarily better, but at least the usual hardships of the fight for survival were arranged in a different way, richer in interest and in hope.

After many generations those who had been nomads and herdsmen became farmers. They settled in valleys and low-lands and took axe and fire to the primeval woods. In the good bottom lands, elm and lime and maple were laboriously thinned to make way for the plough. But on the heavier clays thick oak and ash formed a barrier of tall trunks through which it was still hard to thread a path. On higher land, on chalk and limestone hills, the extensive vivid green of the beechwood gradually bled out into the paler foliage of upland birch.

It was interminable work, the clearing of the woods, as the figure of Adam said in an old play:

> Strong are the roots of the briars,
> So that my arms are broken,
> Working at them again and again.

So many long years of effort, to so little effect. Below the mountains and the untouched moorland, the sea of trees still ran to the horizon, only punctuated by narrow tracks and a few small village-settlements. A mile at most from the village, beyond the little irregular fields of the older tribal practice or the larger open fields of the manorial system, lay the beginnings of the wild. Bog and marsh were undrained. A dozen steps from the path massed tree-trunks awaited the axe. In the fringes of the woods wild pigs and cattle fed on mast and nuts and rough undergrowth. On the borderlands of Europe bison still roamed, and also herds of auroch, the large-horned, fierce cattle that seemed as big as small elephants to Julius Caesar when he saw them in Germany. Throughout the countryside, hardly a house was beyond the range of the wolf and the wild boar. In the thick shade of uncut woods were lynx and wild-cat and bear.

Some space had been made, however. Land was cleared, agriculture and enterprise in a small way were in hand. Trade was underway, following from successful settlement. Thin lines of prosperity ran down valleys and river-routes, a wealth that was enough to attract invasion from new waves of expansionist or plundering wanderers. The peasants and farmers of the West who stood in the path of these invasions were sedentary folk now. They had lost both the nomadic habit and, to a large extent, the practice of arms. They were workers of land, tied to their holdings. The sudden approach of armed marauders raised terror and alarm. Experience soon taught them to expect either ruin or death.

The turn of the ninth century gave the peoples of Europe new, strong reasons for fear. For some two hundred years one chaos followed after another. The pagan Vikings raided coastlines from the Baltic to North Africa, from Ireland to Sicily. They thrust their swift longboats into the rivers of Europe to plunder Kiev, Cologne, York, London, Orleans, Rouen, Bordeaux, Pisa, Florence and many lesser towns. In the same century Magyar tribes flowed from the East into the lands of the middle Danube, and for many years ravaged further west, into the Po valley of northern Italy and into the

German territories of Swabia and Bavaria. In the south, Islam pressed hard against the Christian populations in Sicily and Spain. Arab corsairs commanded the Mediterranean, even subduing the menace of the Vikings. A parcel of Muslim pirates had established themselves on the French coast of Provence and raided far afield, as far as the fertile valleys of the high Alps. They were, as a monk of a raided monastery said in astonishment, as agile as 'real goats'.

Long periods of turmoil in society spread a climate of fear over the people. Small populations, scattered far apart with poor methods of communication, make sound judgments hard, if not impossible. Folk psychology runs behind the course of history. Who could consider that time tamed most monsters, that the pagan Vikings became the Christian Normans of the eleventh century, in the duchy of Normandy or the principality of Sicily or the kingdom of England hardly distinguishable from the rough knights of the rest of feudal Europe? The danger from the Magyars greatly diminished after Otto the Great defeated them roundly at Lechfeld in 955. The old Magyar life of nomadic robbery and destruction became more and more difficult. The tribes gathered together and gradually settled in the land now called Hungary. In 1001 a certain Vaik proclaimed himself king, converted to Christianity under the baptized name of Stephen, and was rewarded by a grateful Church which later recognized him as a saint. Even the troublesome Muslim pirates were cleared from their lair at Le Freinet in 972, after they had made the mistake of capturing and holding to ransom the very important abbot of Cluny. That was too much for the princes of Christendom to bear.

All this was the long unfolding of the story in time, but what remained in the memory of people was the brutal and insecure life under conditions of disorder and invasion. Too often, in the years between 800 and 1050, the everyday sun declined through the smirch of flame and smoke of a monastery or town robbed and burnt. Folk memory recalled that Vikings in a drunken orgy pelted the archbishop of Canterbury with the bones from their feast and killed him. It was recalled that the man in the Icelandic saga who refused to impale babes on his spear was jeered at and ridiculed as a milksop. It was recalled that the wild Magyars, driven on by their chieftains with whips, ransacked rich abbeys in the Vosges and Lorraine and Burgundy, even as far as the Loire. It was recalled that the Muslim raiders from Le Freinet attacked the famous abbey of Saint-Gall and slaughtered the monks with arrows as they walked in procession round their church. These images express the feeling of the times, set out in many agonized accounts. The written record, such as it is, seems fevered, uncritical, lacking in judgment, but what is constant in it is the ground-note of suffering.

The spirit of the Vikings, which cast such a dejected shadow, became well-understood throughout the West. Even after 1000, by which time the pagan Vikings were well on the way to transmuting themselves into settled, Christian Normans, no one doubted their potential for danger and destruction. An Italian chronicler summed up their character in this way:

> They are a most cunning and vengeful race. They leave their native fields in the hope of richer booty – greedy for gain, greedy for dominion, prone to imitate whatever they see. Their princes, balanced between lavishness and covetousness, are only generous when they hope to earn fame by their gifts. These Normans can flatter when they choose, but they are headstrong to excess and must be curbed by the strong hand of justice. They can bear all hardship if need be, patient of cold, of hunger, of pain, of hard endurance. Few things delight them more than hawking and hunting, but their keenest joy is in the splendour of war.

The abbey of Croyland was founded by the Mercian king on the wet English Fenland of East Anglia in 716. Three hundred and fifty years later the then abbot, Ingulph, made it his business to compile the whole history of this religious house, covering all the terrible years of the Viking invasions. This long record is one of the best portraits we have of a community – peaceful, God-fearing, moderately prosperous – under the constant stress of fear, a stress that helped to undermine all attempts by Church and kings to foster a stable, civil society. In the year 870, Ingulph noted the following account:

The mass being now finished, just as the abbot and his assistants had partaken of the mystery of the Holy Communion, the pagans burst into the church. At once the venerable abbot was slain upon the holy altar, as a true martyr and sacrifice of Christ. Then his assistants were all beheaded by the barbarians, while the old men and children, attempting to fly from the choir, were seized and examined with the most cruel torments, that they might disclose the hidden treasures of the church, and were afterwards put to death.

All the monks being thus slain, and yet none of the treasure found, the Danes, with ploughshares and mattocks, broke open all the shrines of the saints in their marble altar-tombs, and yet still found no treasure. Then the barbarians were extremely indignant. In a shocking manner, after piling all the bodies of the saints in one heap, they set fire to them, on the third day after their arrival, and dreadfully burnt the same, together with the church and all the buildings of the monastery, on this day, the seventh before the calends of September.

A hundred and forty years later life had become far more complicated for the unhappy monks as the simple threat of barbarian violence gave way to a new age of competitive extortion between Anglo-Saxon thanes and Danish warlords, both

THE BATTLE OF HASTINGS, 14 OCTOBER 1066
From the Bayeux Tapestry

trying to wring money out of the monastery. The result for the monks and the people of the Fens was still the same – a renewed acquaintance with death and destruction:

> Whereas every year before, 400 marks had been exacted by King Ethelred, now King Sweyn the Dane came with a new fleet and a most fierce army, and laid waste every quarter. Rushing onward from Lindesey, he burned the villages, disembowelled the peasants, and with various torments put to death all the religious. This was in the year of Our Lord, 1013. Many manors of the monastery were at the same time committed to the flames, and all the retainers slaughtered or carried captive away.
>
> At last, in consequence of the expenses within and the exactions without, the entire treasury of the lord abbot was exhausted. The granaries were levelled with the ground. But the king's collectors were daily making assaults for money. They declared that the abbot was a traitor to his country and a supporter of the Danes, who deserved to be hanged in fetters. Stricken with internal grief of heart at so many terrible threats, the venerable abbot Godric summoned his whole convent to inform them that there was nothing left. Thereupon he begged them to advise him what ought to be done against such a wicked age.

Though the abbey of Croyland was in the eye of the storm, being only a short step across the North Sea as the Vikings year by year poured south from their Scandinavian homelands, the plight of the English monastery and its surrounding population was matched over centuries by the fate of hundreds of other communities in marches and borderlands, on the Atlantic seaboard or on the Mediterranean and Baltic littorals, at the line of the Danube or the Vistula or the Elbe, or indeed in reach of any deep-flowing river system.

The folk saw the troubles of Europe as pervasive and universal, expressed in omens, portents, famines and natural disasters which were accepted as God-given signs of the times. In 1086, in the twenty-first year of ferocious Norman rule and just before the death of William the Conqueror, the *Anglo-Saxon Chronicle* found all undone in England, the commonwealth laid waste amid dearth and pestilence and high prices:

This same year was a very heavy and toilsome and sorrowful year in England, through murrain plague of the cattle.
Corn and fruits were at a stand, and so great uneasiness in
weather, as no one can think. So great was the thunder and
lightning, that it killed many men and ever it grew worse.
May Almighty God better it, as He shall will.

After the birth-tide of our Lord Jesus Christ one thousand
and eighty-seven winters, in the one and twentieth year after
William held despotic sway over England, there came a very
heavy and very pestilent year in the land. Such a malady came
on the people that almost every other man was in the worst
evil, that is with fever, and that so strongly that very many
died. Afterwards there came, through the great tempests, a
very great famine over all England, which killed many more.
Alas! what a miserable and rueful a time it was then! Who
cannot feel pity for such a time? But such things befall for
folk's sin, because they will not love God and righteousness.

The king and his chief men loved much and overmuch
covetousness of gold and silver, and recked not how sinfully it might be got, provided it came to them. The king
gave his land for rent as dearly as he possibly could. And
he recked not how sinfully the reeves and stewards got rent
from poor men, nor how many illegalities they did.

Also, in the same year, before autumn, the holy monastery
of St Paul, the episcopal see of London, was burnt, and the
greatest and fairest part of the whole city. Alas, a desperate
and deplorable time was it!

That was the despondent view of the Anglo-Saxon chronicler suffering, as he saw it, under a Norman tyranny. It is not,
perhaps, the considered view of history, but it fully expressed
the feeling of folk throughout the land. This was a true and
deep-seated feeling, as the Norman-French historian Peter of
Blois confirmed when he came to continue Ingulph's chronicle of the abbey of Croyland. This was how Peter summed up
the state of England at the end of the eleventh century:

Confession and the fair graces of repentance fell into dises-
teem, holiness and chastity utterly sickened away, sin stalked
openly in the streets. It faced the law with a bold eye, and
triumphed daily, exulting in its abominable success.

Then the heavens did abominate the land, and the sun and

the moon stood still in their houses, spurning the earth with the greatest noise and rury, causing all nations to be amazed at their numerous portents. There were thunders terrifying the earth, lightnings and frequent thunderbolts, drenching showers without number, winds of the most astonishing violence, and whirlwinds that shook the towers of churches and levelled them with the ground. Fountains flowed with blood amid earthquakes, while the sea overflowed its banks and made infinite calamities of flood. There were murders and dreadful seditions. The Devil himself was seen bodily. There was a pestilence and famine among both men and beasts, so that farming was almost all neglected. There was no care for the living, and no sepulture for the dead.

The material damage, after two hundred years of unrest and invasion, was very great throughout western Europe. The *Domesday Book*, in England, listed a large number of vills that had been abandoned. In Provence, in the south of France, after the desolation caused by the resident Muslim pirates, ancient lands, developed from the time of the Greeks, had to be re-occupied and cleared again. The old boundaries were completely erased, and men took what they wanted 'according to their power'. Even in the centre of France, where the Carolingian empire had once established a civilized peace, things were hardly better. At the village of Martigny on the Loire, for example, a record from 900 relates that only sixteen families remained on the ruined land, and several heads of families had 'neither wives nor children'. The neglected fields needed work and there was plenty of space: 'people could have holdings if only we were at peace.'

But the mental damage, in this time of constant danger, was even greater than the material loss. History is not well-placed to assess the fractures and the wounds of the mind. A cautious reading of old official documents, as one famous historian has complained, gives a very incomplete picture of 'the vicissitudes of the human organism', but there is a kind of indirect evidence that effectively reveals the interior of the mind where hopes and fears are laid bare. This evidence lies in the imaginations and the stories that men and women tell each other concerning the nature of their own society.

In the Old French feudal epic *Raoul de Cambrai,* said to be very loosely based on certain events that occurred in France around the years 940 to 950, there is a grim portrait of a society torn from top to bottom. Hate, revenge, dishonour, pride, greed, cunning, cruelty, vindictiveness seem to be the foremost qualities of mankind. All is false. Rulers, lords, knights, even churchmen, are no better than murderous and treacherous bandits, and the peasants and townspeople whom they brutalize indeed rise no higher than the level of frightened beasts.

In the course of a violent feud, Raoul advances on the town of Origny. When the day's work is done we are left with the picture of a society at its wits' end:

> Then Count Raoul called to his men. 'Take arms without delay,' he said, 'and ride speedily to reach Origny before night-fall. Spread my tent in the middle of the church; tether my horses in the porch; prepare my food beneath the aisles; fasten my falcons to the golden crosses, and make me a rich bed before the altar. I will lean against the crucifix and deliver the nuns up to my squires. This place, which the sons of Herbert hold so dear, I will destroy and ruin it utterly.'
>
> At once, the knights start for Origny, for they dare not refuse. They cross the moats. They cut down the pallisade and trample it under foot. They cross beside the fishpond and rush to the very walls. Great was the alarm when the citizens see that their fortification is gone, and even the bravest of them was much cast down. But they man the walls, throwing stones and sharp stakes, killing many of Raoul's soldiers. By God! if they find Raoul, they will finish him off. Raoul is in a fury at this defence, and he swears that if one and all are not hanged and destroyed he will not give a fig for his own valour.
>
> 'Barons, fire the town,' he cries. And the soldiers obey him, eager as always for booty. The buildings blaze, the roofs fall in, casks catch fire and burst their hoops. All, young and old, are pitifully burnt. The cellars run with wine, the flitches of bacon smoulder in the crash of fiery beams, and the melting fat adds fuel to the flames. And now the towers of the church are alight. The fire mounts to the belfry, in the nave there is a blazing furnace. The nuns are burnt to death, for nothing can withstand that heat.

When the work is done, Raoul returns to his tent. It was at his command that the nuns were burnt and roasted. Raoul dismounted, unlaced his bright golden helmet and ungirded his good sword of steel. He called for the seneschal who was wont to serve him. 'Prepare me food,' he ordered, 'roast peacocks and devilled swans and venison in abundance. Let us eat our fill. I would not be thought mean by my barons for all the gold in the city.' But the seneschal cried out in amazement: 'In the name of Our Lady, what are you thinking of? You are denying holy faith and your baptism and the majesty of God. It is Lent. It is the holy Friday of the Passion, when sinners should always honour the Cross. And we miserable men have burnt the nuns and violated the church. We shall never be reconciled to God unless his pity be greater than our wickedness.'

Then Raoul glared at him and said: 'Son of a slave, why have you spoken to me like that? Did not these people wrong me? They insulted two of my squires, and it is no wonder they had to pay for it dearly. But it is true, I had forgotten Lent.'

So he called for chessmen and sat morosely in the middle of the meadow.

Without trust, without honour, without safety, the peoples of western Europe saw that all government, all polity, all society had failed them, and they despaired.

No community can safely live in a state of continual fear. In desperate times, when kings, lords and feudal knights have failed in their duty to protect society, when the mortification of disease and pestilence lies all around, there seems only one recourse left – the appeal to religion and the supplication to God.

Neither justice nor kindness could moderate Raoul's reckless plunge into slaughter. Only an odd scruple about Lent gave him a moment of doubt. In the midst of barbarian or Muslim invasion, knowing the weakness of their own flesh and the impotence of civil power, people placed their fate in higher, spiritual hands. 'From the savages of the North, who lay waste our lands, O God deliver us,' cried the men and women of the German frontier. 'Against Hungarian arrows,' prayed the

SOLDIERS DEFENDING A WALLED CITY
From an Eleventh-Century Manuscript

people of Tuscany, 'be Thou our protector.' And in Provence they petitioned the Holy Trinity to 'deliver thy Christian folk from the oppression of the infidel'.

To the rigorous rationalism of the twentieth century, invocations in the name of God seem suspiciously like the throwing in of the towel, appeals to magic and wish-fulfilment in the face of a hopeless reality. This opinion, however, would have seemed scandalous and wrong to the Christian West in the tenth and eleventh centuries. No doubt magic, superstition and ritual entered into the forms of thought in this age, but also, in some deep sense, the material and the spiritual ran together as parallel realities, and minds moved with easy familiarity between the two. No one was surprised when the famous scholar and ecclesiastic Rabanus Maurus put forward a plan for a little book that would treat of 'not only the nature of things', but still more 'of their mystical meanings'. There was nothing on earth that did not have some echo or representation in the heavens. 'Who does not know,' wrote a German priest, 'that the wars, the great tempests, the pestilences, indeed all the ills that inflict mankind, occur through the agency of demons?' That was recognized as simple sense – quite uncontroversial. To read the visions of the mystics and the saints – so startling, so vivid, so tangible – is to be assured that their imaginations trod the spiritual realm as firmly and as easily as their bare feet followed the beaten path from cell to altar.

Nor was it only great or saintly minds that had a feeling of the divine. Quite ordinary folk had an intimacy with God, speaking to Our Lord closely, as if He were in the inglenook or at the kitchen bench. Here, for example, is a common prayer, taken from a book of Anglo-Saxon homilies:

> Jesus, true God, true Son of God, true man, and true Virgin's child. Jesus, my holy love, my sure sweetness, my heart, my joy, my soul-heal. Sweet Jesus, my darling, my life, my light, my healing oil, my balm, my honey-drop. Jesus, teach me, thou that art so soft and so sweet, so dear and so lovely that angels look on thee and are never satisfied of the sight. . . .

And it went on, in the same vein, for three more pages.

When material and spiritual are so intermixed, when a conversation with angels is as easy as a talk with friends, an appeal from one realm to the other in times of constant danger is no surprise. God would preserve where men failed, and it seemed very clear, to the people of the age, that the appeal worked. Barbarians became far less dangerous as they became Christian. The influence of religion helped to tame gross appetites which neither force of arms nor government could restrain. From the point of view of the West, a Christian Norman was a far safer and more tractable human being than his pagan Viking forebear. In the eastern marches of the Holy Roman Empire, the citizens breathed more easily when they knew that Vaik, the nomadic Magyar war-chief, had become Stephen, the Christian king of Hungary. It is no wonder that the Emperor Otto the Great declared: 'We believe that the protection of our Empire is bound up with the rising fortunes of Christian worship.'

Since events had to some degree proved the power of Christian faith to improve western society, the Church, the handmaiden of God on earth, redoubled attempts to spread true doctrine and to encourage the practice of Christian morality. Formerly, in times of invasion, these attempts had been intermittent and capricious. The monastic orders, on whom the propagation of faith chiefly rested (the lowly parish clergy were too ignorant, poor and unlettered to be relied on), were busy saving the lives of their monks and securing their property. Slowly, small currents of reform sprang up in many different communities. Out of unpromising land, devastated by marauders, these springs of hope ran together into larger streams of conviction. Quite suddenly, there was evidence of faith. Imposing stone churches rose over the low hovels of villagers whose meagre resources bore the burden of such stately expense.

There was much preaching, much moral instruction, many homilies and admonitions. Everyone was a target for reform, from lords to laity. The chaplain of the Earl of Chester was busy giving 'salutary counsel' to barons, knights and boys: 'He collected tales of combats of holy knights from the Old Testament and from stories of Christian ages for them to imitate. He told them of the conflicts of Demetrius and George, of Theodore and Sebastian, of Duke Maurice and the Theban Legion, all those who had won through martyrdom the crown of heaven.'

Soon the moral education of society and the attempt to set a Christian limit on knightly violence were vigorously taken up by the papacy. In the eleventh century, the popes consciously brought Christian warfare within the sanctity of the Church and instituted that ideal warrior, the *miles Christi*, the 'soldier of Christ'. In 1053, Leo IX himself took command of an army against the Normans in South Italy. He was defeated. One of his successors, Nicholas II, with greater subtlety made those same Normans the support and the guardians of the papacy and prospered under their protection. In 1063, Alexander II granted the first papal indulgence for the remission of the sins of war. This indulgence was given to the Christian soldiers fighting against the Saracens in Spain, and these holy warriors marched to battle under a *vexillum sancti Petri*, a standard of St Peter. The great Pope Gregory VII, a mighty scourge of laxity and ardent champion of religious and papal rights, took this development much further. After 1073, he took the ideal 'soldiers of Christ' and turned these warriors into veritable 'faithful troops of St Peter' – *fideles sancti Petri* – the hammers of heresy, the scourges of secular backsliding, and a warning to all pagans and infidels.

Nothing in this holy enterprise of the Church had such practical and emblematic importance as the contest with the Muslims of Islam. The Saracens (as all Muslims were called, for ignorant and inexperienced westerners were not capable of making distinctions between the various peoples of Mohammed) were not, in fact, the greatest danger to the West. Except in Spain, and to a lesser degree in Sicily and southern France, the Saracens offered less of a threat, and certainly caused less havoc and destruction in society, than restless, bloody-thirsty, plunder-seeking Vikings. The pagan Viking, or Magyar, professing a loose, unreflective polytheism or animism, was, however, ripe for conversion by the superior gravity, mystery and splendour of Christianity – and a barbarian converted was very often a fierce soldier won for Christ's work. This soon became apparent in Sicily where the Christian Normans of the adventurer Robert Guiscard, still showing many signs of their brutal Viking antecedents, slowly cleared the island of its Muslim presence.

The Saracen, however, was hardly ever a candidate for conversion. He possessed a monotheistic faith as strong and as rigorous as Christianity. He was fortified by the Holy Koran, a book on which he could draw with as much hope and satisfaction as a Christian on the Bible. He was a member of a new faith – founded only in the seventh century – which still had an energy and an impetus towards conquest that had largely died away in the 1,000-year-old realm of Christendom.

Islam confronted the Christian West at all points – in theology, in strong belief, in moral authority, in empire. It outran the Christian West as a promoter of civilization. In the great cities of the Middle East, in the Almoravid towns of North Africa, in the small courts of Muslim Spain, trade and industry and agriculture and science and arts flourished to a degree unknown in the West. Islam was as much a rebuke to western Europe as it was a threat. No wonder that the first indulgence of warfare offered by the papacy was to those fighting against the Saracens in Spain.

A state of Cold War (to use a modern term) existed between Islam and the Christian West, with all the paranoia, wish-fulfilment and sense of unreality implied by that term. A clash of theologies – ideologies – as we have learnt in our own day, engages minds as much as strong arms. On both sides, there was God's work to be done. For Christians, there was the immediate matter of Saracen inroads along the southern boundaries of Europe, but this contest had a symbolic value well beyond the rather limited nature of the warfare. Mohammed was seen as Anti-Christ, and resistance to Islam concentrated the will of Europe into a high and holy aim, drawing together rough, lawless peoples demoralized by too many years of invasion. It came to seem, to many of the best reforming minds in the West, that the very stability and safety of their society depended in a large way on a resolute fight against the power and claims of Islam.

In August 778, in the Pyrenean valley of Roncevaux, the rear-guard of Charlemagne's army, returning from Spain, was set upon by a band of Basque guerrillas and destroyed. A certain

Philippe Sly

Sanford Sylvan

PHILIPPE SLY & JULIUS DRAKE
Tuesday, July 23, 7:30pm
Walter Hall

Praised by The San Francisco Chronicle for his *beautiful, blooming tone and magnetic stage presence*, Québecois bass-baritone Philippe Sly performs a glorious program of song by Schubert, Wolf, Ravel, and Duparc.

RIOTS & RITUALS
Friday, July 19, 7:30pm
Walter Hall

Sanford Sylvan (baritone)
Anagnoson & Kinton (piano duo)
Mark Fewer, Axel Strauss (violins)
Paul Coletti (viola); Christopher Costanza (cello)
Pedja Muzijevic (piano)

Don't miss Francis Poulenc's rollicking, surreal cantata, *Le Bal masque*, Jean Françaix's saucy suite *L'Heure du berger*, Bohuslav Martinů's jazz-flavoured ballet *La Revue de cuisine* and Stravinsky's earth-shaking, primeval dance score, *The Rite of Spring* – which this year celebrates its one-hundredth anniversary.

Elly Ameling

ROBERT POMAKOV & GRYPHON TRIO
Thursday, July 18, 7:30pm
Koerner Hall

[Robert Pomakov] is clearly a talent to watch. Embodying the melancholy heft and gloomy conviction of the classic Russian bass voice. - Washington Post Experience Mussorgsky's profoundly moving song-cycle, *Songs and Dances of Death*, in Gary Kulesha's new and masterful transcription for bass voice and piano trio.

ART OF SONG
Masterclass with Legendary Soprano, Elly Ameling
Tuesday, July 16, 1:30pm
Edward Johnson Building, U of T

The world-renowned Dutch soprano has appeared with most major orchestras and conductors across the globe. This summer, see Elly Ameling in person as she works with rising vocal stars – our Fellows in The Art of Song Program! (July 14 – 27) Tickets available at the door or purchase a Festival Insiders Pass.

FOR FULL FESTIVAL DETAILS, VISIT TORONTOSUMMERMUSIC.COM

TORONTO SUMMER MUSIC FESTIVAL

ARTISTIC DIRECTOR DOUGLAS McNABNEY

MUSIC IN THE CITY
IN THE SUMMER

JULY 16-AUGUST 3, 2013

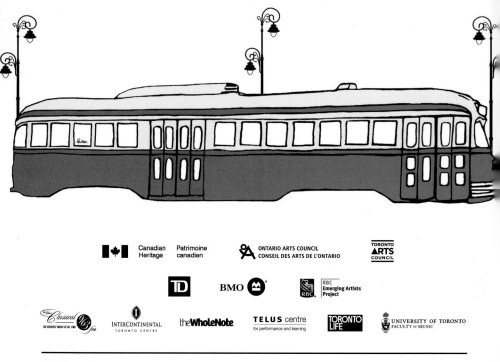

Canadian Heritage Patrimoine canadien

ONTARIO ARTS COUNCIL
CONSEIL DES ARTS DE L'ONTARIO

TORONTO ARTS COUNCIL

TD BMO RBC Emerging Artists Project

The New Classical 96.3 fm THE GREATEST MUSIC OF ALL TIME

INTERCONTINENTAL TORONTO CENTRE

theWholeNote

TELUS centre
for performance and learning

TORONTO LIFE

UNIVERSITY OF TORONTO
FACULTY OF MUSIC

TORONTOSUMMERMUSIC.COM   416-408-0208

Hrodland, captain of the guard and count of the Breton marches, was killed. In time, this brief skirmish under a dusty sun in a remote pass became elevated into the high rhetoric of the *Song of Roland*, a picture of fortitude in defence of Christendom. In the poem, Basques became Saracens. The obscure Hrodland, petty war-chief of a Frankish tribe, became the tragic hero Roland who, in his devotion to his Christian emperor and in his ferocity against the infidel enemy, was a true *miles Christi*, a soldier of Christ.

The Old French text of the *Song of Roland* is, among many things, a tale of barbarian cruelty, of feudal relationships, of chivalry, of treacherous jealousy, of love and heroism, and of plain military stupidity, but a great underlying descant of necessary and enduring resistance against the infidel sounds in the very first verse and punctuates the rest of the poem:

> Charles the king, our great emperor, has been full seven years in Spain. There is nó castle, wall or city left for him to break, except mountain-bound Saragossa. King Marsilie holds it, and he does not love God. He serves Mahomet and prays to Apollo. But it will not keep him from the reach of trouble.

The Christian army decides not to attack the fortress but to withdraw home to France. Out of jealousy of Roland, their plans are betrayed to Marsilie who agrees to ambush the army in the mountains of the north and kill Roland and his fellow twelve champions. Towards the end of summer the armies meet. Each looks resplendent in the sight of the other:

> The day was clear and the sun bright. The gear of the Saracens shines like flame. They march grandly, and blow a thousand trumpets. The noise is huge and the French have heard it. 'My lord and comrade,' says Oliver, 'these Saracens look bold and ready for battle.' Then Roland answers, 'God grant it to us. Let us make a stand here. A man should suffer all distress for his lord, either heat or cold. A man should lose skin and hair. Let us deal great blows so that no ugly song may be made of us. Those infidels have sin, and we Christians have right on our side.'

Preparation is made for battle. Archbishop Turpin spurs his horse to a small knoll and addresses the troops:

'Lord barons, Charles left us here. We should die for our king, and give our help to sustain the Christian faith. Be sure of it, you will have a fight, for the Saracens line up before your eyes. Confess your sins and pray God for mercy, and I shall absolve you to save your souls. If you die it will be as holy martyrs with a place in Paradise.' The French dismount and kneel, and the archbishop blessed them from God.

Then the Saracens fall upon the rear-guard. In his pride Roland will not blow his horn to summon the help of Charles until the very last moment, by which time it is too late. Charles hurries back but finds Roland killed with his companions lying dead around him. Then Charlemagne himself, in rage and grief, chases the Saracens to the gates of Saragossa, and when they see the force of the Christian king, the Saracens begin to despair of their own deity:

'Alas, wicked God,' they cry, 'why visit this shame on us? We serve you well but you give us bad reward.' Then they take away his sceptre and crown and roll him on the ground under their feet. They throw their Mahomet into a ditch, for pigs and dogs to gnaw and to foul him.

The final battle begins, and Charles is hard-pressed. He is sorely wounded, but it is clear that God and St Gabriel are on his side:

When Charles hears the voice of the angel, he has no more fear nor doubt of death. His strength comes back to him. The infidels run, for that is what God wishes. The infidels are dead, and Charles has beaten down the gate of Saragossa. The grey-beard king is proud. A man can do much when he has God's help.

Victory is complete, but the work of Charles is not yet done. His destiny as Christ's champion calls for tears and unremitting toil:

Now the emperor has done justice and his great anger is lightened. He has set Christian faith in the heart of Bramimunde, dead Marsilie's queen. Day passes and the night is dark. The king is lying in his vaulted room when

St Gabriel comes to him from God. 'Charles,' cries the angel, 'what idleness is this? Summon the armies of your empire. Go with your strength to the land of Bire, to the city that the pagans have besieged. Christians call and cry out for you.' The emperor does not wish to go. 'Oh God,' he groans, 'how heavy is my life!' He weeps and pulls at his white beard.

The message of the poem struck home. The Christian admonition in the *Song of Roland* was well understood, even if it was sometimes perverted for base ends in fights between Christian and Christian. It is said that when the Norman jongleur Taillefer went among his troops, to encourage the invaders at the Battle of Hastings in 1066, he was chanting the story of Roland.

Where was the 'land of Bire'? No need to ascend into the imagination, real work enough was waiting to be done nearer home. Saracens were still firmly lodged in the best part of Spain. The re-conquest of Sicily went on at a painfully slow pace, even under leaders as determined and ruthless as Robert and Roger Guiscard. The whole orient crescent, from Egypt to Anatolia, was in turmoil as the Fatimids fought with the Abbasids for control of the Near East. In the second half of the eleventh century the Seljuk Turks joined in the struggle, fellow-Muslims, but as yet not far from an earlier life as plundering Asiatic nomads. These tough soldiers were a threat to both caliphates and to Byzantium as well. In 1071, the Seljuk Alp-Arslan defeated the Byzantine army at Manzikert. Fourteen years later the Seljuk expansion had overwhelmed Antioch, a Christian client-state in northern Syria, and now the eastern flank of Christendom, guarded by the Byzantines, seemed in serious danger.

Even worse, for the Christian West, was the condition of the holy city of Jerusalem. For many years, Muslim and Jew and Christian had lived together in Jerusalem, rubbing together peacefully enough under the undemanding rule of the Abbasid caliphate in Baghdad. European pilgrims found the way to the city clear, and numbers of them made the journey unmolested, but in the first decade of the eleventh century, the Fatimids of Egypt took the city from the Abbasids. The Fatimid caliph al-Hakim, growing steadily insane before he disappeared in 1021, stunned the citizens with a new regimen of prejudice, violence and cruelty. Al-Hakim's conduct seemed odd and excessive even to Muslim historians:

> In the year 1009 he absolutely forbade the making and selling of beer. No one could enter the public baths without a loin-cloth, and women must cover their faces and not paint themselves. He enforced his rules most strictly and many were flogged for disobeying.
>
> He ordered Jews and Christians to wear sashes around their waists and badges on their clothes. Christians dressed in black and hung great wooden crosses around their necks, the length of a forearm and weighing much. In 1013 Jews were compelled to wear bells when they entered the baths.
>
> Al-Hakim liked to roam at night, swathed in a white woollen cloak. He abolished a number of taxes, and he had all the town dogs killed. He banished women from the streets, closed their baths and forbade the shoemakers to make them shoes. On 13 February 1021 al-Hakim disappeared and was never seen again. It is said that he was murdered by religious zealots.

In the onslaught against non-Muslims in Jerusalem many churches and monasteries were destroyed or damaged. In October 1009, al-Hakim had ordered the destruction of the church of the Holy Sepulchre. For many years the church lay in ruins until, in 1027, the Byzantine emperor bribed the caliphate to allow reconstruction. But the security of Christians and Jews was not increased, as Muslim factions fought for control of Palestine. The indignant West cried that 'the navel of the world' was in cruel, impious hands: 'Base and bastard Turks hold sway over our brothers.'

There was reason, in the capitals of Europe and particularly in Rome, for weeping, and for grave men, like Charlemagne in the poem, to tear their beards.

–2–
THE POPE

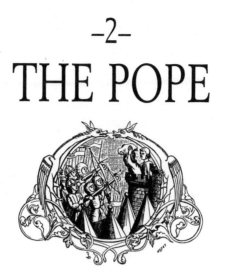

The monk in the papal robes was shivering, in spite of the thick woollen cloak pulled tight about him. He had been more than a week in this place that seemed to him no friend to his health, but he had a task to complete, and a plan to unfold.

On 18 November 1095 he had come to the town of Clermont in the French Auvergne, to take his place at the head of a Church Council. There was much business to discuss: matters of religious reform, relations between church and state, grave questions concerning the chaos and violence in western society, appeals for help from ordinary folk tyrannized by feudal militias, campaigns to be supported against infidel Saracens in southern Europe, support also for the Byzantine empire on the eastern flank of Christendom where barbaric Seljuk Turks were re-invigorating the forces of Islam. All these were matters of great moment and they had attracted to the Council a large congregation of more than three hundred prelates. Very many barons and knights, as anxious for their material possessions as for the state of their souls, were also attending. Their tents and pavilions spilled off into surrounding fields churned muddy in a wet November.

For nine days the Council had talked and made plans. Now, on the 27th, the spiritual head of the Council was about to address the multitude assembled in the market-square. The day was cold and blustery. Veils of sodden cloud drifted from the peaks of the Puy de Sancy, the Puy Mary, the Plomb du Cantal and other rugged lumps of the Massif Central. The vast remote hinterland of smooth tumbled uplands and ragged ravines, from where the south-westerlies were coming, seemed as tight and closed as a gnarled fist squeezing a sponge. In the market-square, above the heads of the crowd, was a platform of stout timber, which served at other times as a scaffold. The man about to mount it was irresistibly reminded of mortality and the needs of the soul. Had he the words that would be a balm for the spirit and a guide out of perplexity?

The man at the foot of the platform was Odo of Lagery, at first a monk and then prior of the great reforming monastery at Cluny in Burgundy. He had been elected pope in 1088 and took the name Urban II. After the first feeling of exaltation on his election, he knew, as an honest man, that he was unworthy of this high and holy office. He was, however, a man of excellent reputation, 'admirable in life and habit, always striving to raise high the honour of Holy Church', and he resolved to be guided by the reforming zeal of Cluny and by the example of his powerful and fiery predecessor, Pope Gregory VII. Urban was learned in scripture and well read in the works of the Church Fathers. He saw all the world under the colour of Christ. He knew there was nothing that did not belong to God, and that the ideal order of society flowed from a divine plan universally mediated through the Roman pontiff, who was the Vicar of Christ. 'God, the ruler of all things,' he assured Christian knights fighting in Spain and Sicily, 'when He wishes, takes away kingdoms and alters the course of the times.'

How could the Lord's dominion be safeguarded here on earth? No one was better placed than the pope, to know the full extent of the task. Even at the moment of Urban's election, Rome was in the hands of an anti-pope, a sorry opportunist from Ravenna puffed up by riches and driven on by the cynical support of the German emperor. Papacy and empire

POPE URBAN ARRIVES IN FRANCE (left) AND CALLS FOR
A CRUSADE AT THE COUNCIL OF CLERMONT (*right*)

were still locked in the long struggle over the investiture to
ecclesiastical offices, a contest that had caused Gregory VII so
much grief. The German emperor, Henry IV, was trying everything that money and secular power could do to frustrate the
will of the Church. Nor was help to be expected from Philip
I of France. This king, on whom a French pope might hope to
lean, was under sentence of excommunication for bigamy.

'If the head is sick,' Urban often told himself, 'all parts of the
body will suffer.' The infection started with princes and
prelates. Then the disease tainted the blood in all the body
politic. That was plain to see, and in case the new pope might
have been inclined to look away, many voices were ready to
instruct him. The devil was abroad, raging like a lion, devour-
ing the people. Peace, goodness, faith were trampled underfoot
all over Europe, both high and low, within the Church and
without. The ideal of Christendom was greatly degraded, and
contentment was nowhere seen, for the princes of the land
were always at strife, first this one and then that one, always
quarrelling and rushing to arms. Who could keep the goods of
the land safe for their owners? In the interminable squabbles
many were taken captive and barbarously thrown into foul

prisons to be ransomed for impossible sums, or tormented there by the three evils of cold, thirst and starvation, or allowed to die unseen. Holy places were violated, monasteries and Church estates attacked and burnt. In short, very many suffered, since both the human and the divine were held in derision.

Urban knew that a pope had a special responsibility within such a wretched society. God's providence in the world could not work without the proper hierarchy of a just and holy order, in which kings, prelates, nobles, knights, clergy and villeins had their appointed places, but all below the pope at the summit of Christian society. 'What wonder then,' the people enquired, 'that the whole world is a prey to disturbance and confusion? For when the Roman Church, which is the source of correction for all Christianity, is troubled by any disorder, the sorrow is communiated from the nerves of the head to the members subject to it, and these members suffer in sympathy. This Church is indeed our mother, as it were, at whose bosom we were nourished, by whose doctrine we were instructed and strengthened, and by whose counsel we were admonished.'

Urban heard too many angry or despairing cries. It was hard to make a policy out of such desperation. He preferred to be guided, both in theory and in practice, by the light of the past, by the positive tradition of the Church. In its better moments the Church had always tried to limit or control the brutality of man, his quickness to fly to arms and make a chaos of the society so laboriously fostered by Christian faith. To avoid warfare altogether was beyond the hope of mankind, for (as many pointed out) battles 'existed first in heaven, so it is no great marvel if wars and fighting arise in this world'. This problem had confronted the Fathers of the Church, among whom was St Augustine. With his powerful and persuasive mind he considered the question of violence in a Christian society and set out the doctrine of a 'just war'. According to the saint, cruelty, vengeance, oppression of the weak, military pride and lust for power were deeply wrong. However, in times of invasion or danger to the faith (Augustine wrote as the Vandals were ripping apart the late Roman Empire), a Christian soldier had a melancholy duty to undertake certain wars for protection or defence, but only 'by command of God and by lawful authority'. Without the licence of Holy Church, 'he who can think of war and bear the thought without great sorrow is indeed a man dead to human feeling.'

At the end of the tenth century, after a long time of troubles, the Church again attempted to set a formal limit on customary violence. Under the terms of the *Pax Dei*, the Peace of God, the bishops tried to place certain classes of people and property – the clergy, the poor and all their goods – beyond the reach of warring factions. At the same time, the *Truga Dei*, the Truce of God, took a lead from an earlier decree by Charlemagne and limited the time available for fighting. By 1050, the period from sundown on Wednesday to midnight on Sunday was, in theory at least, closed to all armed quarrels and private acts of war.

Urban saw that voluntary pacts, like the Peace and the Truce of God, had little success in putting a stop to the dangerous but profitable life of war. In the storm of the times there was easy plunder to be gained amid the wreck and flotsam of damaged communities, but it seemed also to Urban that these agreements, weak though they were, indicated a mood of soul-searching within Christian society. They were a recognition of how humiliated ordinary people were face to face with their own sorrows and disasters. In misery and at the end of hope the people were expressing their sense of loss, their nostalgia for a lost land of contentment, which in reality had perhaps never existed, but was present to them always in the holy rhetoric of the Church. And beyond the grief of nostalgia, the Church thought it saw the glimmer of a true revival of religious feeling in the eleventh century. All his adult life Urban had been part of the large reforming movement that flowed out of the abbey of Cluny. He was certain that a time of better faith was near. The earth, wrote one enthusiastic reformer from Cluny, was clothing itself anew in 'a white garment of churches'.

It was high time for the pope to act. In former years the papacy, trapped in its own troubles, could do little more than give anxious support to voluntary associations, but more and more, in the clearer religious air of the eleventh century, the popes took an active hand to rein in violent men. The papal theologian Ivo of Chartres insisted that all killing needed penance and absolution from the Church, even in a just war. Urban's predecessors in the eleventh century, in particular Gregory VII, that strenuous and irascible defender of papal privilege, tried to put a kind of holy *imprimatur* on all acts of war, licensing this one and condemning that. In this way many outrageous, self-serving rogues were commissioned into 'the army of Christ'.

Pope Urban inherited this policy, and he kept to it in his sober, steady way, avoiding the rows and the clashes with great princes that had made the pontificate of Gregory so lively. Urban supported with all his heart wars that aimed to push back the Saracen advance in southern Europe. The Normans, the soldiers of Pisa, the followers of the legendary El Cid in Spain were overwhelmed with words of praise. 'The island of Sicily has been set free,' Urban exulted with the Normans. 'With these triumphs against the Muslims,' he wrote to the Pisans, 'God's majesty has crowned Pisa with glory.' The fall of Toledo was welcomed with equal rapture: 'With joyful heart we rejoice and give thanks to God, because in our time He has given such a great victory to the Christian people.' All this was the work of God, and it was the proper task of the armies of Christ to defend the faith and lands and liberty of Christendom against the heathen.

To do this, to gird oneself for the battles of Christ, was surely in the main stream of Christian moral thought. Was not the ideal society of Christendom much more than a mere heterogeneous mass of striving, competitive individuals, all with personal intimate aims not to be measured the one against the other? Aristotle had said, and the Church Fathers agreed, that society was prior to the individual. Christian society was a community united in a shared vision of the good of mankind and of the good of the community. An individual should judge his virtue not so much by his disposition towards courage, justice, prudence, etc – though all of these would be needed. Rather, he should consider how his own personal qualities helped and took forward the aims and ends of the Christian community. Yes, Urban thought, that was all very well in theory. The practice among ignorant, grasping men who liked fighting was rather

different. The pope pondered the matter. Campaigns against
infidels, here and there in the south, allowed knights some
moments of virtue, but it did not last. Soon those same knights
were once more turning their bile and agression against fellow
Christians. What Urban needed was an enterprise, clearly
virtuous in serving the ends of Christendom, which would
channel the raw brutal energy of the time into some great and
enduring work of Christian conscience.

In these moments of reflection, the pope's mind turned
towards Jerusalem.

The very thought was enough to make one pause. Who could
know where that journey might end? Was it not enough
that Christian men were united in faith against the Saracens
in Spain? Urban had blessed that war in defence of the West
as a task commendable to the soul, but local campaigns had a
worrying complexity about them. The Church might stress
the needs of true faith, but to the men on the battlefield the
warfare looked strangely familiar, having more to do with invasion, land-hunger, dynastic ambition, military pride, plunder,
and good employment for penniless feudal knights. Not much
there to do with religion. Besides, what did one know of Spain?
Did cannibals live there, or those who wore their heads in their
chests? In these ages, the sense of geography or anthropology
among ordinary people was extremely shaky. To many, the borders of Europe were as remote as the Dawn Palace of the Sun
in old mythology. But Jerusalem! That was a symbol that
burned clear in western consciousness. And as for the actual
place, a surprisingly large number of people from the West –
clergy, pilgrims, merchants – had been to Palestine and could
give first-hand accounts of the Holy Land.

For more than three hundred and fifty years, from the time
when the Caliph Omar made a treaty with the Patriarch
Sophronius until 1009, when mad al-Hakim began attacks on
Christians and Jews, the city of Jerusalem and the Holy Land
were open to the West, with an easy welcome, and the way
there was no more dangerous than a journey from Paris to
Rome. Westerners went eagerly, and there were many curious
wonders for their eyes:

Now Syria is a land of blessing, a country of cheapness, abounding in fruits, and peopled by holy men. The upper province, which is near the dominion of the Greeks, is rich in streams and crops, and the climate is often cold. The lower province is even more excellent, and more pleasant, by reason of its luscious fruits and in the great number of its palm trees. Unequalled is this land of Syria for its dried figs, its plentiful olive oil, its white bread, and the veils of Ramleh; also for quinces, pine-nuts, raisins, antidotes against poisonous bites, herbs of mint, and Jerusalem roses. And further, know that within the province of Palestine may be found gathered together six-and-thirty products that are not discovered thus united in any other land.

Who in the West had met the like of these things before – the Kuraish pine-nuts, quinces, the Ainuni and Duri raisins, the Kafuri plum, the As Sabai fig and the fig of Damascus? There were waterlilies and sycamores and the carob from the locust-tree, lotus-fruit, artichokes, sugar-cane, and Syrian apples. Add to those fresh dates and olives, shaddock, indigo, juniper berries and luffahs, oranges, Nabk fruit from the Sidr tree, almonds, asparagus, bananas, sumach, cabbages, truffles, lupins, and the early prune called at-Tari. If all this did not overwhelm the senses, then there were the special delights: snowy sherbet, buffalo milk, acacia-scented honeycombs, the Asimi grape, the Tamri fig, and Kubbat made from carob-sugar, almonds and pistachio nuts.

Sated amid the luxury of this land, the pilgrim then came to Jerusalem itself. In all sober judgment here was a city worthy of its place in the three great monotheistic religions of Judaism, Christianity and Islam:

The buildings of this Holy City are of stone, and nowhere will you discover finer or more solid construction. Here there is neither defect nor deficiency. Wine is not publicly consumed and there is no drunkenness. The city has no brothels, public or private. The people also are noted for piety and sincerity. Provisions are most excellent, the markets are clean, the mosque is of the largest size, and nowhere are holy places more numerous. The grates are enormous, and the quinces without equal. In Jerusalem are all manner of learned

men and doctors, and for this reason the hearts of men of
intelligence yearn towards her. All the year round, her streets
are nevery empty of strangers.

In this demi-paradise of Syria and Palestine, all needs were
satisfied. How could a traveller hunger, thirst, or be weary
when everything was fruitful? 'I heard from a certain person
whom I can trust,' wrote a Persian visitor in 1047, 'that the
Prophet Mohammed (peace be upon him and the blessing of
Allah!) was seen in a dream by a saintly man, who spoke to
him saying, "O Prophet of God, give me assurance forever that
I will find my daily bread." And the Prophet replied, "Truly, I
shall warrant this unto you, even by the bread and the oil of
Syria."'

The land satisfied the body, but Jerusalem was a balm for
the spirit. There were so many holy places to be visited, so
much praying to be done, so many saintly and learned people
in attendance. Of all places on earth, here body and soul might
be joined in harmony. 'When you have passed out of the great
mosque,' wrote the Persian, Nasir-i-Khusrau, 'there lies before
you a large level plain called the Sahirah, which is said to be
the place foretold for the Resurrection, where all mankind
shall be gathered together. For this reason people come from
all parts of the world to stay in the Holy City till death over-
takes them, to be ready at the appointed place for the Day
fixed by Allah (may He be praised and exalted!).' Was not this
a parallel tale to the Christian story, first expressed in a late
Roman Sibylline prophecy much discussed by western churchmen around 1000, at the turn of the millennium, that at the
world's end the last emperor would be crowned in Jerusalem?

People of many nations, and of three religions, came to
the Holy City to pray, to study, to do business, to live well, to
grow rich in body and soul, perhaps even to die in the odour
of sanctity. The Muslim geographer Mukaddasi, himself
Jerusalem-born, watched the changing crowd go confidently
across the wide stone slabs of his well-loved streets, under the
shadow of temple, church and mosque, and he summed up
their happiness: 'Now, as to my saying that Jerusalem is
the most illustrious of cities, is she not the one that unites the

advantages of This World with those of the Next? He who is of the sons of This World and yet is ardent in the matters of the Next, may with advantage seek her markets; while he who would be of the men of the Next World, though his soul clings to the good things of This, he too may find these here!'

However, beware of approaches to perfection. Even in Jerusalem there were flaws. Mukaddasi quoted an old saying from the Torah: 'Jerusalem is a golden basin filled with scorpions.' The baths were filthy, and provisions very expensive. Visitors were heavily taxed and regarded with suspicion by the guards at the gates. It was in many respects a heartless place. 'In this city,' said Mukaddasi, 'the oppressed have no help, the meek are molested, and the rich envied.' He commented darkly that, if there were scorpions amid the precious places, it was to a large extent the fault of the Christians and the Jews. So brazen and numerous were these people that the Muslim could hardly get to the mosque. 'Everywhere the Christians and the Jews have the upper hand, and these same Christians are rude and without manners in public places.' The brick-red countenance, the all-consuming appetite, the cheerful squalor of Saxon pilgrim or Frankish foot-soldier! Whatever the conduct of these Christians, certainly they jostled in large numbers in the streets of Jerusalem. Yet this was a Muslim city in an eastern land that had been for almost 400 years under the rule of Islam. What rights could Christians possibly have here, except by permission of Islam?

Mukaddasi completed his account of the Holy Land in 985. Within twenty-five years the good life changed for Jews and Christians. In 1009 Caliph al-Hakim destroyed the Church of the Ressurection [the Holy Sepulchre] (in Arabic, by a play on words, it was called the 'Church of the Dunghill'). Christians were harried and punished, restraints and penalties were placed on their way of life. Christians suffered but not outrageously so, at least according to the standards of danger and insecurity in the contemporary life of the West. In any case, the worst oppression did not last long. Even with al-Hakim himself, the sharpness of his bite was not as bad as his crazed barking. The Byzantine emperor felt safe enough to visit Jerusalem incognito:

Al-Hakim having news of this visit, sent for one of his cup-
bearers and said, 'There is a man of such and such a look
whom you will find seated in the Holy Place. Approach him
and say that al-Hakim has sent you to him, lest he should
think that I, the Caliph, knew not of his coming. But tell
him to be cheerful, for I have no evil intention against him.'

Soon the panic was over. In 1037 al-Mustansir came to an
amicable agreement with Emperor Michael IV. The Greek
emperor released five thousand Muslim captives and then was
permitted to rebuild the Church of the Resurrection. The new
church was wonderful to see. Nasir-i-Khusrau commented on
its marbles, its ornaments, its statues, its pictures, its brocades
and coverings in cloth-of-gold. It was large enough for eight
thousand people. And in 1047, when Nasir saw it, the
Christian worshippers had returned in strength: 'I saw seated
in this church great numbers of priests and monks, reading the
Scriptures and saying prayers, both by day and by night.' The
flow of pilgrims from the West hardly faltered, not even when
Muslim quarrels and the arrival of the Seljuk Turks from far-
ther east began to make all Syria and Palestine dangerous to
travellers. In 1064, a very large body of German pilgrims, said
to number some seven thousand, set out for the Holy Land,
led by two archbishops and two bishops. The journey did not
go well for these pilgrims. For their defence they had committed themselves into God's hands, ineffectively aided by
staves and stones. In the disturbed lands of northern Syria they
were attacked and easily robbed, losing many lives, but the
remainder struggled on to Jerusalem and many other pilgrims,
despite all the hazards, were only too ready to follow them
out of Europe.

Yet gradually, in Christian eyes, what had seemed certain was
made doubtful. Was the Holy City, the very centre of the earth,
to remain open for Christians? An al-Hakim, a dynastic quarrel
between Fatimids and Abbasids, an incursion of rough nomads
such as the Seljuks, might in one moment kick the beam off
balance and put Christian lives in jeopardy. Western pilgrims
continued to make the journey, but at what cost? Pope Urban
was aware that Archbishop William of Trier, one of the leaders
of the German pilgrims in 1064, had been attacked, stripped

naked, and left half-dead. On the same pilgrimage a stately and noble abbess, not young in years, was captured, robbed, and raped in the sight of all until she died.

Was it not the duty of the pope to try to secure the safety of Christian lives, particularly in the holiest places of Christendom? Immediately after the attacks by al-Hakim in 1009, a forged decretal, supposedly issued by Pope Sergius IV, pleaded with the West to help Jerusalem: 'Look out across the sea. Think of the Day of Judgment, when the joys of Christ will be possessed by those who act in His name here on earth. Come, my sons, defend God and win an everlasting kingdom.' The knights of the West, poor, fragmented, war-bound, were not yet persuaded and by the mid-century it no longer seemed so urgent, as the different religions slipped back towards their old easy accommodation. Then, in a whirlwind of fierce energy, the Seljuk Turks dragged thunderclouds into the calm air.

In 1071, at Manzikert, the Byzantine army suffered a catastrophic defeat by the Seljuks. In the same year the Turks captured Jerusalem. It was at once apparent that a new, strong, unpredictable Muslim power threatened, not just the road to the Holy Land, but a part of Christendom itself, whose eastern flank was secured by the Greeks of the Byzantine empire. Quickly, appeals went out from Byzantium to Rome. There was no love between the eastern and western branches of Christianity. Even a man as shrewd and sensible as Abbot Guibert, soon to be in the thick of crusading effort, could find no kind words for the Greeks. From the Greek mind, he wrote, 'come heresies and a portentous crop of various plagues, which have grown so high and into such an inextricable labyrinth, that the most neglected soil could never produce a wilder crop of thorns or nettles.' They were more 'ill-conditioned than brute beasts', and the good abbot hoped they might be left to stew in their own mess.

Even so, the papacy was not so blind that it missed the danger to Christendom posed by the weakness of the Greek empire. When Emperor Michael VII begged help from Pope Gregory VII in 1073, the firebrand pope offered a grand 'army of liberation' which he would lead himself as *dux et pontifex*. This body of fifty thousand western soldiers might even push on (the language is deliberately vague here) from the Greek border to the relief of Jerusalem. Nothing further was heard of this plan, for Gregory had troubles enough in Europe, but when Alexius Comnenus repeated the appeals at the beginning of Urban's reign, and early in 1095 sent emissaries to badger the pope at the Council of Piacenza, Urban was determined to help. Simple questions of policy, trade and safety dictated his help, whatever tears he might shed from heartache over Jerusalem. Even at Piacenza, the pope was beginning to give shape to a visionary scheme, exhorting the West to 'take an oath' to help the Greeks: 'When he heard also that interior parts of Romania were held oppressed by the Turks, and that Christians were subjected to destructive and savage attacks, he was moved by compassionate pity. Prompted by the love of God, he got ready to cross the Alps and come into Gaul.'

He was planning for another, more thorough discussion of the difficult eastern problem, to be held at another Church Council in November. Eight months later, as Urban journeyed to Clermont in France to begin that Council, his thoughts were almost in order. His mind would not let go of a certain theme. Again and again he heard the words of Psalm 79: 'O God, the heathen are come into thine inheritance; thy holy temple they have defiled; they have laid Jerusalem on heaps.'

On 27 November, when the moment came, Pope Urban was ready for it. He mounted the platform with firm, deliberate steps, indicating a firmness of purpose. The sea of faces below did not intimidate him. His voice against the sharp wind was distinct, and loud enough to carry to the end of the crowd.

'Dearest brethren,' he began, 'I, Urban, invested by the permission of God with the papal tiara, and spiritual ruler over the whole world, have come here in this great crisis to you, servants of God, as a messenger of divine admonition.'

It was a bold beginning. The crowd stirred. The times were hard and dangerous, as all mankind knew; but what great crisis was this, that drew from the pope a message of divine admonition? Surely some revelation was at hand! First, however, the pope had some preliminary matters to dispose of, for no religious work could be accomplished except by those with clean hands and pure hearts.

'If there be in you,' Urban continued, 'any disposition or crookedness contrary to God's law, because you have lost the moderation of reason and justice, I shall earnestly try to correct it at once, with divine assistance.

'For how can he make peace who hates it? If anyone has soiled hands, how can he cleanse the spots from the contaminated? For it is written, "If the blind lead the blind, both shall fall into the pit." Accordingly, first correct yourselves, so that without reproach you can then correct those under your care. If you wish to be the friends of God, do generously those things that are pleasing to Him.'

No one doubted that many were present, both clergy and laity, who showed only too clearly in their lives a 'crookedness contrary to God's law'. As they dropped their eyes it seemed as if the pope's words picked out each wrong-doer and confronted that man or woman with intimate sins. Urban did not intend to let them off easily:

> See to it that the rights of Holy Church are maintained, and root out the heresy of simony. Let the buyers and sellers of church offices be struck by the lash of the Lord, and disgracefully driven through narrow ways into utter confusion. Above all, keep the Church in all its orders entirely free from the secular power of princes. Whoever lays violent hands on a bishop, let him be considered excommunicated. Whoever seizes monks, or priests, or nuns, or pilgrims, or traders, to despoil them, let him be accursed. Let thieves and robbers and arsonists be driven from the Church and accursed. Consider how great will be the punishment for those who steal, and how the damnations of hell await the rich who give no alms.
>
> Dearest brethren, you have seen the world disordered by these and other evils for a long time. In some places in your provinces one scarcely dares to travel for fear of being robbed, or kidnapped, or taken by bandits, by force or by trickery, night or day, within doors or without. Let us renew the Truce of God, long ago established by our holy fathers. If anyone, by pride or ambition, infringes this injunction, let him be condemned by God and by this Council.

All that Urban said was true, only too true. In shame, the lords and prelates of the western world heard his words and recognized the extent of their failings. But the wise reformer, together with the indictment of sin, offers the chance of redemption. The psychology of sinners was no mystery to the Church, for had she not for a thousand years, in the confessional, learnt when to lash and when to soothe the Christian conscience? Now, before his repentant audience, Pope Urban began to unfold his grand idea, his plan that would save the honour and the soul of Europe:

> Now that you have promised the Lord, O you sons of God, to keep peace more earnestly than before, and faithfully to sustain the rights of Holy Church, there still remains for you a very necessary work. For you must hurry to aid your brethren in the East, who have often begged and certainly need your help. They are under attack from the Turks, and these heathens have advanced as far into the territory of Christendom as that part of the Mediterranean known as the Arm of St George. These Turks have conquered the Christians in battle, killed and captured many, destroyed the churches, and devastated the kingdom of God.
>
> So I exhort you with earnest prayers – not I, but God – that as heralds of Christ you urge all men of all ranks, rich as well as poor, knights as well as foot-soldiers, to hasten to exterminate this vile race from the lands of your eastern brethren. I call on those present here. I proclaim it to the absent. Moreover, Christ commands it!

There was something noble in this appeal, but also a promise of escape. The direction pointed out by the pope led away from the bleak bare hills of the Auvergne, from the lowering weather, the flying clouds undershot with dark as chill as death, from the soaked and winter-rutted lanes of western Europe. In the sun of the East richer plans and bolder ambitions might flourish, shooting up in an unaccustomed warmth, and all by permission of Holy Church. When there was little to lose at home, it was not so hard to wager on the chance of prosperity for the body and a reward for the soul in the East. Urban had caught the mood of the crowd. He hurried on with his message:

O what a disgrace if a race so despised as the Turks, so base and full of demons, should overcome a people faithful to the All-powerful God, and resplendent with the name of Christ! O what reproaches will be charged against you by the Lord Himself if you do not help our fellow Christians! Let those who delight in making private wars against the faithful turn their wrath against infidels, who should have been driven back before now. Let robbers become soldiers of Christ. Let them fight barbarians, not brothers. Let those who will fight and kill for any low wage now labour instead for an eternal reward. Let those dejected in mind and body offer themselves to the glory of heaven. And if any who goes should lose his life, by land or sea, or in fighting the pagans, his sins shall be remitted. This I will grant by the power invested in me by God.

The general picture was clear, but it was time for the pope to fill in the details, in particular to put some flesh on the enemy. What did his audience know of the Seljuk Turks, this strange, remote race? Ignorant westerners needed to be

CHURCH OF THE HOLY SEPULCHRE, JERUSALEM

reminded of the infamous heathens, their cruelty and hatred of Christians. Did not these Turks (the pope claimed) use the blood of circumcized Christians to stain the altars and pollute the baptismal fonts? They killed captives by torture, slitting the stomach and hooking the end of the intestine, which they attached to a stake. Then the poor captives were whipped into motion until the viscera burst from the body and the victims fell dead in the mess of their own guts. Others they bound to a post and used as a target for arrows. Still others were forced to extend their necks, to see if a pagan scimitar could sweep off a Christian head with a single blow.

Such was the nature of the Turk, a foe who deserved no mercy. The first part of Urban's oration had been addressed to sinners, that is to say the people of the West. Now men noted that more brusque, steely and violent notes were entering into his language, for the great task that he had in mind needed the participation, not of sinners, but of soldiers: 'Let the Holy Sepulchre of the Lord, our Saviour, which is possessed by unclean nations, especially move you, and likewise the other Holy Places, which are now treated with ignominy and polluted with filthiness.'

Pope Urban had come to the heart of his discourse. Here was the extraordinary and blessed task that he was offering to those he called 'most valiant soldiers, descended from invincible ancestors'. He was giving them the chance to redeem Jerusalem, the Holy City, from heathen conquerors and cried out:

> Enter upon the road to the Holy Sepulchre, wrest that land from the wicked race and make it subject to yourselves. Jerusalem is the navel of the world; the land is fruitful above others, like another paradise of delights. The Redeemer of the human race has made it illustrious by His advent, has beautified it by His presence, has consecrated it by His suffering, has redeemed it by His death, and has gloried it by His burial. Now this royal city is held in subjection by those who do not know God. Therefore, she cries out to be liberated and implores you to come to her aid. She calls to you in particular, because God has given you, above all nations, great glory in arms.

The plight of Jerusalem was hammered home by Urban, for he knew that the imagination of his audience stopped well short of the shores of Palestine. Think, he implored the crowd, of the holy body of the Blessed Mary, lonely and abandoned in the valley of Jehosaphat. Think of the monstrous impiety of those who raised idols in the Temple of Solomon, or who committed abominations in the church of the Lord's Sepulchre. Who were these but the enemies of God, idolaters who scattered the bones of God's servants and gave the remains of the saints to the beasts of the field?

> Woe unto us, brethren, we who already suffer the scoffing and derision of our neighbours! We have become the scorn of all people. Let us bewail the unexampled devastation of the Holy Land. This land is rightly called holy, for there is not even a footstep that does not give witness to the body or the spirit of the Saviour. Here also in this land were the Mother of God and the apostles. Its earth drank up the blood of martyrs. How blessed are the stones that crowned you, Stephen, the first martyr! How holy are the waters of the Jordan, in which our Saviour was baptized! Take note, O soldiers of Christ, of the children of Israel who prefigured you, those who crossed the Red Sea and took that land by the strength of their arms. With Christ as our leader, let us emulate those children and drive out the unclean ones who are the Jebusites of our own day, and enter into the earthly Jerusalem, which is the image of the Celestial City.

It was soldiers that Urban wanted, an army of the Lord. A Frenchman himself, he appealed to his hosts and fellow-countrymen in Clermont. Were not the Franks, he told them, a race chosen and beloved by God, set apart from all other nations by the bounty of their land, by their true faith, and by the honour that they paid to Holy Church? The Franks had a duty to defend the faith beyond that of other less favoured nations. Perhaps there was something conventional in this appeal – one Frenchman flattering others – but behind the words to the Franks was a more important appeal to a turbulent group of men throughout Europe who had it within their power to make peace at home or successful wars abroad.

No great scheme for change or conquest could go forward

without the support of western knighthood. The knights, in their violence and contempt for civil society, lay at the root of the problem in the life of the West, but their very strength, and the tatters of ideal chivalry that still clung to them, made it possible for them to be part of the solution. If only they could be spurred into good and righteous action! This thought brought forth all Urban's arts of persuasion. If the knights were not tempted by virtue, then they might be shamed by guilt. Roundly, and without mincing words, he began to condemn their usual habits and conduct:

> Listen and learn! You, girded with the badge of knighthood, you are nothing but puffs of arrogance and pride. You rage against your brothers and cut each other in pieces. But the true soldiery of Christ does not rend asunder the sheep-fold of the Redeemer. The army of Holy Church is a friend and a protector of her people. But you knights debase her wickedly.
>
> Confess the truth. Truly, your way does not lead to life. You, oppressors of children, robbers of widows. You, guilty of murder, of sacrilege, thieves of another's rights. You, hired to shed Christian blood. As vultures smell corpses, so you sniff out battles and run to them with open arms. In truth, this is the worst way of man, utterly removed from God.
>
> But now, if you wish to care for your souls, either lay down the girdle of knighthood, or boldly advance as knights of Christ and rush as quickly as you can to defend our brothers in the East and to preserve the Church. For she it is from whom the joys of your whole salvation have come, who poured into your mouths the milk of divine wisdom, and who set before you the holy teaching of the Gospels. Restrain your murderous hands from the destruction of your brothers, and fight the heathens for your faith.
>
> Under the banner of Jesus Christ, our Leader, struggle for your Jerusalem. In Christian battle-line, most invincible line, more dire and dreadful than any of old, assail and drive out the Turks, those who are more wicked than the Jebusites. May you deem it a beautiful thing to die for Christ, in that city where He died for us.

Great efforts deserve extraordinary rewards. In the stories

of chivalry, the knight errant was a wanderer, one who sought out injustice, always in the saddle, ready to fly at a moment's notice to the aid of the oppressed. Pope Urban knew the large literature of chivalry, the tales of love, of foot-loose travel, of excitement and the clash of arms, and the journey that the pope offered to real western knights might encompass all of these. To some extent, the reward of the expedition to the Holy Land lay in the experiences of the adventure itself. It was a hazard into the unknown that relieved the boredom and squalor of everyday life. Other familiar rewards (always implied but better left unsaid) would come from the plunder, loot and ransom-money that filled the coffers of a successful army. Feudal knights were no strangers to this source of wealth. The lands of the East were rumoured to be exceptionally rich, so they might be expected to yield exceptional profit.

Besides the material rewards, there was also the promise of a spiritual reward. Death was inevitable, but should it strike in the course of the pope's great work it would be an end very close to martyrdom. It was not difficult, even for hardened campaigners, to believe that a death for Christ in Jerusalem would be a 'beautiful thing'. And it was particularly pleasing to those same campaigners that such a state of grace was able to go hand in hand with the joy of battle and the plunder of victory:

> If it befall you to die this side of Jerusalem, be sure that Christ shall still number you in His army. God pays with the same shilling, whether at the first or at the eleventh hour. To kill Christians is a matter of horror; but it is not wicked to flourish your sword against Saracens. That is righteous warfare, and it is charity to risk your life for your brothers. Do not trouble about the concerns of tomorrow. Those who fear God want nothing, nor those who cherish Him in truth. Moreover, the possessions of the enemy will be yours, since their treasures will be the spoil for your victorious arms. Or if your blood gushes out, and you die, you will have gained everlasting glory. For such a commander as Christ you ought to fight. Short is the way, little the labour, which will repay you with the crown that does not fade. Accordingly, I say to every one of you: gird yourselves, and

be valiant sons. For it is better to die in battle than to behold
the sorrows of your race and the distress of the Holy Places.

Carried away by the passionate words of Pope Urban in the
chilly market-square, the crowd below the platform heaved
and stirred, like a great slothful beast rising from sleep. The
people who heard the pope were moved. A broad and attrac-
tive avenue of vision, redemption and profit had opened up
before them, and they were ready to take it. As they listened,
there was something for every ear. For the ambitious soldiers,
there were the clang of steel and the cries of death or triumph.
For the astute or the greedy, there was the rustle of gold and
precious coins; for the pious, the hints of immortality. But the
learned and sharp-witted Abbot Guibert of Nogent heard the
key-note that supported all the pope's divergent and wide
appeals as Urban begged the audience:

> Consider therefore, that the Almighty has provided you for
> this purpose, that through you He may restore Jerusalem
> from such debasement. Ponder, I implore you, how full of
> joy and delight our hearts will be when we shall see the
> Holy City restored with your little help, and the divine
> words fulfilled in our times. Let your memory be moved
> by what the Lord Himself says to the Church: 'I will bring
> thy seed from the East, and gather thee from the West.'
> God has already brought our seed from the East, since in
> a double way that region of the East has given the first
> beginnings of the Church to us. But He will also gather it
> from the West, since He will make good the wrongs of
> Jerusalem through you, the people of the West. With God's
> help, you can do this. And believe without question that in
> your battles Christ will be your inseparable standard-bearer.

Pope Urban finished his oration. Then, by the power vested
in him as the successor to St Peter, he gave an apostolic blessing and absolved from sin all those who vowed to save
Jerusalem. As a sign of their adventure he ordered them to
wear an emblem in the shape of the Cross, in memory of the
Passion. Under this sign they became soldiers of Christ, and
because every man wore a Cross, this holy expedition was
called a Crusade.

At once, cloth crosses of every size and colour were cut out, to be sewn to the shirts and the tunics and the cloaks and the *byrra* of all those who now clamoured to set out. When the sewing was done, Urban decreed that if any were false to the Cross or their vow, if any should fall away even through love of family or affection for their native lands, then they should be outlawed forever, or until they repented and completed their vows.

Then all kinds of men, rich and poor, began to prepare for the hard task that the pope had set out for them. They were eager to be on their way, for now, in the eyes of the Church, and perhaps for a little while in their own estimation, knights and villeins, a great rabble of fighting men, were no longer bandits, robbers and peace-breakers, but the new Maccabees, heroes of God and guardians of Jerusalem.

−3−
Via Dei −
The Path of God

In the spring of 1096, after several years of drought, the heavens opened on France. That autumn, the harvest was as good as folk could remember. It was taken as a sign, one among many. In the previous year, shortly before the Council of Clermont, a shower of meteorites rained in the night sky. In February 1096, as the French king and his nobles met to discuss the crusade, the moon in eclipse turned blood red. In March, a sudden aurora drove the fearful into the churches. In August, the moon was again in eclipse. A little later, the winter night was pierced by the blaze of a comet. A scourge of St Anthony's Fire swept France, leading to death for many, or a poor, crippled life. Was it punishment or warning? On the flesh of the most fervent crusaders appeared the brand of a burning cross. As the Holy Land beckoned, the heavens spoke often, and the people were disposed to listen:

> There were also clouds the colour of blood rising both east and west, darting up into the zenith to meet each other. Again, about midnight, fiery splendours flushed the sky of the north, and often we saw torches of fire flying through

the air, as we proved by many witnesses. On a certain day, at about three of the clock, a priest of exemplary life called Sigger saw two knights rushing at each other in the air, and after they had fought for a long time the one who carried the large cross bore down the other and was the victor.

Some men who were keeping watch in a horse pasture said they saw the semblance of a city in the air, with many companies hurrying to it on horse and foot. And some showed the sign of the cross stamped by divine power on their clothes, and even on their foreheads or other parts of their bodies. By this sign they believed that they had been predestined for the army of the Lord.

I may mention also that a certain woman was pregnant for two years and brought forth a boy who could speak from birth. By these and like signs all creation was summoned into the army of the Lord.

Few in the West doubted the message from the skies. For many, it heralded the arrival of the millenarian prophecy of the end of time. The trumpet was sounding for the coming of the Just Judge, a portent confirmed for the Church by signs and wonders throughout the world. For others, unready for this prophetic doom, the signs were at least marks of divine approval for Urban's crusade:

> When it was God's will and pleasure to free the Holy Sepulchre from the power of the pagans and to open the way for Christians to travel there for the redemption of their souls, He showed many signs, prodigies and portents to sharpen the minds of Christians, so that they would eagerly hurry there. For the stars in the sky were seen through the whole world to fall to earth, as dense as hail or snowflakes. A fiery way spread through the heavens, and in a short while half the sky turned the colour of blood. Dreams and visions were seen, too many to count.

Like the aurora, a mood of expectation hung in the air, insistent and powerful in effect, but unclear in meaning. In the face of these wonders, the people needed guidance and direction. Immediately after Clermont, Pope Urban set out to broadcast his appeal and to make its meaning plain. He hurried about central and southern France, preaching widely, in Limoges, Angers, Le Mans, Nîmes, Tours and in several lesser towns. Though he was very much the Frenchman calling to his fellow-countrymen, he stayed clear of the heartlands belonging to the French king, who was still under sentence of excommunication. Urban spent a year wandering through France, and no one could doubt the energy and force with which he put forward his message. He himself wrote, without exaggeration, that he had 'urged most fervently the lords and the people of the land of the Franks to free the eastern churches'.

Later, Urban extended his appeal. In church councils up and down the land the crusade was promulgated and promoted. The pope sent embassies to the Christian courts of Europe. In particular, he wooed the rulers of the Italian city-states, where the dexterous bankers lived who were best able to raise the funds for such a gigantic enterprise. The pope was eager to proclaim his crusade as the duty of all Christendom, but it was tacitly acknowledged that the French were the chief supporters and enthusiasts. Bishop Adhemar of Le Puy, from that part of France where the crusade was first preached, was the pope's vice-regent who, when the official army of the princes finally got under way, 'prudently and wisely led the whole army of God and vigorously inspired them to accomplish the undertaking'. Another strong supporter and promoter was Hugh of Die, the powerful archbishop of Lyon. Beyond the pulpits of these great men, a myriad small voices made themselves heard: priests and monks, itinerant friars, saintly men, visionaries, madmen, harbingers of doom, prophets, hotheads, entrepreneurs of folly or violence, stirrers in the great cauldron of discord, hoping to pluck from it some advantage. It is no surprise that the message became garbled, in an age of poor communications, where word of mouth was as important as, and far quicker, in effect, than official instruction or papal documents.

It was a world of wild words and implausible promises in which, as the German chronicler Ekkehard of Aura discovered, the French were most affected by rash enthusiasm:

The West Franks could easily be persuaded to leave their lands, since for several years Gaul had suffered at one time from civil war, at another time from famine, and always from too many deaths. Then they were greatly alarmed by the disease that began near the church of St Gertrude of Nivelle – that affliction known as 'St Anthony's fire' – which made them fear for their lives. This was the form it took. The patient was attacked in some part of the body by invisible burning, with unspeakable torment and without remedy, until he either died in agony or lost the limb that was the seat of the suffering. Today, we still see so many witnesses to this scourge, in maimed hands or lost feet.

If the French rushed to the crusade out of despair, Ekkehard also noted that many others were moved by a variety of impure motives, tricked or duped or cajoled, fleeing from the burden of debt, or from family troubles, or from the arm of justice. He knew that, although the French might show an unsteady and foolish optimism, the path to crusading in northern Europe, for sound political reasons, was likely to be long, doubtful and stony:

> For the Teutonic peoples, this trumpet call sounded only faintly, particularly because of the schism between the empire and the papacy, from the time of Pope Alexander II even to this day. This, alas, has strengthened the mutual hatred and enmity between the Romans and us! So it came to pass that almost all the Teutonic nations, at first ignorant of the reason for this setting out, laughed to scorn the motley throng of knights, soldiers, peasants, women and children that passed through their lands. They regarded them as crazed, victims of unspeakable folly, striving for danger in the place of safety, and leaving their birthlands for nothing but disaster on the way and the vicissitudes of chance in the land of promise. They gave up their own possessions while coveting those of strangers!

It took time and some idealism to overcome the ingrained prejudice of the German nations. 'Although our people,' Ekkehard admitted, 'are more perverse than other races, yet because of the promise of divine pity, the enthusiasm of the Teutons was at last fired by Pope Urban's proclamation, for they were finally taught what the message really meant by the crowds passing through their lands.'

The appeal had an effect – immediately in France, more slowly and with some misgiving elsewhere – but to whom was it addressed? Obviously to princes, great lords and warriors, especially if they were French, but Urban, fearing the faithless and self-serving ambition of princes, was anxious to get behind the life of courts and enter into the hearts of the people. The need for a wider appeal gave a certain lack of clarity to his message. Knights, of course, were needed in large numbers, for they were the professionals of war, and the crusade itself was in part an attempt to tame the lawlessness of knights, to set them a task worthy of their fighting spirit. Both in his words at Clermont and in his letters afterwards Urban did his utmost to encourage knights, 'since they might be able to restrain the savagery of the Muslims and restore the Christians to their former freedom'.

Yet this crusade was much more than a campaign of conquest, or a warlike adventure in a far land. It was thrust forward as a holy work, and as such was likely to attract all people of faith and hope, and in particular churchmen who yearned to follow in the very footsteps of Christ. However, some people, as the pope knew well, would be nothing but a hindrance to a military expedition. The poor, the peaceful, the untrained and unarmed, women and children had no place in the pope's plans. Nor did he want to impoverish the spiritual life of the West (fragile enough as it was) by a mass exodus of clergy. As shepherds of the western flock, priests and especially monks could not be released. Urban had been a monk himself and knew the need for monastic hands to sow the seeds and tend the shoots of religious reform. In his address at Clermont he had made himself plain:

> We do not command or advise that the old, or the feeble, or those unfit for bearing arms, undertake this journey. Nor ought women to set out at all without their husbands, or brothers, or legal guardians. For they are more of a hindrance than help, more of a burden than an advantage. Let the rich aid the needy, taking with them, according to their means, experienced soldiers. Priests and clerks of any order are not to go without the consent of their bishops; for this journey would profit them nothing if they go without

permission. Also, it is not fitting that even laymen should
go without the blessing of their priests.

All that was clear enough, but against wandering monks the
pope was even more severe: 'We do not want those who have
abandoned the world and avowed themselves to spiritual warfare either to bear arms or even to go on this journey. We go
so far as to forbid them to do so.'

Despite warnings, many in the general populace, from top
to bottom, clamoured to go. Fulcher of Chartres, who had
witnessed the events at Clermont, wrote: 'After the determination of the council and the papal blessing, those present
withdrew to their homes to make known what had been done.
When these tidings were proclaimed throughout the
provinces, people agreed under oath that the peace called the
Truce should be kept mutually by all. Finally, then, many
persons of every class vowed after confession that they were
going with a pure intent wherever they were ordered to go.'

Pope Urban wanted an army of seasoned soldiers for arduous
military duty. He got instead Everyman's army, not only a
military expedition of knights and foot-soldiers under warrior-
lords, but also an army of the poor, the humble, the hopeful
and the faithful, as well as the rogues, the wide-eyed fanatics
and the desperate, plus their wives and children in many cases.
Their feet were firmly set on the *via Dei*, the path of God.

The pope had offered them a meritorious pilgrimage, and
they intended to take up that offer. This crusade, Urban
promised, would be a *recta oblatio*, a worthy sacrifice, and an
act of devotion that would count towards the salvation of the
soul. The sewing of the cross on the clothes of the crusaders
was a powerful penitential gesture, recalling in the mind the
Gospel words of both Matthew and Luke: 'If any man will come
after me, let him deny himself, and take up his cross, and follow
me. For whosoever shall save his life shall lose it: and whosoever
shall lose his life for my sake shall find it.' And again: 'Whosoever
doth not bear his cross, and come after me, cannot be my
disciple.' What, to people of simple faith, could be clearer than
that? The reward for such a sacrifice, also promised in the
Gospel of St Matthew, was equally clear: 'And everyone that

BYZANTINE MOSAIC OF CHRIST ON THE
WALK OF ST SOPHIA

hath forsaken houses, or brethren, or sisters, or father, or mother, or wife, or children, or lands, for my name's sake, shall receive an hundredfold, and shall inherit everlasting life.'

Encouraged to see the crusade as a pilgrimage, the ordinary

people willingly did so. 'We go,' said two brothers in a typical statement of intent, 'on the one hand for the grace of the pilgrimage, and on the other under the protection of God to wipe out the defilement of the pagans and the immoderate madness through which numberless Christians have already been oppressed, made captive or killed in barbaric fury.' The pope kept faith with their intentions, promising to absolve 'all penitents from all their sins from the hour that they took the Lord's cross, and he lovingly released them from all hardships, whether fasting or other mortification of the flesh'. The indulgence to the crusaders was quite clearly laid out in a papal decretal: 'Whoever for devotion only, not to gain honour or money, goes to Jerusalem to liberate the Church of God can substitute this journey for all penance.'

Uplifted by the promise of salvation, folk crowded the churches where the priests, in a new rite, distributed swords along with pilgrims' staves and a blessing. This eruption of the people, particularly in France, was like a sudden fever in society, a large epidemic with odd economic and social consequences. These effects were noted by the scholarly Abbot Guibert of Nogent:

> So many men were in haste to make their affairs ready for this journey that seven sheep were sold for five *denarii*, to give but one example of the sudden cheapening of all goods. The former scarcity of corn was turned into plenty; for each pilgrim, eager to raise money at all hazards, parted with his goods, not at his own price but at the buyer's, lest he be delayed from treading the *via Dei*, the way of God. So we saw this marvel, that all men bought dear and sold cheap, and a few coins would now purchase the possessions which neither prison nor torture could have wrung from the peasants but a short while before. Nor was it less laughable that the very men who had hitherto derided this foolish selling by their neighbours would then, of a sudden impulse, also sell up for a few pence and march forth side by side with those they had previously mocked.
>
> Thus God Almighty, who is wont to bring many vain beginnings to a pious end, led these simple souls into salvation merely through their good intention. Then you might

see a marvellous and most curious sight: a troop of poor folk with two-wheeled carts drawn by oxen which they had shod after the manner of horses. In these little carts were their scant possessions, and often their families also; and their little children, as soon as they came to some walled town, would ask again and agaian if this was the place to which they were travelling, a place called Jerusalem.

Now, at that time, before this great movement of the nations, the whole of France suffered the cruellest conflicts, with robbery, fire and arson, brigands and bandits on almost every road. Men fought pitched battles for no other excuse but insatiable greed. In a sentence, whatsoever was open to sight was coveted and taken by these rogues. Then, of a sudden, there was a marvellous and incredible change of spirit, by reason of the decree of Pope Urban. Men sought out bishops or priests to invest them with the sign of the cross. And even as the wildest winds are often laid by a little fall of rain, so we beheld this immediate peace, and cessation of customary fights and tumults, by means of a breath that passed invisibly from man to man. And this breath – we cannot doubt it – was of Christ.

All this time, in the winter of 1095 and the early spring of the next year, while the common people were working themselves into a ferment of ill-directed enthusiasm, the princes and the great lords of the expedition were preparing with slow and orderly caution, needing as they did 'large funds and the support of numerous followers'. The main body of the crusade was not due to set out until the Feast of the Assumption, 15 August 1096, and even this deadline seemed unlikely to be met, but the common folk, having cast their goods and livelihoods to the winds, must march or starve. For all the frailty of knowledge and purpose implicit in their adventure, when the poor and ignorant set foot on the long, perplexing road to Jerusalem, it was a brave moment of hope, and those who saw it were moved:

O, how fitting and pleasing to us all to see those crosses, so beautiful whether of silk or of woven gold or of plain cloth, which these pilgrims by order of Pope Urban sewed on the shoulders of their mantles or cassocks or tunics. It was indeed proper that soldiers of God, prepared to fight for His honour, should be signed and fortified by this fitting emblem of victory. Since they wore this symbol as a mark of faith, they very truly obtained the Cross whose sign they carried.

What further shall I say? The islands of the sea and all the regions of the earth were shaken under foot, so that the psalm of David seemed to be fulfilled: 'All nations whom thou hast made shall come and worship before thee, O Lord, and shall glorify thy name,' so that later they might justly say, 'We will worship in the place where his feet have stood.'

But O what grief, what sighs, what weeping, what lamentation among friends, when the husband left his dear wife, and his children, and all his possessions, his father, his mother, his brother, and all his relatives! Those who remained shed many tears, but the departing pilgrims still did not weaken. For it was the love of God that made them leave all they possessed, firmly convinced that the return would be a hundredfold to those who loved Him.

Then the husband commended his wife to God and he kissed her tenderly, and weeping he promised to return. But she, fearing that she would never see him again, was unable to stand and with many howls fell senseless to the ground. Though the one she loved was living, for her it was as if he were already dead. But he, like one who had no pity, moved neither by the tears of his wife nor the grief of his friends, trod firmly on to the path, though his heart was wretched as if clenched in ice. What can one add? Only this: 'It is the Lord's doing, and it is marvellous in our eyes.'

Out of the French countryside, prepared by the strength of papal idealism and watered with the sorrow of so many preachers and moralists, there sprang up a flourishing crop of demagogues, fanatics, charlatans and opportunists of all kinds. In their hurry to be on the road, these men side-stepped all authority. Burdened with folly more than with arms and knowledge, they each caught up a flock of pilgrims and adventurers and drove forth into an unknown world. The German chronicler Ekkehard, from a land that supported emperor rather than pope, watched with suspicion this ferment of French enthusiasm:

While all creation was being summoned into the army of the Lord, the enemy of man, the Evil One himself, did not delay to sow his own tares, to rouse false prophets, and to mingle, under the guise of religion, false brethren and shameless women amid the army of the Lord. And so, through the hypocrisy of some, the falsehoods and the gross immorality of others, the army of Christ was polluted to such an extent that, according to the prophecy of the good shepherd, even the elect were led astray.

About this time, a legend concerning Charlemagne was invented, that he had been raised from the dead for this expedition, and other great men from the past were also resurrected by rumour. And many foolish stories abounded, such as a goose that guided its mistress on the pilgrimage, and other tales of that kind. Yet since each person may be known by his fruits, even as wolves are recognized under sheep's clothing, so those same deceivers may be questioned and found out by their acts and effects. And those who have no answer to account for the alms so hypocritically taken from the faithful, or for the many ignorant bands of pilgrims that have been misled and murdered for plunder, these men I say may be compelled to do hard penance.

Among several men who needed a rigorous 'questioning' – in the manner recommended by Ekkehard – the best-known was the French preacher called Peter the Hermit.

He was from the city of Amiens, if I am not mistaken, and we learned that he lived as a hermit in monk's clothing somewhere in northern Gaul, I know not where. We beheld him leaving there on some unknown mission, going about cities and towns under the pretext of preaching. He was surrounded by such great throngs, received such enormous gifts, and was so praised for holiness, that I do not remember any other man held in such honour.

From his sudden wealth he was very generous to the poor. He reclaimed whores and gave them husbands, and not without a dowry which he provided. Everywhere, with amazing authority, he restored peace in place of strife. He wore a plain woollen shirt with a hood, under a sleeveless cloak extending to his ankles. His feet were bare. He lived on wine and fish and hardly ever, or never, ate bread. What he said and did were regarded as little short of divine, so much so that the very hairs were plucked from the tail of his mule as relics.

That was how Abbot Guibert saw Peter, and in the eyes of this fastidious cleric there was not much to explain in the upstart preacher: 'His effect we ascribe not so much to the popular love for truth as for novelty.' However, a later chronicler,

ILLUSTRATION FROM *Le Chevalier Du Cygne*,
SHOWING A CITY BEING ATTACKED AND BESIEGED

Albert of Aix, who knew the devastation that the first peasant armies had caused in his own Rhineland, saw the irrational strength of the popular movement: 'In every admonition and sermon, with all the persuasion he was capable of, Peter urged the start of the journey as soon as possible. In response to this flood of noise, all the common people, sinful as well as chaste, adulterers, murderers, thieves, perjurers and robbers, every kind of person indeed called Christian, nay women and penitents also, all joyfully entered upon this expedition.'

By the end of March 1096, ragged battalions were beginning to spill out of northern France, heading through Germany towards the eastern borderlands of Europe. As the mob moved on, new recruits stuck to it, like burrs to wool. Different factions interwove, embraced, quarrelled and separated, led by several men besides Peter the Hermit. There was a knight known as Walter the Penniless, the German monk Gottschalk, a priest called Folkmar and, worst of all, the German nobleman Count Emich of Leiningen. The mass of people following after these men was not in any true sense an army, but rather disparate bands of the trained and the untrained, some knights and many foot-soldiers, peasants and rabble, clergy, camp-followers, women and even children. Some were properly armed, others had sickles and pitchforks. In the waggon-train were wheelbarrows and farm carts drawn by mules and oxen. In every band there was perhaps a small leavening of military men. Walter the Penniless, a competent soldier, was said to have in his command (if that was the right word) eight knights and no less than fifteen thousand foot-soldiers. Peter the Hermit, once he was beyond France, soon attracted a strong, warlike body of Swabians under Duke Walter of Tegk and Count Hugh of Tubingen. Emich, himself a feudal lord, was accompanied by knights of his own kind and was joined in Germany by several companies of French, Burgundian, Flemish and English adventurers, properly armed and led by experienced campaigners. However, because of lack of co-ordination, discipline, planning, integrated command and settled purpose, these muddled and often riotous forces amounted to little more than Christian ruffians on the loose.

When the worst of the winter weather had cleared, the

Christian armies began to advance into Germany, and the first to feel the edge of their weapons were the peaceful Jewish communities long-settled in the trading cities along the river-valleys of the Rhineland and the Danube. Christian chroniclers had the grace to lament these bloodthirsty acts, though not without hints of malice and prejudice against Jews. The chief culprit, all agreed, was Count Emich of Leiningen:

> Just at that time there appeared a certain soldier, Emich, a count of the lands around the Rhine, a man of very ill-repute because of his tyrannical way of life. Called by divine revelation, like another Saul as he maintained, to the practice of religion of this kind, he usurped to himself the command of almost twelve thousand bearers of the cross. As he led them through the cities of the Rhine and the Main and the Danube, they utterly destroyed the hateful race of the Jews wherever they found them (claiming in this matter a zealous devotion to Christian faith) or forced them to convert into the bosom of the Church.

It was not just Emich who was at fault. Albert of Aix blamed the whole rabble of Christians who followed Peter the Hermit and Gottschalk, while the Jews themselves implicated bishops and princes in the slaughter and looked on the deliberate terror as nothing less than a pogrom:

> In the year one thousand and twenty-eight [1096] after the destruction of the Temple, this evil befell Israel. The nobles and the lords and the common people of the land of France united and decided to soar up like an eagle, to wage war, and to clear a way to Jerusalem, the Holy City. They wished to go to the tomb of the crucified one, a rotting corpse that avails nothing and cannot save, being of no worth or significance.
>
> They said to each other, 'Look now, we are going to a distant country to make war against mighty kings. Our lives will be in danger to conquer these kingdoms that do not believe in the crucified one, when actually it is the Jews who murdered and crucified him.' Then they stirred up hatred against us in all quarters and declared that we should accept their abominable faith or else they would annihilate us, even to the suckling infants. So they marched toward us – the lords and the common people – wearing an evil

symbol of a vertical line intersected with a horizontal line on their garments, and with special hats on their heads.

When these errant ones arrived in our lands about the Rhine, they were so impoverished they sought money to buy bread. We gave it to them, remembering the verse: 'Serve the king of Babylon, and live.' But this did not help us. Because of our sins, whenever the errant ones came to a city, the local townsmen would begin to worry us, for they quickly joined in the intention of those on the road to destroy root and vine all along the way to Jerusalem.

Battalion after battalion, like the army of Sennacherib, the errant ones came, and some of the lords in our kingdom said, 'Why do we sit? Let us join them, for every man who goes to clear the way to the unholy grave of the crucified one will be qualified and ready for Hell.' Then the gatherings of the errant ones became as numerous as the sands of the sea. They issued a proclamation that read, 'Whosoever kills a Jew will receive pardon for all his sins.' And to encourage them along this path there was a man called Dithmar or Folkmar who swore that he would not depart from this kingdom till he had killed at least one Jew.

The Jewish communities of the Rhineland had been warned of the Christian advance by brethren in France. As early as December 1095 anti-Jewish riots had taken place in Rouen where crusaders muttered among themselves, 'Great tracts of country stand between us and the enemies of God whom we wish to conquer. It is absurd to begin this enterprise when before our eyes are the Jews, more hostile to God than any other race.' Most men who wore the cross made little distinction between Jew and Muslim. It was as praiseworthy to get rid of one as the other, and the former was closest. When crusader spoke to Jew, said the chronicler Solomon bar Simson, it was in this manner: 'You are the children of those who killed the object of our veneration, hanging him on a tree. And he himself had said, "There will yet come a day when my children will come and avenge my blood." We are his children and it is therefore our duty to avenge him against you who disbelieve in him.'

At first, the Christian army passed through with little damage, being successfully bribed by the Jews to turn aside, but at the beginning of May the bigoted and brutal Count Emich killed twelve Jews in Speyer who would not convert to Christianity. Two weeks later, Emich attacked the community at Worms and slaughtered 500 Jews, even though they were under the protection of the local bishop. Then, exhilarated by the shedding of blood, Emich and his followers burst into the city of Mainz amid scenes that remained forever terrible in the memory of Solomon bar Simson:

> On the New Moon of Sivan, Count Emich, the oppressor of all the Jews (may his bones be ground to dust between iron millstones), arrived outside the city with a mighty horde of errant ones and peasants. They camped in tents since the gates of the city were closed. Emich was chief of them all, for he claimed to have a branded cross upon his flesh, made by an apostle of the crucified one as a mark of singular favour. This man showed no mercy to the aged, or youths, or maidens, or babes, or sucklings, not even the sick. He made the people of the Lord like dust to be trodden underfoot, putting all to the sword and disembowelling pregnant women.

The Jews of Mainz prepared as best they could. They bribed as many Christians as they could reach, giving 400 *zekukim* of silver to the local count and the bishop and the city fathers, and sending Emich seven pounds of pure gold. The city and the bishop promised them protection, but Emich was not moved. The Jews armed themselves and retreated to the inner courtyard of the bishop's palace. After two days the intimidated townspeople opened the gates to Emich's horde and the Jews awaited their fate. They were ready to defend themselves, but they were not soldiers and were no match for Emich's mob:

> The hand of the Lord rested heavily on His people. Then the Gentiles rose against the Jews in the courtyard and began to exterminate them. The bishop's men, who had promised help, being like broken reeds, were the first to flee, and the bishop himself ran from his church since the enemy wanted to kill him too, for speaking in favour of the Jews. The enemy entered the courtyard on the third day

of Sivan, a day of gloom and clouds and thick darkness. Alas for this day on which we saw the torment of our soul! O stars, why did you not withhold your light?

When the people of the Sacred Covenant saw that heaven's decree was issued against them, and that the enemy were entering the courtyard, they cried out together in a great voice, 'Let us stay no longer, for the enemy is upon us. Let us hasten and offer ourselves as a sacrifice before God. Let us examine our knives to see that they are not defective and then kill ourselves in sanctification of the Eternal One. Friends, cut your throats, or thrust the knife into the belly.'

The foe hurled missiles and arrows at them, but our people did not flee. The enemy rushed in and put all they could find to the sword, in slaughter and destruction. Then our women girded their loins with strength and resolution. They slew their own sons and daughters, and then themselves. Many men also took courage into their hearts and killed their wives and children and babes. The most gentle and tender of mothers killed the little one of her delight. Young and old, men and women, arose and killed one another. From the windows of the courtyard, maidens and brides and bridegrooms called out: 'Look and behold, O Lord, what we are doing to sanctify Thy Great Name. We will not exchange You for a crucified scion who was despised, abominated, and held in contempt in his own generation, a bastard son conceived by a menstruating and wanton mother.'

On that day, the third of Sivan, one thousand and one hundred holy souls were killed and slaughtered, the souls of innocent poor people. Wilt Thou restrain Thyself for these things, O Lord? It was for You that innumerable souls were slain!

After the massacre at Mainz the crusaders moved on quickly. Chaotic, predatory bands surged and eddied balefully through southern Germany, overwhelming Jewish communities in Cologne, Neuss, Eller, Xanten, Trier and Metz. No doubt Count Emich was the chief instigator of these disasters, but he was not the only Christian leader with a hatred and contempt for Jews. As the armies headed eastward, away from the Rhineland, there were further attacks by Folkmar on the

Jews of Prague, and by Gottschalk and Peter the Hermit in Ratisbon and Regensburg where both men tried to force wholesale conversion on the Jewish communities.

In summer, after several weeks of terror against Jews, the capricious whirlwind of crusaders blew away to the east, leaving inconsolate elders to reflect on the long tragedy of Jewish history: 'God, maker of peace,' wrote Solomon bar Simson with unconscious irony, 'turned aside and averted His eyes from His people, and consigned them to the sword. No prophet, seer, or man of wisdom was able to understand how the sin of the people was deemed so great as to cause the destruction of so many Jewish lives in so many communities. These martyrs endured the extreme penalty normally reserved only for murderers. Yet it must be stated with certainty that God is a righteous judge, and we are to blame.'

If Jews bowed their heads, humble in the face of an inscrutable God, certain Christians, at least, were horrified and ashamed. What could one expect, wrote Albert of Aix, from 'foolish and insanely fickle wandering people', who believed that a goose was inspired by the Holy Spirit, and followed a nanny-goat as a mascot? Their guilt was manifest in their failure. 'So the hand of the Lord is believed to have been against the pilgrims, who had sinned by excessive impurity and fornication. They had slaughtered the exiled Jews out of greed for money, not for the sake of God's justice, although the Jews were opposed to Christ. Our Lord is a just judge and orders no one unwillingly or under compulsion to bear the yoke of the Catholic faith.'

Loaded with spoils from the Jewish communities in Germany, the Christian mobs hurried on to the borders of Hungary. They were heading eventually for Constantinople, where they hoped, with the help of the Byzantine emperor, to cross into Turkish territory. Then their real trials would begin. Now success and easy plunder were gradually left behind. The eastern borderlands of Europe, in late summer, were fertile and able to support an army on the move, but it was remote land, sparsely populated by peoples who knew very little of the Franks and their western allies. The country

was wild, the road unclear, provisioning difficult. The crusaders pressed on with their usual high-handed insolence.
Abbot Guibert wrote:

> Our men, strangers as they were, came to such a marvel-
> lous pitch of madness that they began to tread the people
> of the country underfoot.
> These Hungarian folk willingly offered all things for
> sale, as Christians to Christians. Yet our wanton pilgrims,
> forgetful of the hospitality they had received, fought their
> hosts without any cause, thinking that they were peaceful
> folk who would not resist them. Thus, with execrable mad-
> ness, they set fire to the public stores of wheat, violated
> girls, carried away wives, plucked the beards of the men or
> singed them with fire. Now there was no longer any talk
> of buying the things necessary for life, but everyone set
> himself to robbery and bloodshed with all his might, shout-
> ing such boasts as, 'Thus will we do against the Turks.'

The further the armies went, the worse was their conduct,
unshackled entirely from the restraints of their own lands and
customs. When they were held up by the Danube, the followers of Peter the Hermit tore apart a wooden village, to
make rafts for their crossing. At Semlin, Peter's men were
enraged to see crusader arms and armour hanging from the
town walls, as a warning to other marauders to stay away. This
was only an added incitement to violence, and the army of
Peter stormed and ransacked the town. Advancing into
Bulgaria and the Balkan mountains, a land already notorious
for banditry and sudden death, the undisciplined western
armies became so fragmented, wilful and lost that they were
soon easy prey to the fierce bands of mountainmen of the
region. By the beginning of August the tattered remnants of
the expeditions led by Walter the Penniless and Peter the
Herbit were straggling into the suburbs of Constantinople,
'with a certain number of recruits from Germany, and with
the last dregs of our own Frankish army, saved but barely alive
after the slaughters on the way'.
At first, Emperor Alexius received the woebegone western
mob with sympathy, providing the remains of the army with

lodgings and supplies. However, he refused permission to cross the Bosphorus into Asia Minor, saying – rightly – that the poor Christian force would be no match for the large warlike masses of the Turks. This prohibition was received with ill-grace and soon, as Abbot Guibert reported, the crusaders reverted to their familiar, violent, destructive ways:

> They tore down palaces in the city, set fire to public build-ings, stripped lead off the churches and sold it to the Greeks. Then the troubled Emperor forgot his former rea-sons for delay and absolutely commanded them to cross the Bosphorus. On the other side of the strait their conduct in no way improved. Vowed to fight the heathens, they every-where plundered Christians, unrestrained either by the heavy hand of a king or by the fear of God. Therefore they fell into sudden ruin, for it is written, 'Death cometh to meet undisciplined folk, and short-lived are all things that lack thought and moderation.'
>
> There were in the army some recruits from southern Italy, Lombardy and Germany who became impatient of the pride of the Franks, and so they separated themselves. For these Franks, as their very name signifies, are extremely vivacious, but unless they be strictly curbed and controlled they are fierce to excess amid other nations. Therefore the men from across the Alps parted from the Franks, chose a certain Rainald as their leader and marched into the king-dom of Roum. Four days' march beyond Nicaea they found a deserted town, which they occupied and took their fill of the stores laid up there. Soon after, at Michaelmas, the Turks came up with them and attacked, pressing the siege so hard that our men were closely shut in without any water. They thirsted till they were forced to bleed their horses to drink the blood. Others dipped kerchiefs and linen into sewers, to squeeze the moisture into their mouths. Others, to cool their burning flesh, dug pits and lay under the fresh-turned earth.
>
> After eight long days the town fell. Many of our men fled over to the Turks and abode with them forever. But very many of our army were taken captive. Some, when commanded to deny Christ, with lips and soul refused and were beheaded. Others had the curse of a slower death, sent to slavery under savage masters, or set up as targets

ALEXIUS I COMNENUS BEFORE CHRIST

for enemy arrows. These were the first martyrs for God under our new and almost desperate conditions.

Meanwhile Peter the Hermit, being oftentimes vexed with the great madness of his companions and troubled by their frequent defeats, had given over the leadership of his own Frankish army to Walter the Penniless. He was a man of great personal courage, better able, or so Peter thought, to restrain the foolish by military authority. Therefore Walter, with that army of madmen, went by forced marches to Civitot, a city beyond Nicaea. But the Turks, following swiftly on the heels of our soldiers, caught Walter midway and slew him with the greater part of his men. By then, Peter the Hermit had already departed to Constantinople, unable to restrain our people and fearing to be part of their unbridled and foolish levity.

Some of Walter's men escaped to Civitot. Others, unable to fly, preferred to be drowned in the sea rather than fall into Turkish hands. Some ran into the wastes of the mountains to hide amid the rocks, and others fled into the forest. When the Turks had chased and captured all they could find, they laid siege to Civitot, trying to burn out the defenders, and then storming the walls. When the town was taken our men were treated as before, facing death or a new life of slavery in some remote province belonging to the enemy. This was done in October 1096.

The Emperor, when he learnt of this disaster among the faithful, allowed the survivors back across the Bosphorus into Greece. But he insisted that they should wander no more, and he made a law to the effect that they must sell their arms. Such was the fate of the peasants' army, the company of soldiers and pilgrims that followed Peter the Hermit. And certain it is that they gave no hope to the true pilgrims of the Cross, but rather inspired the Turks with boldness and pride.

It was a lesson for the West, among many to be learnt, that it would take more than a rabble of Christian adventurers to defeat the Turks. The road to Jerusalem was not so easily won.

4

MARCHING EAST

'Off we go now,' they sang on the road, 'selling our fiefs, to win God's Temple, and lay the Saracens low.'

Marching feet stirred the late summer dust. The sun beat down on breathless days, awaiting the autumnal turn. The countryside had a wan, defeated look, washed out by heat and dryness. Day by day, the mass of people went on steadily. Few knew the length, or even the direction, of the road, but the marchers swung along in good order, full of energy and hopes and coarse humour. At last, the princes and their armies were on the move.

The first act in the service of God, for nobles and knights, was the raising of money. A knight was ashamed to take the field without the accoutrements of his class and calling. The violent power of western knighthood in battle rested on the charge and terrific onrush of heavy cavalry, and a knight needed many expensive things to maintain this grip on the battlefield. Immediate funds had to be found for weapons, armour, horses, servants, and the fitting out of retainers. Further sums were required, continually and sometimes in desperate measures, for the supply and support of a large number of followers and their animals on a journey of more than fifteen hundred miles across alien territory hardly known to the West. At the end of that journey was a campaign against a strong enemy in a hostile land. No one could know how much it would all cost, but after hard experience knights began to see that the expense, each year, might be three or four times as much as a man's annual income from his land.

Land, in most cases, was all a knight had. The nobles of Europe were members of an agrarian economy and even the greatest had few material possessions beyond his landholdings. To raise money a man must sell, mortgage, alienate or arrange loans on land. If he were to be a crusader, to dispossess himself became a holy duty, and Pope Urban himself had tried to smooth this path of necessity by threatening to excommunicate all those who prevented, or extorted gross profits from, the sale or mortgage of feudal lands. The ideal commitment to the crusading task was shown by two great lords of northern France, the brothers Godfrey of Bouillon and Baldwin of Boulogne, who, 'seized by the hope of an eternal inheritance and by love, prepared to go to fight for God in Jerusalem by relinquishing and selling all their possessions'.

A crusader's vows, if resolutely kept, came at a high price. Yet hardly less was demanded, in integrity and ingenuity, from those who provided the money needed by the knights. In the enthusiasm of the time, to make the journey to the Holy Land, there was a surplus of every commodity from corn to castles, and prices were seriously depressed. Few financiers and merchants had the cash to make large loans. A great lord might raise funds by imposts and taxes on his tenants, but it was not in the spirit of the crusade to win the Holy City on the backs of pauperized peasants. So the best and sometimes the only source of funds was the enduring and ever-accumulating Church, whose adventure this was in any case. Bishoprics and monasteries, particularly in France, scoured to the very bottom of their treasure-chests. To raise the money to pay for Godfrey's castle at Bouillon, the bishop of Liège stripped his diocese of relics, plate and jewels. Monasteries, sometimes with reluctance, acquired by purchase or mortgage more property than they knew what to do with. It seemed as if a

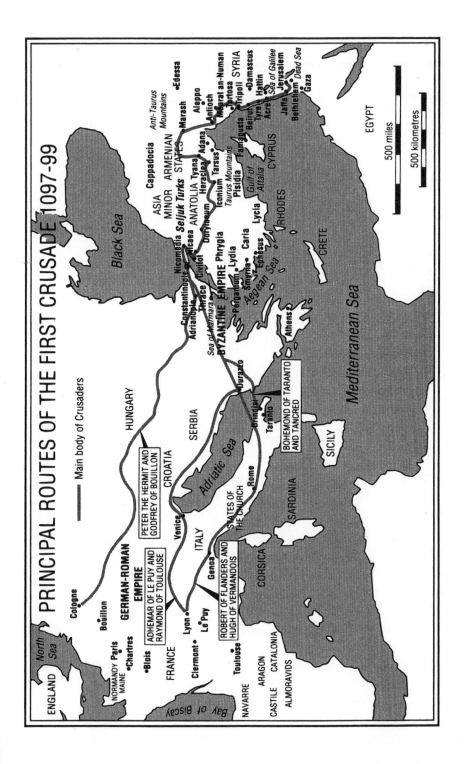

PRINCIPAL ROUTES OF THE FIRST CRUSADE 1097-99

——— Main body of Crusaders

PETER THE HERMIT AND GODFREY OF BOUILLON

ADHEMAR OF LE PUY AND RAYMOND OF TOULOUSE

ROBERT OF FLANDERS AND HUGH OF VERMANDOIS

BOHEMOND OF TARANTO AND TANCRED

ENGLAND
North Sea
Bay of Biscay
NORMANDY
MAINE
Paris
Chartres
Blois
Clermont
FRANCE
Lyon
Le Puy
Toulouse
NAVARRE
ARAGON
CASTILE
CATALONIA
ALMORAVIDS
Genoa
Rome
ITALY
STATES OF THE CHURCH
Venice
Corsica
SARDINIA
SICILY
Brindisi
Taranto
Adriatic Sea
CROATIA
SERBIA
HUNGARY
GERMAN-ROMAN EMPIRE
Bouillon
Cologne
Durazzo
Mediterranean Sea
Black Sea
Constantinople
Adrianople
Thrace
Sea of Marmara
Nicomedia
Nicaea
Civitot
BYZANTINE EMPIRE
Pergamum
Smyrna
Ephesus
Athens
Aegean Sea
CRETE
RHODES
Lydia
Caria
Lycia
Phrygia
Dorylaeum
ASIA MINOR
Seljuk Turks
ANATOLIA
Cappadocia
Anti-Taurus Mountains
Pisidia
Gulf of Attalia
Attalia
Taurus Mountains
Iconium
Tyana
Heraclea
Adana
Tarsus
Marash
ARMENIAN STATES
Edessa
Aleppo
Antioch
CYPRUS
Famagusta
Beirut
Tyre
Acre
Jaffa
Bethlehem
Jerusalem
Hattin
Sea of Galilee
Dead Sea
Gaza
Tripoli
Tortosa
Ma'arat an-Numan
Damascus
SYRIA
EGYPT

500 miles

500 kilometres

spectacular financial transaction was as much a badge of the crusade as the cross worn on the clothes. When Duke Robert of Normandy, the brother of the English king, needed money for his journey, he gave a five-year mortgage on the whole duchy of Normandy to King William II for the very large sum of 10,000 silver marks.

The burden of debt laid on the land was heavy for the crusader to bear but often even heavier for the family left behind. If two or more members of a family set out, such was the expense of the preparation, and so much land was disposed of, that there was very little left at home for their households to live on. Yet these occasions were not rare. In companionship, many relatives departed together, even among the highest families of the land. There was even some competition within families not to be outdone in the service of the Lord. Godfrey, Baldwin and Eustace, three powerful sons of Countess Ida of Bouillon, all started together for the Holy Land. Bohemond of Taranto, the leader of the Normans from southern Italy and Sicily, had in his entourage his three nephews Tancred, Robert and William. Even the papal legate, Adhemar of Le Puy, was accompanied by his brother William of Monteil.

Where the great men led, many lesser bands of brothers and relatives followed. They were willing to risk immediate impoverishment, not only for themselves but also for their families. They put the future in jeopardy, for the sake of an uncertain destiny in a far-off land. Often their motives are cloudy to history. Who would not expect wilfulness and ambition in these headstrong, ignorant men? Whatever their sins, however, they were not lacking in idealism when they set out.

Abbot Guibert of Nogent saw the armies leave, marching under colours of hope and faith: 'These men left their illustrious wives and beloved children, making light of all men hold dearest for the sake of an exile on which they had set their hearts. To abandon honours and possessions is nothing. These things are no part of our true selves. But it fills us with amazement that the mutual love of husband and wife, firmly fixed by their tenderness for their offspring, could be torn apart by this departure without peril to either side.'

After the Feast of the Assumption, 15 August 1096, with the early harvest showing an abundance of grain and the grapes hanging thick and full on the vines, the four chief armies of the crusading princes began a slow, unco-ordinated drift towards the East. Among the first away was Hugh of Vermandois, brother of the French king and the standard-bearer for the kingdom of France since his brother Philip was still excommunicated by the pope. Anxious perhaps to establish his pre-eminence, Hugh the Great (as he was known) hurried down the leg of Italy to Bari and immediately took ship. 'He landed,' wrote Fulcher of Chartres, 'at the city of Durazzo with his own men. But having imprudently departed with only a scant army, he was seized by the citizens there and brought to the Emperor Alexius at Constantinople, where he was detained for a considerable time, not altogether free.'

It was a warning. Life in the eastern lands of Europe, where Alexius and the Greeks held the ground between Christ and Mohammed, was more difficult and strange than simple westerners realized. So when the main body of crusaders from Provence and southern France set out under the legate Adhemar and Raymond of St Gilles, they followed the same Italian route but they did not rush. Raymond, Count of Toulouse, was already over fifty, the oldest, richest and most experienced of the crusading nobles. Often, by advice or wealth, he was able to put right a bad situation. Though his campaigning instincts were sound, and his importance was recognized, he was not well liked, being cold and aloof, nor was he beyond suspicion for avarice and too much pride. His army went steadily down Italy, gathering many Italian knights and foot-soldiers on the way, and in the autumn sailed in good order to Ragusa in Dalamatia.

Two contingents set out from northern France. The first, under Godfrey of Bouillon and his brothers Baldwin and Eustace, followed the route already taken by the people's crusade of Peter the Hermit. This road went through southern and eastern Germany, into Hungary and Bulgaria, and entered the territory of the Byzantine Empire. Many Germans attached themselves to the army as it passed, their initial distaste for this papal adventure overcome by the extraordinary

A SIXTH-CENTURY MOSAIC SHOWING A FLEET
AND FORTIFICATION

pageantry of an army that marched, under the sign of the cross, in the name of Christ. The reputation of the leader, Duke Godfrey, may also have persuaded knights to risk all on a foreign field. He was a noble of many virtues and some genuine piety, respected, brave and moderate, but still capable of falling into temptation, as he did when he extorted bribes from the Jewish elders in Cologne and Mainz, though the western emperor, Henry IV, had given him orders to leave the Jewish communities alone. Contradictions of character were nothing new in crusaders. Even in men of worth and religious feeling, it was not possible to find unsullied goodness.

The second army from northern France got away late, in October, and then tried to make up time. It was impressively led by some of the most powerful princes of the West, the chief one being the eldest son of William the Conqueror, Robert of Normandy, who had pawned his duchy to pay for his crusade. He was joined by Robert of Flanders, lord of many wide acres, and by Stephen of Blois, the Conqueror's son-in-law. He was a man noted for careful words which seemed to the bolder spirits more like timidity than wisdom, but he was certainly rich and well-connected, being master, 'if fame speaks truly', of as many castles as there were days in the year.

Hurrying after their late start, these men took the Italian route, hoping to take ship before the winter storms. Pope Urban met them and blessed the army near Lucca. Then, going on to Rome, these crusaders found a crowd loyal to the anti-pope ready to confront them in St Peter's Cathedral. As the crusaders prayed before the altar, certain ruffians 'ran up and down on the roof of the church itself, throwing stones at us as we lay prostrate and prayed'.

'We were very grieved when we saw such a great atrocity,' Fulcher wrote, 'but we earnestly wished for nothing to be done except as the Lord would punish them. But many who had come this far with us, without hesitation, now weak with cowardice, returned to their homes.' Pilgrims had set out to face the Muslims. To be caught in Church rivalries, and put under a rain of stones in St Peter's precinct, was for many more than faith could stand.

Hardly two months had gone by and already the realities of the journey and the limits of idealism were becoming apparent. Fulcher found it a painful process of learning: 'Then going through the middle of Campania, we came to Bari, a wealthy town on the edge of the sea. In the Church of St Nicholas we prayed to God effusively. Then, approaching the harbour, we thought to cross the sea at that time. But with the sailors and fickle fortune against us, and with winter weather threatening danger to us, it was necessary that Robert of Normandy withdraw us to Calabria, to spend the severe winter weather, though Count Robert of Flanders with his men did risk and get across the sea. Failed by their leaders and fearing the future, again many of our people sold their bows, took up their pilgrims' staves, and returned home like cowards. For this, they were held worthless by God as well as men, and they became utterly disgraced.'

Great princes, however honourable their first intentions, were not excused from folly and misjudgment. Nor was it likely that all crusaders would share the high aspirations and fervour of the leaders. In the ranks of the armies were, as usual, many men of dubious virtue and poor intentions, with little to lose and much to gain, for whom the crusade promised a change of fortune. The English chronicler William of Malmesbury, writing shortly after the First Crusade, commented drily: 'Then the Welshman left his forests and neglected his hunting. The Scotsman deserted his fleas with which he is most familiar. The Dane abandoned his drink and was temporarily sober. And the man of Norway turned his back on raw fish.'

For men such as these, the crusade was intended to lead to a better life, and progress in that direction was subject to a daily calculation. At any moment it was always possible to cut one's losses and return to fleas, drink or raw fish.

The religious foundation of the crusade, real but insecure and laid in haste without deep footings, carried a large superstructure of ambition and self-interest. And nowhere was this more apparent than in the fourth of the crusading armies. In the summer of 1096 a force of Normans from southern Italy and Sicily was besieging Amalfi under two tough soldiers, Roger of Sicily and Bohemond of Taranto. Bohemond, younger, more energetic and daring than his uncle Roger, was also the nephew of Robert Guiscard and was not far short of that famous general in the arts of war. He had already twice defeated armies of the Greek emperor. In the dog days of summer, as the siege dragged on under the idle sun of the south, it came to his notice that a more glamorous and worthy venture was afoot. That was sufficient for Bohemond. As if on a whim he rallied his Norman knights, enthused them with unexpected Christian spirit and abruptly broke away from Amalfi.

> As for Bohemond, that great warrior, he was besieging Amalfi when he heard that an immense army of Frankish crusaders had arrived, on their way to the Holy Sepulchre and ready to fight the pagans. So he began to make careful enquiries as to the arms they carried, the badge which they wore in Christ's pilgrimage, and the war-cry which they shouted in battle. He was told, 'They are well-armed, they wear the badge of Christ's cross on the right arm or between

the shoulders, and as a war-cry they shouted all together: "God's will, God's will, God's will."' Then Bohemond, inspired by the Holy Ghost, ordered his most valuable cloak to be cut up forthwith and be made into crosses, and most of the knights who were at the siege began to join him at once, full of enthusiasm, so that Count Roger was left almost alone, and when he had gone back to Sicily he grieved and lamented because he had lost his army.

A small skirmish was abandoned, a greater opportunity grasped. The strong Norman instinct for the spoils of war scented more glorious prey and larger rewards in the Holy Land. This sudden, bold step was typical of Bohemond. His progress, so full of imagination and swift colourful strokes, was narrated with wonder and appreciation by an anonymous knight of his army in a book called the *Gesta Francorum* – 'The Deeds of the Franks' – a blunt, soldierly account that follows the crusade in all its tragic, foolish and courageous adventures down to the triumphant conquest of the Holy City three years later:

All our Norman knights crossed the sea at Bohemond's expense. They reached western Macedonia, where they found plenty of wine and things to eat, and going down into the valley of the Drina they waited for their men to come to them. Then Bohemond called a council to encourage his

THE CRUSADERS FIGHT THE TURKS AT CONSTANTINOPLE

army, and to warn them to be courteous and to refrain from plundering that land, which belonged to Christians. No one was to take more than he needed for his food.

Then we set out and travelled through very rich country till we came to Kastoria, where we held the feast of Christmas. We stayed for some days trying to buy provisions, but the inhabitants would sell us none, because they were much afraid of us, thinking us to be no pilgrims but plunderers come to lay waste their land and kill them. So we seized oxen, horses, asses and whatever else we could find and went on to Monastir, where there was a castle of heretics. We attacked this place from all sides and it soon fell. So we set fire to it and burnt the castle and all the inhabitants together. After this we reached the river Vardar. My lord Bohemond crossed over with some of his men but left others behind.

Then the army of the emperor of Constantinople came and attacked those left behind. When Tancred, Bohemond's nephew, heard this, he dived into the river and swam back to the others with two thousand men following him. They found Turcopuli and Patzinaks, pagan mercenaries of the Greeks, fighting our men. So they made a sudden, gallant charge, and since they were good and experienced soldiers they routed the enemy, captured many and took them bound to my lord Bohemond. He said to them, 'Rogues, why do you kill Christ's people and mine? I have no quarrel with your emperor!' And they answered, 'How can we do otherwise? The emperor commands and we must obey.' So Bohemond let them go scot-free. This battle was on Ash Wednesday, 18 February 1097. Blessed be God in all His works.

Here, in a few paragraphs, was another catalogue of crusader misconceptions. Local Christian inhabitants, from whom the westerners expected help and provisions, feared soldiers who looked like, and too often acted like, a band of invading brigands. Though the Muslims were the enemy, it was not easy for crusaders to differentiate between kinds of religious error. Christian heretics such as the unlucky folk of Monastir, who were most probably followers of the Manichee sect, were as likely as Muslims to feel the deadly bite of western swords. Nor was it clear whether the Greeks of the Byzantine Empire, allies of the West in name, resented the crusaders more than they needed them. Conflict was always but a short step away between these two branches of the Christian faith. However, the crusade could hardly proceed without the goodwill and active help of the Greeks. Bohemond, the most politic and astute of the western leaders, and a man who knew the Greeks well since he had twice defeated them, was careful at this early stage not to antagonize Emperor Alexius.

While most crusaders were following the route into Italy and making a sea-crossing of the Adriatic, the northern French contingent led by Godfrey of Bouillon was marching along the blood-marked land route to the East, following hard on the heels of the Christian rabble of Peter the Hermit and Walter the Penniless. Very soon, to the surprise of the knights, they came up against the virulent animosity aroused by the passage of the people's crusade. At the Hungarian border, Godfrey and his army were forced to stop and take stock. 'They remained there three weeks in the month of September,' wrote Albert of Aix, 'to hear and to understand why sedition had arisen; why that army had perished but a little time before; and why those whom they met returning in despair had been turned from the road to Jerusalem with their chiefs and leaders.'

The Hungarian king forcefully made his displeasure known to the crusaders and insisted on taking hostages to ensure good conduct as the army passed through Hungary. To show that he had the best of intentions Duke Godfrey left his own brother Baldwin, together with his wife and children. 'Then after camp was pitched, and all were settled at rest, Duke Godfrey sent heralds to say at each habitation and tent that, under sentence of death, no man should touch or take by force anything in the kingdom of Hungary, nor stir up quarrels, but that everything should be exchanged for a just price. And so, day by day, in peace and quiet, with full measure and just sale, the duke and his people crossed the kingdom of Hungary and arrived at the river Drave.'

At the Bulgarian border, passing over into the lands of the eastern empire, Godfrey was met by envoys from Emperor Alexius backed by an intimidating display of Greek force. Again, promises were made and exchanged, and the crusaders marched on to Philippopolis, provided by the emperor with 'a wonderful abundance of food, grain, barley, wine, oil, and very much game'.

It was too much to expect that these pleasantries would last:

> At this time, a message was brought to the duke that Hugh the Great, brother of the king of France, was being held by the emperor in prison and in chains. When he heard this, Duke Godfrey demanded liberty for the prince, or he himself would not keep faith with the emperor. Then hiding his wrath, the duke set out for Adrianople. After swimming his horses across a river, he camped for the night. On the next day, the citizens barred the bridge to the duke's people, so they hastened to Salabria and pitched tents in pleasant meadows. There a messenger returned to say that the emperor had not released the captive prince. Thereupon the duke and his followers burned with anger and refused to keep the treaty of peace any longer. By the command of Duke Godfrey, all that land was given over to be plundered by the knights, who delayed there for eight days, laying waste the whole region.

Then Alexius was quickly brought to his senses. Subtle and accommodating man that he was, he was learning that it was no trifling matter to upset the crusaders of the West.

Alexius learnt fast, but among the western armies it seemed that each group repeated the mistakes and trials of those who had gone before. The army led by Count Raymond of St Gilles and the papal legate Adhemar, whose importance made this body of soldiers the heart of the crusade, had crossed the sea to Ragusa in October without trouble. Winter closed upon them, and soon they were lost and puzzled in the Balkan mountains. Raymond of Aguilers, chronicler of this expedition and chaplain to his namesake Count Raymond, had many complaints about the loathsome country.

> Slavonia was such a desert and so pathless and mountainous that we saw in it neither beasts nor birds for three weeks. The people of this land were so boorish and rude that they would neither trade with us nor guide us, but vanished from

their villages. They even butchered the feeble aged and the weak poor who, out of infirmity, followed our army. The bandits who harried us on the road knew the country, so it was not easy for our knights to pursue and correct them amid steep mountains and thick woods. On a certain occasion, when Count Raymond and some knights were hedged about and attacked by the men of that land, he felt compelled to make an example of six captives, in order to escape from their fellows who violently assailed him. He ordered the eyes of some of the prisoners to be torn out, the feet cut off some, and the noses and hands of the rest to be slashed. Then while the enemy was pre-occupied with sorrow, by the grace of God the count and his knights could escape.

We were in Slavonia about forty days, during which time we met clouds so dense we could feel them and push them before us. At length, through the compassion of God, our army crossed out of that land without losing a single person from hunger nor any in open battle. So I bear witness that God wanted His army to cross safely, in order that the brutes who did not know Christ might, through the valour and patience of His knights, lose something of their wildness or be brought without excuse under God's judgment.

It was painful enough to suffer the savagery of the mountainmen, but these westerners had as yet not met the Greeks. When this happened, there were more dire surprises:

> We came to Durazzo. We believed we were in a country like our own, thinking that Emperor Alexius and the peoples under him were our brothers and helpmates. But these servants of the emperor raged like lions, attacking peaceful pilgrims who, at that moment, had war far from their thoughts. We were butchered in secret places. They stole what they could, by night, in the woods, in places remote from the camp. Although they raged thus, their leader promised peace. We chose to continue the journey and not to avenge our wrongs. On the way we had letters from the emperor about peace, brotherhood, and, as I may also say, about alliance. But this was a snare in words. For all about us Turks, Cumans, Uzi, Tanaces, Patzinaks and Bulgarians, all mercenaries of the Greeks, were lying in ambush for us.
>
> On a certain day, when we were in the valley of Pelagonia,

the legate, Bishop Adhemar of Le Puy, withdrew a little from the camp to rest. Some Patzinaks caught him, knocked him from his mule, robbed him and beat him severely on the head. But since so great a priest was still necessary to the people of God, by divine mercy one of the Patzinaks drove off his fellows, intending to have the spoils to himself, and thereby saved the bishop's life. But the noise of the tumult was heard in the camp, and the legate was rescued.

Chased and attacked on the road, repulsing raiders with powerful retribution, burning whole towns for the loss of a few men, the army of Count Raymond came within easy reach of Constantinople. Here the count was met by messengers from Alexius. The envoys said that it was the wish of other western leaders, already in Constantinople, that Raymond should go to the city for consultation, unarmed and with few attendants. Time was flying, plans had to be made, a battle was surely imminent. The emperor was well-disposed, and he himself would take the cross and lead the crusaders, to ensure that supplies were made available. All the allies needed was the wisdom and experience of the Count of Toulouse. Full of his own importance, Raymond went unarmed into Constantinople.

Now the crusading army was almost complete. Only one contingent was still absent, the one made up of the unlucky knights who had missed the autumnal sailing and had wintered miserably in Calabria. On Easter Day, 1097, under Robert of Normandy they set sail from Brindisi to find that chance was still against them. One of their ships, hardly out of the harbour, split and foundered, killing some four hundred men and women, with the loss also of horses, mules and much money. Seeing the hand of God against them once more, many abandoned the pilgrimage and went home.

'But with hope in Almighty God deep within us, with topsails raised again, and with a great trumpet sound, we thrust ourselves upon the sea when the wind was blowing gently. On the fourth day we reached land about ten miles, I judge, from the city of Durazzo.'

At last God was merciful. The peoples of the region, so bitter and treacherous against the first waves of crusaders, kept out of sight. The only injuries suffered were from the enmity

PLAN OF CONSTANTINOPLE MADE FOR PILGRIMS OF THE CITY

of nature, from landslip and rock-falls, exposure, or the force of water in the crossing of mountain torrents. The march itself went swiftly, and within five weeks these crusaders were ready to camp in front of Constantinople.

By April 1097, with the various strands of the crusading army camped in the suburbs and surrounds of Constantinople,

Emperor Alexius had cause to worry. He did not like or trust westerners. He was distressed by their gross habits, their smell, their uncouth manners, their violence and rowdiness, and most of all by their courage and power in battle. He had reason to fear the crusading princes. He knew they were men of high ambition, and he had no reason to think that their idealism would survive the test of time. Much of what they hoped to gain was likely to be at the expense of the Greek empire. Though all were Christians, his religion was not quite their religion. The western campaign so far had made the crusaders weary, angry, frustrated, quick to take offence, and deeply suspicious of the Greeks and their mercenaries. Ordinary knights and foot-soldiers, camped within sight of many wonders but restricted and policed within Constantinople, were bored and resentful at what they could see but not touch.

'O, what an excellent and beautiful city!' cried Fulcher of Chartres. 'How many wonderful and grandly built monasteries and palaces! How many marvellous things in every district and all the streets! It is tedious to recite the wealth of the goods found here, of gold, silver, precious cloth and holy relics. In every season, the busy ships of the merchants bring here everything that men might need. I judge that almost twenty thousand eunuchs are kept here continuously.'

A priest, such as Fulcher, might be content only to wonder, but the curiosity of simple western soldiers, dazzled by a display of opulence that was beyond their dreams, could take more rapacious forms. Alexius wanted the crusaders safely across the Bosphorus as quickly as possible, but not before he had tried to extract oaths of loyalty from all the chief nobles. He succeeded with all except Raymond of St Gilles, and he had to be content with that. Then with forceful courtesy, and with many gifts, he sent his awkward guests into the land of the Seljuk Turks.

We crossed the sea which they call the Arm of St George. Then we hastened to the city of Nicaea, which Lord Bohemond, Duke Godfrey, Count Raymond and the Count of Flanders had already surrounded in siege by the middle of May. This city was in the possession of the eastern Turks, who were very keen archers and bowmen. These Turks had subjugated the whole land of Roum as far as the city of Nicomedia.

'As we went into this land, O how many severed heads and bones of the dead did we find lying on the plains beyond Nicomedia. In the preceding year, the Turks destroyed the inhabitants of this region, who were not used to this kind of archery. We shed many tears at this sight.

Robert of Normandy and Stephen of Blois brought the last division of the army up to Nicaea. The crusaders were now one force, united in the field for the first time. In their march they had seen the heads and bones of a defeated people, and they knew that a strong, hard enemy awaited them. The serious task of the crusade was about to begin.

We took up station in front of the city, which was so closely besieged by land that none dared go out or in. For the first time, our men were all collected together in this place, and who could count such a great number of Christians? I do not think that anyone has ever seen, or will ever again see, so many valiant knights.

On one side of the city was a great lake, on which Turkish boats went to and fro, bringing food and wood and many other things to the city. So our leaders took counsel and sent to Constantinople to ask the emperor to dispatch boats to Civitot where there was a harbour, and to have oxen to drag these boats over the mountains to the lake. The emperor did this, and sent his Turcopuli with them. Then at a certain daybreak there were the boats, in good order, sailing across the lake towards the city. The Turks, not recognizing these boats, were surprised. But when they realized that the fleet belonged to the emperor, they were afraid almost to death. They began to wail and lament, while the Franks rejoiced and gave glory to God.

We besieged this city for seven weeks and three days, and many of our men suffered martyrdom there. They gave up their blessed souls to God with joy and gladness, and many of the poor starved to death in the Name of Christ. All these entered heaven in triumph, wearing the robe of martyrdom, saying with one voice, 'Avenge, O Lord, our

blood which was shed for Thee, for Thou art blessed and
worthy of praise for ever and ever.'

Nicaea fell on the day of the summer solstice, 19 June 1097.
In this test of arms the Turks had made themselves known as
warriors who knew their business. Victory had gone to an army
vastly superior in numbers. The long attrition of the siege had
worn down the garrison, and the fall of the city was no great
triumph for the West. The crusaders went away from Nicaea
in a sober mood, with much to reflect on.

Before dawn, our men arose, and because it was dark they
could not see to keep together, but divided into two bands.
And thus they travelled for two days. On the third day the
Turks made a sudden and fierce attack on Bohemond and his
comrades. The enemy began all at once to howl and roar and
shout, bellowing in their own language some devilish words
that I do not understand. In the midst of innumerable Turks,
valiant Bohemond ordered all his knights to dismount at once
and quickly form a defensive camp. 'Men,' cried he, 'brave
soldiers of Christ, you can see that we are encircled and that
the battle will be hard, so let the knights advance and fight
with courage while the foot-soldiers pitch a camp.'

As we prepared ourselves, the Turks came upon us from
all sides, throwing darts and javelins and shooting arrows
from an astonishing range. Under the weight of the charge
from so many foes still we went forward as one man. The
women in our camp were a great help to us that day, for
they carried water to the fighting men in that heat, and gave
comfort and encouragement to our hard-pressed soldiers. My
lord Bohemond sent hasty messengers to find the leaders of
the other band, to Count Raymond and Duke Godfrey, to
Hugh the Great and the bishop of Le Puy, to summon them
to the battlefield with all speed, saying, 'If any of you wants
a fight today, let him come and play the man.' Duke Godfrey,
reckless and brave, and Hugh the Great came first, followed
by the Count of St Gilles and the bishop.

Whence came this great cloud of Turks and Saracens,
people whose names I do not know? The whole country,
from the mountains to the valleys, was covered with this
accursed folk. For our part we sent a secret message along
the line, praising God and saying, 'Hold fast, trust in Christ,

and in the victory of the Holy Cross. Today, please God, we will all gain much booty.'

That description was from the anonymous knight of the *Gesta*, a stout-hearted Norman for whom fighting was the familiar task of manhood. He gives little impression of the panic and fear overwhelming the band of crusaders. The more timorous priest Fulcher, who was also there, gives a truer picture of ordinary folk staring at death in the heat and dust of an alien land:

> All of us, huddled together like sheep in a fold, trembling and terrified, were fenced in by the enemy on all sides, so that we could not turn in any direction. It was evident that this had befallen us because of our sins. For dissipation had polluted certain ones, and avarice or some other iniquity had corrupted others. There was a vast cry smiting the heavens, of men and women and little children, and also of the heathens who rushed upon us. No hope of life remained.
>
> Then we confessed that we were culprits and sinners, humbly begging mercy from God. The bishop of Le Puy, our Protector, and four other bishops were there. There were also many priests, clothed in white vestments, who besought the Lord most humbly to overthrow the strength of our enemy and pour the gifts of His mercy on us. They sang weeping, and they wept singing. Men, fearing immediate death, ran to them and confessed their sins.

All that, no doubt, reflected the wider context of the crusade, as a pilgrimage of faith directed by religion, but for an account of the battle it is better to follow the plain words of the *Gesta*:

> Our line of battle formed up at once. As soon as our knights charged all the barbarians, their allies and mercenaries took to their heels and fled. There were more than three hundred thousand pagans, not counting the Arabs, and God alone knows how many there were of them. They fled very fast to their camp, and then they continued their flight and we pursued them, killing them, for a whole day. And we took much booty, gold, silver, horses, asses, camels, oxen, sheep, and many other things which we have no name for.

If God had not been with us in this battle and sent us the other part of our divided army, none of us would have escaped. The fighting went on from the third hour to the ninth, but Almighty God, who is gracious and merciful, delivered his knights from death.

What man would dare to write of the skill and prowess of the Turks? They thought they could strike terror into the Franks by means of their arrows, as they have done to Arabs, Saracens, Armenians, Syrians and Greeks. Yet, please God, their men will never be as good as ours. They have a saying that they are of common stock with the Franks, and that no other men are naturally born to be knights. This is true, and nobody can deny it. Had they but affirmed the faith of Christ, you could not find stronger or braver or more skilful soldiers. And yet by God's grace they were beaten by our men. This battle was fought on 1 July 1097.

Praise from the author of the *Gesta*, a man who knew war and saluted a worthy enemy, was praise indeed. This battle of Dorylaeum, the first contest in open battlefield between the crusaders and the forces of Islam, was a trial for both armies. It showed the likelihood of the westerners to be taken by surprise, and their notorious difficulty in forging a single army out of various bands led by wilful, independent nobles. None of the chroniclers, neither the author of the *Gesta* nor Fulcher nor Raymond of Aguilers, really knew why the crusaders had divided after Nicaea. What was Bohemond doing on one road, with Godfrey and Count Raymond on another? The explanation of the *Gesta*, that they had blithely marched apart in the darkness before dawn, hardly convinces. It was, in any case, a most unmilitary action. As a result of that separation Bohemond was nearly lost, and he was only saved in the nick of time.

On the other hand, the western knights, when they did manage to form line and put their characteristic battle-plan into action, were clearly more powerful than the Turks. They showed the ability of heavily armed knights, well protected by chain-mail, to rout, at least in open field, the fast, agile, skirmishing horsemen of the Turks, with their quick-shooting but light bows.

Yet for all their power, the Christians at Dorylaeum came within moments of disaster, thanks to their own muddle and lack of co-operation. A soldier, such as the author of the *Gesta*, might attribute the victory to courageous hearts and military virtues, but Fulcher, the priest, knew better. The victory was God's reward to men of faith. It validated the idea of the crusade, and showed the knights of the West that their cause was just:

> The Lord does not give victory to the pomp of nobility, nor to brilliance in arms, but out of pity He aids the pure in heart who are fortified by divine strength in time of need. Therefore the Lord, perhaps pleased with our supplication, slowly restored our vigour and weakened the Turks.
>
> Alas, how many of our laggards and stragglers did they kill that day! From the first hour to the sixth great difficulties encompassed us. But then, little by little, after we were spurred on and strengthened by the arrival of our allies and friends, divine grace was miraculously present. Suddenly, we saw the backs of the Turks as they turned in flight.

Fulcher wrote of a miraculous shift of fortune, but another priest, Raymond of Aguilers, spoke openly of an actual miracle:

> A wondrous miracle was reported, though we did not see it. Two knights in shining armour and of marvellous appearance advanced before our army and so threatened the enemy that they were not able to fight. Indeed, when the Turks tried to strike them with their lances, these two knights were invulnerable. As a testimony to this, we add as follows: for two days, far from the passage of arms, we found enemy horsemen and their horses dead along the road.

In truth, Dorylaeum was an unexceptional battle, though the knights were caught at a disadvantage and came dangerously close to defeat. The Christian mind did not see it like that, however. The battles of the crusade were part of no ordinary venture. They belonged to God's plan, against which the pagan and the infidel could not prevail.

5

THE EMPEROR

The palace was vast, many rambling stately buildings with linked courtyards and pavilions, set on the side of a hill where sweet breezes came off the water. There were sounds of fountains, and running water, and a cool cover of leaves shaded against a sun rising hot out of Asia. In the northern part of this complex, in the great hall called the Magnaura, the emperor awaited envoys from the outer world. It was certain that the envoys would be barbarians, for that was the name bestowed upon all peoples who did not speak Greek. Their languages were like the barking of dogs or bleating of sheep, noises that seemed only to say 'bar-bar'.

As the stranger from one of these nations advanced over the porphyry and Carian marble of the palace floor, his hands resting on the shoulders of two eunuchs, gilded birds in the branches of a golden tree began to sing, each one singing the natural song of its species. At a distance, raised up on six steps, was a throne, bronze and gilded wood, enclosing in the large embrace of its arms more space than any ordinary man required. Guarding the throne were golden lions, beating the floor with their tails, and roaring. Their tongues leapt in the snarl of their mouths.

Then the envoy performed the *proskynesis*, throwing himself to the ground three times before the emperor on the throne, and when he lifted his head after the last abasement he saw that the throne and the emperor had risen from the modest height of a man's waist up into the rafters of the ceiling, and the emperor's clothes had changed in the wink of an eye in style and colour, going from brilliant to yet more brilliant.

The illusions, the tricks, and the cunning of the engineering had their effect. To the envoys from the outer world, Constantinople was indeed a city of wonders, a place calculated to impress and confuse. The man on the throne, the ruler of the city and the empire who changed even the glamour of his clothes with the dazzling rapidity of a chameleon, seemed to his theorists, and perhaps to himself, a man more than human: 'Some affirm that the emperor is not subject to the law but is the law. And I say the same. Whenever he acts and legislates, he does well, and we obey him. Blessed lord, God has raised you to the imperial authority and by His grace has made you, as you are called, a god on earth, to do and act as you will.'

That was the constitutional opinion given by a Greek scholar about the time of the crusade, but this small blasphemy only echoed the celebrated advice given to Emperor Justinian in the sixth century:

> You are truly emperor, since you have the authority of an imperial ruler and are master of your passions, and also since you are adorned with the crown of temperance and are clothed in the purple of justice. Other kinds of authority have death as their heir, but such imperial authority lasts forever. Other powers find their end in this world, but the power you have is saved from eternal punishment. The emperor is equal to all men in the nature of his body, but in the authority of his rank he is similar to God, who rules all.

In the eyes of the emperor there were good reasons for a god-like pride. Rome had declined, in the dark ages of invasion, into a broken ant-heap of faction and sedition, displaying only a decrepit grandeur and the memory of empire. Paris was little more than a country town, and London was a graceless huddle on a muddy estuary. However, to gaze from the summit of the palace hill in Constantinople, where the eastern point of the long city promontory slid abruptly into the waters of the Bosphorus, was to look on a splendour and an achievement of an entirely different kind.

Inland, sheltered north and south by the arms of the Golden Horn and the Sea of Marmara, and protected in the west by the mighty wall of Anthemius, a city of some 750,000 inhabitants tumbled off seven hills in a glittering array. Thoroughfares marched out to the city walls, beginning their journey towards all points of the empire from the pillar called the Milion, just below the palace hill. At first, before many divisions, the great road drove west into the Augusteum, the central piazza of the city, where five other large pillars celebrated the founders of the empire, in particular Constantine and Justinian, and their families. Then the arcaded highway went from forum to broad forum decorated with further pillars, memorials to other heroes and numerous triumphs. From the vantage points on the hills, the tops of the many pillars thrust skyward interspersed with the bright domes and tiled roofs of palaces, churches and monasteries said to number more than three hundred.

The city, though huge, was planned and regulated, far more so than any other city outside China, but it was too vital and energetic a place to remain completely ordered. Widths were ordained for certain streets, building heights were specified, balconies permitted or not, domestic architecture approved. A bold aqueduct and handsome cisterns looked after the water supply, and careful provision was made for drainage and sewage. However, tenements sprang up like sudden mushrooms, mixing cheek by jowl with the palaces and the churches and the many houses of commerce, insinuating into the civic spaces with all the hurry and babble of large cosmopolitan immigrant communities. Arabs, Syrians, Jews, Kurds, Armenians, Slavs, Bulgars, Russians, Khazars, Patzinaks, Cumans, dark seamen from North Africa, Venetian traders, fair-haired Scandinavians of the emperor's Varangian guard, even men of unnamed tribes with caravans from the lands of the Tarim or the Irtysh or the Hwang-ho – all were welcomed to the entrepot of the city and the *oikoumene* of the empire, which demanded from them little more than peace, a respect for the faith of the Byzantine Church, and a willingness to speak Greek.

Nothing was lost by the presence of the foreign communities, and the rash of tenements spoilt little in the grand vistas of the city. Starting at the silk-market of the House of Lights, where the illumination of sunlight from huge windows competed with the brilliance of the merchandise, the fashionable shops went in ordered rows down the arcades on both sides of the broad Mese, dividing at the Forum Amastrianum then flowing serenely on, one branch to the southerly Golden Gate and the other to the northern Charisian Gate, close by the new palace of Blachernae, much favoured by Emperor Alexius as a safe place for the entertainment and bemusement of crusaders. In streets and public places statuary was everywhere, so it seemed that marble was just another clothing of the citizens. The great number of churches gave religion an importance and a public face, at least, not equalled even in Rome. The glorious bulk of Hagia Sophia, Hagia Eirene and the huge Church of the Holy Apostles, by their very presence, caused a sudden intake of breath and a lifting of the heart. A bewildering host of more modest churches, chapels, little monasteries and hermit cells spoke of more reticent holiness and real devotion. At the other end of the moral scale, Aphrodite in marble advertised the large brothel in the Zeugma district, down by the raffish quays of the Golden Horn harbour.

It was a breezy city, too, with many open spaces acting as lungs between the dense crowd of certain areas. There were parade grounds, on which the army had stamped a destiny for several insecure emperors. There were parks and trees and olive groves, wide squares for recreation, and away towards the city wall in the southwest, in rolling country where the small stream of the Lycus ran into the sea, there were orchards and vegetable gardens and even cornfields. Everything was a testimony to confidence, energy and taste but particularly to wealth.

In the temperate climate of the Black Sea edge, at the narrow strait of the Bosphorus where Europe and Asia met, Constantinople mediated exchange and drew commerce from

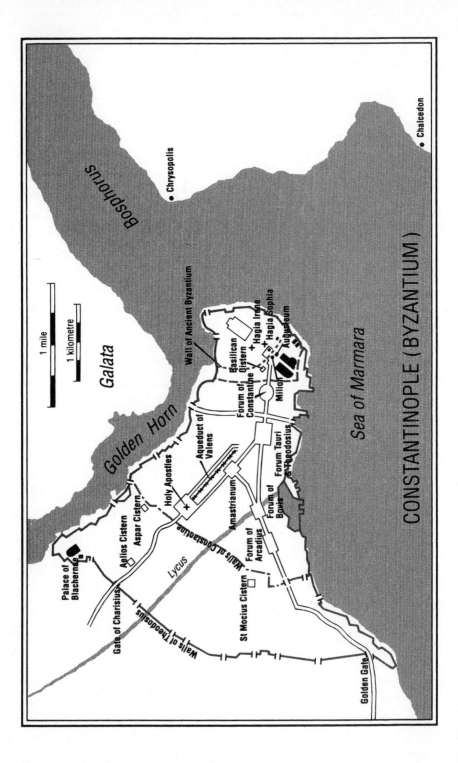

CONSTANTINOPLE (BYZANTIUM)

all over the known world. The wealth of empire and the profit of trade accumulated, and over many centuries it was spread with a bountiful hand. A widow in the age of Basil I, towards the end of the ninth century, was able to bequeath the emperor 3,000 slaves. A bastard son of an emperor, even in disgrace, thought it becoming to his dignity to travel with more than 2,000 servants and attendants. A farmer and landowner, born poor but grown rich on property and the feeding of the city, was said to own 12,000 sheep, 800 horses and 600 oxen, and the land to support these numbers. When he gave feasts, a whole regiment of guests sat down to eat, served on tables of ivory and gold.

However, wealth cannot be put to work unless it is safe. The rich aristocrats of Constantinople were notoriously factious and jealous, but as one family rose and another fell the riches that passed from losers to winners were still circulated and maintained within the city and the empire. As for trade, the merchant houses of Constantinople were almost assured against the shock and calamity of outside invasion, for the great virtue of the city – perhaps its greatest – was its security. Protecting it, along the two arms of the sea, were fourteen miles of sea-walls. At their western ends these walls joined with the wall of Anthemius, a four-and-a-half-mile construction worthy of a Titan, extending from the Golden Horn in the north to the Sea of Marmara in the south and sheltering the city from the landward side. This wall, of dressed stone and brick filled with rubble, was 30 feet high and 16 feet thick, and it was fronted by a 60-foot ditch paved in stone. There were 188 towers commanding every approach and about a dozen gates, some for civic traffic and others for the military alone. From the fifth century for just over a thousand years, until well into the age of gunpowder and cannon, all invaders of Constantinople came up against this defence and recoiled. Hopes of conquest by Huns, Avars, Arabs, Bulgars, Patzinaks, Russians and Turks, as well as Frankish crusaders, stopped at these battlements.

Truly, a place of wonders! A French historian, writing at the very beginning of the thirteenth century, expressed the sense of amazement felt by every stranger who visisted the city from the time of Constantine himself to the fall of the city in 1453:

> Indeed they stared well at Constantinople, those who had never seen it, for they could not believe that any city in the world should be so rich. When they saw the tall ramparts and mighty towers that shut around the city, and those rich palaces and lofty churches, of which there were so many they seemed uncountable, and the length and the breadth of this city that was sovereign among all others, not one of these people could believe his eyes.

Great wealth and splendour cause jealousy in poorer, less fortunate men. Admiration for the city was usually mixed with greed and desire, as the Byzantines knew well. Hatred and spite against Constantinople were common emotions, particularly from the people of the West when they compared the failing world of the old Rome with the resplendent empire of the city on the Bosphorus which men called the New Rome. Shortly before the arrival of the first wave of the crusaders, one of the city's poets wrote:

> This is the city by the wide world desired,
> Which seized the royal garland of the globe
> And grasped the sceptre and the crown of Rome.

The old Roman Empire had been one entity, in culture and society and religion. In dangerous times, for administrative ease and military safety, Diocletian had split the empire into two, with a western branch based on Rome and an eastern branch based on the ancient Greek city of Byzantium. Under Constantine and his successors, the eastern subjects of the empire, clustered around the city now renamed Constantinople, had resisted barbarian invasion and had prospered. The western fabric, however, had begun to fall apart under the pressure of the Germanic tribes. In time, the empire in the East became Greek in language, culture and Christian religion, though still claiming to be the true inheritor of the old Roman tradition and even calling itself, most confusingly, 'Roman'. Western Christianity, under the papacy, remained Latin in language and doctrine and gradually accepted protection and patronage from the Germanic tribal chiefs who had overwhelmed and re-ordered the old empire in the West. When the pope crowned Charlemagne on Christmas Day, AD 800, and invested him with the title of Roman Emperor, in western eyes the empire was now translated to the king of the Franks by authority of the pope. To the Byzantines, this coronation was an act of barbarian outrage, of no value, and broke the inalienable unity of the historical Roman Empire, whose legitimate sovereign now could only be the emperor in Constantinople.

The break between western and eastern empires developed into settled opposition, in polity and in religion. Time and distance encouraged many subtle differences in Christian doctrine between the pope in Rome and the patriarch in Constantinople, and these became reasons for anger and name-calling and recrimination. In 1054, after arguments of much heat but little light, each side anathematized the other, and the two Churches were formally in schism. This had only confirmed long years of acrimony and petulance that gave rise to much vindictive propaganda, which was as amusing as it was serious. Like parties to a bad divorce, both sides lost all shame and restraint. The comments were virulent:

> I came to Constantinople on 4 June and was treated igno-miniously and harshly, as a studied insult to yourself. I was shut up in a palace that was indeed vast and open, keeping out neither cold nor heat. To add to my tribulation, I found the Greek wine undrinkable because pitch, resin and gypsum had been added to it. The house was without water, which I could not even buy to quench my thirst. This was bad enough, but I had an extra affliction in the rogue sent to guard me and look after my needs. Wherever you searched, you would not find his like here on earth, but only in Hell.

That was how Bishop Liudprand of Cremona began his report of an embassy to Constantinople in 968, taken on behalf of the western emperor Otto the Great. The account is a rich history of prejudice and disgust, a distillation of centuries of animosity between West and East:

> That day, the emperor invited me to join him at dinner. As

he thought me unworthy to take precedence over any of his own lords, I sat fifteenth from him, with no tablecloth. At this vile and disgusting banquet, swimming in oil like a drunkard's feast, and sprinkled with the most dreadful fish brine, he asked me many questions about your power, lands and armies. When I replied reasonably and truthfully, he retorted, 'You lie. Your master's soldiers cannot ride, and do not know how to fight on foot. They are weighed down by huge shields and heavy armour, and their long swords only get in the way. Besides,' he added with a malicious smile, 'they are hampered by the insatiable greed of their stomachs. The belly is their god. For these soldiers, boldness lies in satiety, courage in drunkeness.' And the emperor threw in as a further insult, 'You are not Romans, but Lombards.'

What a contrast there was, in the eyes of Liudprand, between this rude, despicable fop and his own noble master, the western Otto:

The sovereign of the Greeks is long-haired, wears a tunic with long sleeves and covers his head like a woman. He is a liar, deceitful, lacking in compassion, wily as a fox, arrogant but with an air of false humility, mean and greedy. He feeds on garlic, onions and leeks, and drinks bathwater. The king of the Franks, on the other hand, has a manly, neat haircut. His clothes are the very reverse of feminine. He wears a proper hat. He is truthful, guileless, compassionate when need be, severe when it is required, always truly humble, never mean. He does not live on garlic, onions and leeks.

Before Liudprand fled away from 'that city full of perjury, lies and deceit, grasping and avaricious, a place of empty pomp', he etched on the wall of his 'hateful dwelling' a warning to the Latins against the Greeks, and one last fierce outburst against the emperor, Nicephorus Phocas:

Greeks cannot be trusted. Don't trust them, O Latins, and don't believe a word they say. A Greek will perjure himself most piously for the slightest advantage. In this lofty house, open to the sky but with walls of variegated marble and vast windows, a house without water, a vicious house that lets in frost but does not keep out summer heat, I,

Liudprand, bishop of Cremona in Italy, led here to Constantinople by my desire for peace, have been shut up for four months of summer.

In his anger at Nicephorus, the bishop ended with a dire prediction: 'The day is looming when, unless God prevents it, Mars, urged on by cruel Furies, will rage through all the world, and the peace we long for will be silenced, through *your* fault.'

Before the end of the next century, it may have seemed to the Greeks that the bishop's prediction was coming true. Disastrously, they had lost the battle of Manzikert, and Turks were cutting away the empire. Then armies of Frankish crusaders were trampling towards Constantinople, with who knew what treacherous plans and bestial appetites? Not that the emperor of the moment, Alexius Comnenus, would ever have thought it was *his* fault. West and East held each other to blame, for the loathing between them was mutual. Frankish contempt for the sly and effeminate Greeks was matched by Greek horror of the brutal, barbarian Franks. In this respect Alexius was no different from his countrymen, as Anna Comnena, his daughter and his biographer, made clear:

> Alexius had no time to relax before he heard a rumour of the approach of innumerable Frankish armies. He feared their arrival since he knew their uncontrollable passion, their unstable and erratic character, and all the other peculiar traits of the Celtic temperament, with their inevitable consequences: how greedy they were for money, which led them to break agreements for the slightest whim and without scruple. He had heard this said of them, and it was quite true.

Yet Alexius, an effective and intelligent ruler, saw clearly the threat to his empire from the Seljuk Turks, and as early as 1082 he had appealed for help, in the name of Christianity, to both the papacy and the princes in the West. For some years, divided and muddled, they were deaf to any appeal. Then suddenly, the great upsurge of crusading enthusiasm that followed the speech of Pope Urban at Clermont caught Alexius by surprise and was far worse than anything he had expected. 'Alexius did not despair,' his daughter wrote, 'but made every effort to prepare

for war if need arose. But the actual events were more fright-
ful even than the rumours, for the entire West and all the barbarians who lived between the Adriatic and the Straits of
Gibraltar moved in a body to Asia, marching across Europe
country to country with all their households.'

The undisciplined Christian mob of the people's crusade
was on the borders of the empire, and Emperor Alexius was
in a state of alarm. The march of the crusaders was accompanied by a plague of locusts, 'which did not attack the wheat
but played havoc with the vines'. The Greeks took this as a
sign that the Franks would leave Christians alone but would
bring affliction to the Turks, 'who were the slaves of wine and
drunkenness and Dionysus'. Alexius, however, was too canny
a ruler to be governed by superstition or let the run of events
be dictated by luck.

While the poor people's crusade of Peter the Hermit was
following the long land-route, Alexius heard that the first parties of the princes' crusade were crossing the Adriatic. These
western soldiers were not enemies, but being 'exceptionally
hotheaded and passionate' they could not be trusted. Alexius
took sensible precautions. He sent trusted officers to Durazzo
and Avlona on the Adriatic with instructions to treat the westerners respectfully and to arrange supplies for them along the
road, but also to watch them with an eagle eye, 'so that if they
saw them making raids or plundering the country, they could
check them with light skirmishes. And with these officers
were certain interpreters in the Latin tongue whose duty it
was to prevent misunderstandings and conflict between
Byzantines and Latins.'

Alexius had done what any prudent and competent king
would do. Now, in the face of such a large influx of unpredictable but powerful strangers, he could hardly push his
authority further. He could try to bend events to his advantage, using his famous cunning and intelligence, but he could
not control them. His best policy was to observe and wait.
From the first, what he saw he did not like. The history of
Peter the Hermit's foray into Asia seemed like a brutal
epitome of troubles ahead. The Byzantine view was forcefully
stated by Anna Comnena. She was horrified by the cruelty of

the wild Norman troops at Nicaea, who 'cut in pieces some of the babes, impaled others on wooden spits and roasted them over a fire, and subjected old people to every kind of torture'. Then she noted the quarrels, the disorganization, the selfish greed of the westerners. Those who were proper soldiers were powerful fighters but indiscipline, greed and foolishness made them vulnerable to a general who knew his business, such as the sultan Kilij Arslan at Nicaea:

> So many Franks and Normans died by the Turkish sword that the heaped remains of the fallen made a mountain of considerable size, so huge was the mass of bones. Later, some men of the same race as the slaughtered barbarians, when they were building walls like those of a city, used the bones of the dead as pebbles to fill the cracks, so the city became their tomb. To this very day, the wall stands, built of mixed stones and bones.

Anna showed little sympathy for this decimated rabble, the followers of Peter the Hermit and Walter the Penniless. When the stragglers returned to Constantinople, Alexius disarmed them and banished them as quickly as possible, but the emperor knew that the western leaders and their armies could not be handled in the same brusque, simple way. He had to pay careful attention to the crusading princes, both individually and collectively, and give them the benefit of all his Greek guile. His plan was to take the leaders aside, one by one, and draw from each an oath of loyalty to himself as emperor. In Byzantine eyes, this would be nothing more than the customary oath of a vassal to the legitimate ruler of the Roman Empire.

Hugh the Great, the over-proud brother of the king of France, was the first of the western princes to land on Byzantine territory. According to Anna Comnena, he had already written to Alexius in insulting terms: 'Know, Emperor, that I am the King of Kings, the greatest of all beneath the heavens. It is my will that you should meet me on my arrival and receive me with all the ceremony and deference due to my noble birth.'

By happy chance, when Hugh was shipwrecked near Durazzo, the officers of the emperor were close by, but they hardly received him in accordance with his own wishes. They feasted him and flattered him but did not let him free. He was firmly taken on a roundabout route to Constantinople where he was welcomed and honoured by Alexius, 'who soon persuaded him by large gifts and every show of friendship to bind himself to the emperor by the customary oath of the Latins'.

The simple, candid conceit of Hugh was easily satisfied, but Anna was apprehensive of the other leaders. She had been informed that Godfrey of Bouillon was very rich, and extremely proud of his birth, his valour and the glory of his family. The ordinary folk of the crusade she was inclined to forgive, for she thought them either truly bound in the service of Christ or led astray by more villainous characters, in particular Bohemond and his like, 'for they hoped to seize Constantinople itself on their journey, regarding its capture as a natural aim of the expedition'. The Norman knight Bohemond was greatly feared: 'He disturbed the mind of nobler men, and still held a grudge against the emperor.'

As the crusading armies slowly converged on Constantinople, Alexius worked hard. He sent out spies, intercepted messages, arranged obstacles, diversions, warnings. He was trying to influence the movements of the Franks, but he did not want to antagonize them beyond a certain point. That was a question of nice judgment. The leaders from the West, awkward, proud men, were touchy and easily gave way to violence. Disliking the Greeks, they misunderstood gestures and suspected the worst:

> Some of the lords with Godfrey were invited to meet the emperor. He wanted to persuade them to urge Godfrey to take the oath of allegiance. But the Latins wasted time as usual with their long-winded speeches, and a false rumour went back to the Frankish ranks that Alexius had arrested these lords. At once, the troops marched on the city, starting with the palaces near the Silver Lake, which they demolished completely. An assault was also made on the city walls. Trusting to their great numbers they had the effrontery to try to set fire to the gate below the Blachernae Palace, near the sanctuary of St Nicolas.

The citizens defended the walls, though Alexius was reluctant to kill the crusaders, fearing further provocation to their leaders, so he ordered his archers to shoot low, to kill the horses and dismount the knights. Only when the imperial guards sallied out of the gates did the crusaders retreat. Such a dangerous confrontation, with loss of life, helped to persuade Godfrey, reluctantly, to take the oath. 'Then Godfrey came to the emperor and swore an oath as he was directed, that all the cities, lands or castles he might win, if they had in the first place belonged to the Roman Empire, he would hand them over to the officers of the emperor. Having taken this oath Godfrey was given generous rewards and was invited to share Alexius's palace and table.'

Honoured, feasted, soothed and rested, Godfrey soon crossed over the Bosphorus and pitched camp, with plentiful supplies provided by the emperor. Thus, by a mixture of force, cunning and diplomacy, Alexius tried to make terms with all the different parties among the crusaders. His daughter Anna was full of admiration for his subtlety:

> It was typical of Alexius, that he had uncanny foresight and knew how to seize an advantage before his rivals. Meanwhile, the Frankish forces were eagerly pressing on the capital, as numerous as the stars of heaven or the grains of sand. I desire to name all their leaders, but I cannot do so. Words fail me, partly because I cannot make the barbaric sounds – who can pronounce them? – and partly because I recoil before their great numbers.'

The work of persuasion was slow. Alexius took men aside, lapped them in the luxury of the Blachernae Palace, let them see what they too might have, flattered them, tempted them. 'Privately, he talked with them, and used the more reasonable to put pressure on the reluctant. When they hung back – they were anxiously waiting for Bohemond – and evaded his requests with new demands, he answered their objections with no difficulty and worried them in a hundred ways till they were driven to take the oath.'

After some time and much effort only Bohemond and Raymond of St Gilles had yet to take the oath. Bohemond was the difficult case. He had fought against the Byzantines before, and had defeated them. He was known to be brave, ambitious and ruthless, and Alexius feared him. The net of wiles that had caught the others was spread for Bohemond, with special attention to the promise of riches and principalities. Then he was asked to take the oath:

> Understanding his position, he agreed gladly enough, for he was neither of noble family nor of great wealth. In any case, Bohemond was a liar by nature. After the ceremony Alexius had a room set apart and the floor covered with all kinds of riches: clothes, gold and silver coins, precious things of every variety filled the room so completely that you could not walk in it. When the door was thrown open, Bohemond was amazed. 'With such wealth,' he said, 'long ago I would have mastered many lands.' 'All this is yours,' said the official of the palace, 'a present from the emperor.' Bohemond was overjoyed. But after he had rested and thought a while, when the wealth was brought to him he changed his mind. 'Away with it all,' he cried, 'why do you insult me?' This Latin moodiness was familiar to Alexius, and he quoted this popular saying: 'His mischief shall rebound on his head.' When Bohemond heard this, and saw the riches quickly disappearing, he switched again, like a sea-creature that transforms itself in a minute.
>
> The truth is that Bohemond was an habitual rogue, quick to take advantage of any circumstance. He was braver, but far more of a rascal, than all the other Latins who came to Constantinople at that time. But he was also far poorer in money, influence and men. He was a supreme mischief-maker. As for inconstancy, that was to be expected – a trait of all Latins.

Alexius had drawn the net and within it, bound by oath, were nearly all the chiefs of the crusade. Only Raymond of St Gilles remained unfettered. He was the richest and most influential of the westerners, a man Alexius needed to control more than most, but the emperor allowed him to slip away unburdened by the oath of fealty. There was much sympathy between the two men, alike perhaps in age, in pride of possessions, in great responsibilities. Anna Comnena made it clear that her father had a 'deep affection' for Raymond, on account of his 'superior intellect, his unspotted reputation, and the purity of his life'. Alexius thought that Raymond 'outshone all Latins as the sun is brighter than the stars', and he valued his friendship and advice. Raymond was the one foreigner to whom the emperor could unpack his heart, lamenting his tribulations, speculating on the real motives of the other princes, discussing future plans of action. To Count Raymond, wrote Anna, her father 'unreservedly opened the doors of his soul'. This intimacy was of great benefit to the crusade, for the emperor knew the character of the Turks and their methods of warfare. It did not matter very much that Raymond had evaded the oath, since he repaid the emperor's confidence with a pledge of friendship and support. 'As far as I am concerned,' he told Alexius, 'I will always try to the best of my ability to keep your commands.' The emperor was content with that. Then Raymond crossed to the other shore and prepared to face the enemy who were, after all, not Greeks but Turks.

With the departure of the crusaders Alexius sighed with relief to have rid Constantinople, with so little pain, of so many troublesome men, but now he was in some doubt as to his next step. Should he join the crusade? It would be a fine thing for him to prove his authority and his generalship. In any case, it would be wise to keep an eye on these unpredictable western rogues. As usual, he decided to keep a watching brief:

> Alexius would have liked to share in the expedition against the infidels too, but he feared the enormous number of the Franks. He did think it wise, however, to move across the water to Pelekanum. If he made his headquarters near Nicaea, he could get information about the progress of the Franks and at the same time learn of the Turkish activities in and around that city.

Caution, watchfulness, careful judgment based on the fullest possible knowledge – that was the way Alexius Comnenus conducted affairs of state.

After the first shock of the meeting between crusaders and the Byzantines at Constantinople, the prejudices of both parties remained on the whole undisturbed. Alexius and the Greeks were able to congratulate themselves on a modest success. There had been clashes, but only a few lives were lost, and the city itself survived with little damage. The dangerous foreigners had been hurried over the sea, and the emperor had won from the western leaders at least a formal acknowledgment of ascendancy, which might be put to good use later.

As for the crusaders, they grudgingly admitted the skill with which Alexius had handled events, but they did not like him and they never trusted him. He was a deceitful double-dealer, and the cause of calamities that began with Peter the Hermit. The chronicler Raymond of Aguilers roundly put the whole blame for Peter's failure on Alexius:

> We recognized then that the emperor had betrayed Peter the Hermit, for he compelled him, ignorant of the place

A MOSAIC PORTRAIT OF EMPEROR ALEXIUS
From Hagia Sophia in Constantinople

and of all military matters, to cross the strait with his men and exposed them to the Turks. When the Turks saw that unwarlike multitude, they cut them down without effort to the number of 60,000. This made the Turks bold and proud, and they sent captured arms and prisoners to the Saracens and other nobles of their own race, and they boasted far and wide that the Franks were poor fighters and of no account in battle.

This was a telling criticism, for it made Alexius the reason for a loss of face in battle, and there was nothing the Franks prided themselves on more than their courage and prowess in war. Once the dislike between the two peoples was based on this ground, the distance between them could hardly be bridged.

Yet western chroniclers could not deny that the emperor was a central figure in crusading plans. Fulcher of Chartres knew it and bluntly spelt out Alexius's importance:

> It was necessary for all our leaders to confirm friendship with the emperor, without whose aid and advice we could not have completed our journey, nor could those who wished to follow us on that road. To our leaders, then, the emperor himself offered money and silken clothes, as much as anyone could want, and also horses and supplies, which they needed to complete their great travels.

Nor were several of the crusading princes entirely reluctant to be wooed by Alexius. To unsophisticated soldiers of the West, the emperor, with a high lineage extending back to the heroic age of Constantine, with his culture, wealth and lands, was an almost mythological figure of grandeur and refinement. It was flattering indeed to have such a man trying to ingratiate himself. Stephen of Blois was a great lord in his own territory, the son-in-law of William the Conqueror and master of many castles, but he was as giddy as a schoolboy under the warm sun of the emperor's charm. Stephen wrote to his wife Adele:

> Truly, the emperor received me with dignity and honour and with the greatest affection, as if I were his own son, and he loaded me with most bountiful and precious gifts. In the whole of our army of God there is neither duke nor count

nor other noble person whom he trusts or favours more than
myself. And truly, my beloved, his Imperial Highness has
very often urged, and still urges, that we commend one of
our sons to him. He promises that he will give the boy such
great honour that the lad will have no reason to envy even
ourselves, his parents. So I say to you that there is today no
man under heaven like the emperor, for he is enriching all
our princes most generously, relieving all our knights with
gifts, and refreshing all the poor folk with feasts.

We smile at this innocence, seeing a fox at work among
lambs. It is small wonder that the princes fell, one by one,
into the web of the emperor's design. Only Bohemond had
the worldliness and the calculating eye to see through the
emperor's tricks, but the Norman knight was biding his time,
and allowed himself to be bought off for the moment. His
attitude towards all the Byzantines seemed to be one of studied contempt, though day by day he would play their games,
if it pleased him. Had he not already beaten them on the
battlefield, and could do so again? Something of this insulting
confidence also rubbed off on Bohemond's chronicler, the
anonymous knight of the *Gesta*. For him, Alexius was 'that
wretched man', or 'that abominable emperor', or 'a fool as
well as a knave', and the Greek officers and troops were no
better. The *Gesta* expected nothing good from Greeks and
was always ready to put the worst interpretation on their
actions:

> When the emperor heard that Bohemond, that most dis-
> tinguished soldier, had come, he ordered him to be received
> with fine ceremony, but took care to keep him outside
> the city. After a while the emperor invited him to a private
> meeting, with Duke Godfrey and Raymond of St Gilles
> also present. Then the emperor, angry and troubled,
> planned how to entrap these Christian knights by fraud and
> cunning, but by God's grace neither he nor his men found
> an opportunity to harm them. At last, all the nobles of
> Constantinople, who were afraid of losing their country,
> devised a crafty plan to make the dukes, counts and all the
> leaders of our army swear an oath of fealty to the emperor.
> At first our leaders flatly refused to do this, saying, 'Truly,

this is unworthy of us. Why should we swear an oath to him at all?'

But perhaps we were fated to be misled often by our leaders, for what did they do in the end? They will say that they were constrained to do it by need and willy-nilly had to humble themselves to the wishes of that abominable emperor.

Now, the emperor was much afraid of the gallant Bohemond, who had often chased his army from the field, so he told Bohemond that he would give him lands beyond Antioch, fifteen days journey in length and eight in width, if he would swear fealty freely, and he would keep his promise if Bohemond would keep his oath. But why should such noble knights submit to a thing like this? It must have been because they were driven by desperate need.

Then the emperor for his part guaranteed good faith and security to all our men. He swore also to come with us, bringing an army and a navy, and faithfully to supply us with provisions both by land and sea, and to restore all those things that we had lost. Moreover, he promised that he would not cause or permit anyone to trouble or vex our pilgrims on the way to the Holy Sepulchre.

After the negotiation in Constantinople, it was the view of the parties that a large but vague contract had been struck. Alexius would give the crusaders every practical form of help and assistance, and would even accompany the crusade in some high honorific role, just so long as the western leaders would acknowledge his imperial authority, keep discipline among their men and their own ambition in check, and indirectly help to secure the Byzantine Empire against the Turks. After his relief that the city was free of the ruffians, Alexius began to see how unrealistic was his ideal picture, but he crossed the Bosphorus with good intentions and for the first weeks of the campaign fulfilled his part of the bargain. Then at the long siege of Nicaea the grand plan began to go awry. Alexius began to think that these barbarians were irredeemably vicious and beyond control. There was, if nothing else, the question of their brutality. At the fall of Nicaea, Anna Comnena wrote: 'So the Franks won a glorious victory. They impaled the heads of many Turks on the ends of their spears and carried these back like standards, so that the infidel might not be so eager for battle in the future. Such are the ideas and actions of the Latins.'

Events like this made Alexius reconsider his place in the enterprise. Anna went on,

> He would have liked to accompany the expedition against the godless Turks, but abandoned the project after a careful weighing of the arguments. He noted that his Byzantine army was hopelessly outnumbered by the enormous host of the Franks. He knew, too, from long experience how untrustworthy the Latins were. Nor was that all. The instability and treacherous nature of these people might sweep them again and again, like the tides of Euripus, from one extreme to the other. These were men who for love of money were ready to sell their wives and children for a pittance. For these reasons the emperor was prevented from joining the journey. However, if wisdom dictated his absence, it also suggested to him that he should give the Franks as much material aid as they needed.

Though their supplies and support from the Greeks continued, the crusaders noted the cooling of the imperial enthusiasm, and the *Gesta* was again ready to condemn another piece of malicious double-dealing. When the besieged Turks in Nicaea surrendered to the emperor, and he treated them leniently, the *Gesta* was in a rage: 'The emperor, who was a fool as well as a knave, told them to go away unhurt and without fear. He had them brought to him at Constantinople under safe-conduct, and kept them carefully, so that he might have them ready to injure the Franks and obstruct their crusade.'

Who, finally, is to judge between West and East? Alexius himself was quite certain of the justice and rightness of his actions. In 1098, when the abbot of Monte Cassino in Italy wrote asking again for help for the crusaders, the emperor replied, not without a weary note of self-justification:

> Let your Venerable Holiness be assured on that score, for my empire has been spread over them and will aid and advise them on all matters. Indeed, we have already cooperated with them to the best of our ability, not as a friend

or ordinary relative, but like a father. And had not my empire so supported and aided them, who else would have afforded them help? Nor does it grieve my empire to assist them a second time.

There was much truth in what the emperor said, which even the *Gesta* might have acknowledged with a blush. Considering the troubles of his state and time, Emperor Alexius resolved his problems with dexterous skill. In doing this he was, in the later opinion of Greek historians, a credit to illustrious predecessors, showing those qualities of intelligence, flexibility and judgment expected in the best imperial successors to Constantine and Justinian:

> Reflecting that by himself he was unable to keep up the all-important fight against the Turks, Alexius understood that it was necessary to make an alliance with the Latins. He did this by dissembling, shrewd manipulation and cunning. Luckily he found a heaven-sent pretext, in that these Latin peoples thought it quite intolerable that the Turks should rule in Jerusalem and control the Sepulchre of Our Saviour Jesus Christ. For this reason very many Latins, numbering in the thousands and tens of thousands, came as fast as they could to Constantinople.
>
> After Alexius had exchanged oaths of loyalty and made treaties with them, he went off to the East, and through divine assistance, the aid of his allies, and his own efforts, he quickly forced the Turks to abandon the lands of the Byzantines. He freed the cities and restored imperial power in the East to its former glory. Such a man was Emperor Alexius: great in making plans and great in performing deeds.

6

THE ROAD
BLOCKED

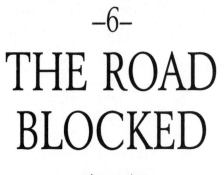

Towards the end of June 1097, some ten months after setting out from France, Stephen of Blois wrote home to his wife Adele celebrating the first success against the Turks on the march to Jerusalem:

> God has triumphed and the very large city of Nicaea was surrendered on the 13th day before the Calends of July. We read that the holy fathers of the primitive church held a synod at Nicaea. After the defeat of the Arian heresy, they were led by the teaching of the Holy Spirit to confirm there the faith of the Blessed Trinity. And this city, which because of its sins later became a mistress of error, now by the mercy of God has been made, through His unworthy servants, a disciple of truth. I tell you, my beloved, five weeks after leaving Nicaea we will be in Jerusalem, unless Antioch resists us. Farewell.

This letter was in its way a characteristic crusading document, made up of piety, ignorance, enthusiasm and unfounded hopes. The name Nicaea was indeed famous in the annals of the Church, but Stephen might have remembered that the very definition of the Trinity given at Nicaea, in 325, was the cause of the most painful theological difference separating Christian Latins and Christian Greeks. As for the hope to be in Jerusalem in five weeks, two years later the Holy City, though tottering on the brink of capitulation, still had not fallen. Stephen was right about one thing, however. Antioch was the place where the march stalled and hopes began to crumble.

After the success at Nicaea, followed almost immediately by the victory at Dorylaeum, the crusaders had reason to be cheerful. Their army, when all the different groups were gathered together, was formidable. The priest Fulcher, with a medieval awe for large numbers and no means to count them, thought there might be 600,000 western soldiers at Nicaea. A later German historian, who ingeniously computed the numbers by the time it took the army to cross a certain bridge, suggested 105,000. Cautious scholars often divide large medieval numbers by ten, and modern estimates put the army at between 45,000 and 60,000, with perhaps five thousand mounted knights and the rest foot-soldiers. In any case, the army was very large for the time, and it had proved itself in two victories over the Turks.

The crusaders were fortunate, too, in the disarray of their opponents. The Turkish conquest of Anatolia, less than thirty years old, was little more than a thin military superstructure imposed on a restless population, mainly Christian Greeks and Armenians, who had been part of the Byzantine empire since time out of mind. The vast Seljuk sultanate, in Anatolia and elsewhere in Asia Minor, was already beginning to fragment under the press of distance, loose organization, political incompetence, and individual ambitions. Independent regional governors, with their own standing armies, went their own way unless forcibly restrained by a strong prince. After the fiery royal general Tutush was killed in battle in 1095, there was no unifying authority in the whole ramshackle empire. The Turks held the cities and prowled the countryside. They had many tough captains with good fighting men under their command, able to give the crusaders a sharp lesson on the tactics of hit-and-run, but jealousy and dissension among

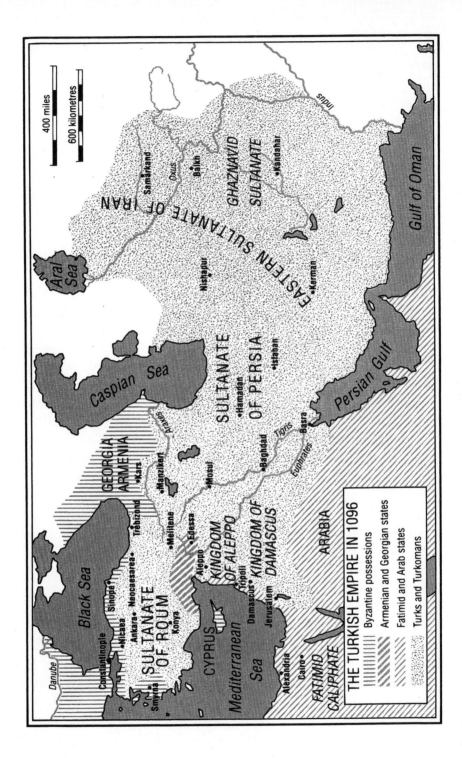

THE TURKISH EMPIRE IN 1096

||||||| Byzantine possessions

/// Armenian and Georgian states

/// Fatimid and Arab states

Turks and Turkomans

FATIMID
CALIPHATE

ARABIA

SULTANATE OF PERSIA

EASTERN SULTANATE OF IRAN

GHAZNAVID SULTANATE

SULTANATE OF ROUM

KINGDOM OF ALEPPO

KINGDOM OF DAMASCUS

GEORGIA
ARMENIA

CYPRUS

Mediterranean Sea

Black Sea

Caspian Sea

Aral Sea

Persian Gulf

Gulf of Oman

Danube

Constantinople
Nicaea
Smyrna
Sinope
Neocaesarea
Ankara
Konya
Trebizond
Kars
Manzikert
Melitene
Edessa
Aleppo
Tripoli
Damascus
Jerusalem
Alexandria
Cairo
Mosul
Baghdad
Basra
Hamadan
Isfahan
Nishapur
Kerman
Samarkand
Balkh
Kandahar

Araxes
Tigris
Euphrates
Oxus
Indus

400 miles
600 kilometres

the leaders made them unable to combine against a western army that might be stung but could hardly be defeated by ambush and sudden raids.

Two swift blows had overcome Kilij Arslan, ruler of the principality of Roum, which covered most of the middle and the south of modern Turkey. His capital at Nicaea had been taken, and his army was defeated at Dorylaeum. 'When the news was received of this shameful calamity to the cause of Islam,' wrote the Damascus historian Ibn al-Qalanisi, 'the anxiety of the people became acute and their fear and alarm increased.' From Nicaea to Antioch, where the Mediterranean turns the corner towards the Holy Land, is about five hundred miles. So long as the crusaders took a southerly route within the borders of Roum, they would meet no serious opposition.

In retrospect, it had not seemed so easy. In the words of Abbot Guibert, the whole adventure of the crusade was an agony. 'There never had been,' he wrote, 'among the princes of the world, men who exposed their bodies to so much suffering, solely in the expectation of spiritual reward.' He did not add that most of their troubles arose, not from the enemy Turk, but from their own deficiencies. Their itinerary was unplanned, the way ahead a blank map etched with a few sparse indications grudgingly marked by Greeks or Armenians. Relations with the Greek emperor were not good, being soured by suspicion, jealousy and mutual hatred. The unified western army was huge and unwieldy, ill-prepared, ill-provisioned, burdened with families and camp followers, harangued by churchmen, riven by squabbles, composed of many nations that could barely speak to each other. 'Whoever heard such a mixture of languages in one army?' Fulcher wrote in understandable perplexity. 'Here we have French, Flemings, Frisians, Gauls, Allobroges, Lotharingians, Allemani, Bavarians, Normans, English, Scots, Aquitanians, Italians, Dacians, Apulians, Iberians, Bretons, Greeks, and Armenians. If any Breton or Teuton wished to question me, I could neither understand nor answer.' It was as if they were not members of the army of God, but the conscripts of Babel.

For the crusaders, provisions and lines of supply were a puzzle that they never solved. In the first weeks of the campaign, besieging Nicaea which was within easy reach of Constantinople, the army had supplies provided by Emperor Alexius, who to this extent at least kept his word, but on the march, in the manner of the times, the crusaders expected in the main to live off the country, which was in many places fertile enough. Later, ships of the Italian city-states were able to bring supplies to the eastern Mediterranean ports. However, the western army, surrounded by enemies, found it hard to make the link with the supply-ships.

After Dorylaeum, at the beginning of July 1097, the western army set off in good heart. It was high summer in a hot land:

> Meanwhile we were coming in pursuit of those abominable Turks, who were fleeing before us every day. And when they came to castles or towns they used to deceive and mislead the inhabitants, saying, 'We have defeated all the Christians and now none of them will ever dare to oppose us again. So let us enter.' Then they burned or destroyed everything that might be helpful or useful to us, as they fled in great terror at our approach. We therefore pursued them through a land that was deserted, waterless and uninhabitable, from which we barely emerged or escaped alive. For we suffered greatly from hunger and thirst, and found nothing at all to eat except prickly plants which we gathered and rubbed between our hands. On such food we survived wretchedly enough.

That was the complaint from the author of the *Gesta* who was, like many professional soldiers, an inveterate grumbler. However, the gentler and more temperate Fulcher agreed with him: 'We very often suffered from the lack of enough bread and food in these places; for we found the land of Roum, which is very good land and specially fertile in all crops, excessively devastated and ravaged by the Turks.'

Heat and weariness, lack of water and thin rations, poor hygiene, and the stress of the march day by day caused many crusaders to sicken and die. To begin with, this was an expectation of campaigning in a far country and was hardly worth mentioning. Later, illness, starvation and infectious disease depleted the army in an alarming way, but even in the easier

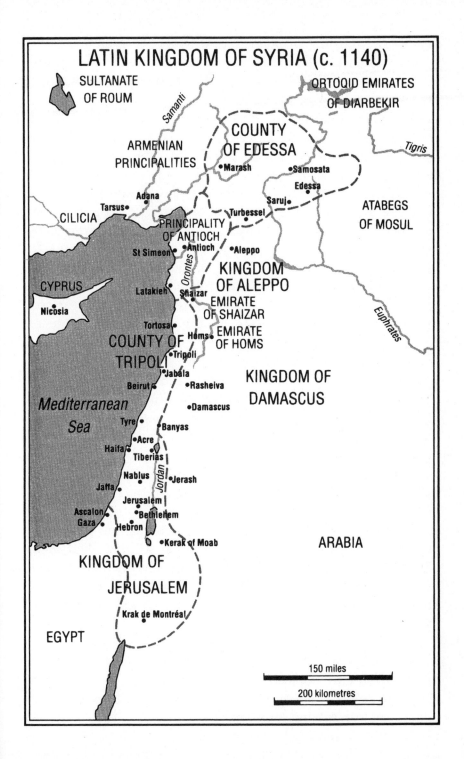

LATIN KINGDOM OF SYRIA (c. 1140)

SULTANATE
OF ROUM

ORTOQID EMIRATES
OF DIARBEKIR

Samanti

COUNTY
OF EDESSA

Tigris

ARMENIAN
PRINCIPALITIES

•Marash

•Samosata

Edessa

Adana

Tarsus•

Saruj•

ATABEGS
OF MOSUL

CILICIA

•Turbessel

PRINCIPALITY
OF ANTIOCH

St Simeon•

•Antioch

•Aleppo

Orontes

KINGDOM
OF ALEPPO

CYPRUS

Latakieh•

Shaizar•

EMIRATE
OF SHAIZAR

Nicosia•

Tortosa•

Homs•

EMIRATE
OF HOMS

COUNTY OF
TRIPOLI

•Tripoli

•Jabala

Euphrates

Beirut•

•Rasheiva

KINGDOM OF
DAMASCUS

*Mediterranean
Sea*

•Damascus

Tyre •

•Banyas

•Acre

Haifa•

Tiberias

Jordan

Nablus•

•Jerash

Jaffa•

Jerusalem

Ascalon•

•Bethlehem

Gaza •

Hebron•

•Kerak of Moab

ARABIA

KINGDOM OF
JERUSALEM

Krak de Montréal

EGYPT

150 miles

200 kilometres

days of the journey through Roum, when the men were still fit and the enemy no great danger, the incidence of sickness was a warning of terrors to come. When Anselm of Ribemont, in November 1097, sent the archbishop of Rheims a report of the progress so far, he asked for prayers for the knights of his entourage who were dead. Seven of his companions had been killed in battle, at Nicaea or Dorylaeum, but six others had died of sickness, or as Anselm put it, 'in peace'. The proportion between the loss to war and the loss to sickness was about even. Desertion was another cause of loss. The support of the poor people of the crusade was ever fickle. If they were content and well maintained by their lords they would go on. In the face of starvation, or sickness, or just lack of progress and success, many would fall by the wayside or turn tail. Later, several knights of reputation and some lords, both great and small, abandoned the crusade, to the sorrow and shame of Christendom.

Disease and poor food soon began to take a toll on the animals as well. Pack-animals struggled and suddenly collapsed. Ill-fed horses, used to the hayfields of Europe, declined and died under the onslaught of flies and ticks and the Cilician sun. 'We lost most of our horses,' lamented the Gesta 'so that many of our knights had to go on as foot-soldiers, or for lack of horses we had to use oxen as mounts. And our great need compelled us to use goats, sheep and dogs as beasts of burden.'

Again, this was confirmed by Fulcher: 'Truly, you would either laugh or perhaps shed tears of compassion, when our people, lacking beasts of burden because so many had died, loaded wethers, nanny-goats, sows or dogs with their possessions. We saw the backs of these little animals chafed by the heavy loads. And from time to time even armed knights used oxen as their mounts.'

The loss of horses had serious consequences, which became worse as time went on. By November 1097, there were less than a thousand horses in the whole army. The chronicler Raymond related that his namesake, the rich Raymond of St Gilles, set up a fund with his own money to replace the mounts lost by his knights. Raymond's party of Provençals was the largest group in the army, yet his knights had only a hundred horses. Horses were given extra rations, even when the men themselves were doing so poorly. A starving man might open the vein of a horse to drink the blood, though many refused for fear of weakening the mounts. In one of the many skirmishes below the wall at Antioch, the western knights broke off the engagement to chase a riderless horse and as a result lost the fight. To these knights, it was more important to capture a stray horse than to drive back the enemy. Even the great lords Godfrey of Bouillon and Robert of Flanders found themselves for a time without horses.

The truth was that the crusading army without the overwhelming force of its heavy cavalry lost much of its power, and the foot-soldiers, unprotected by the armoured knights, were an easy target for the fast-riding, agile Turkish archers. Even more important, a Christian knight, a member of the order of chivalry, forced to fight on foot, or red-faced with indignation on an ox, was a man ashamed. In the eyes of others he was reduced in feudal rank, and in his own eyes he lacked self-respect. To have to endure such a condition was a grave indignity, amounting almost to a loss of manhood.

After a month's hard travel across the arid lands of central Anatolia the road became easier. The *Gesta* noted:

> At last we began to reach fertile country, full of delicious things to eat and all sorts of provisions. Finally we came to Iconium [Konya], where the citizens gave us advice, warning us to carry skins full of water, which is very scarce for a day's journey from that city. This we did, and then we came to a river where we camped for two days while our scouts took the road before us to Heraclea [Ereghli], where a large Turkish garrison was waiting to ambush us. But our knights, trusting in Almighty God, attacked these turks boldly. That day, the enemy was defeated and fled as quickly as an arrow shot from a bowstring by a strong hand. We rushed into the city at once and stayed for four days.

There was consternation among the Turks at this steady Christian advance. Ibn al-Qalanisi recorded the alarm among the leaders:

Yaghi Siyan, lord of Antioch, therefore hastened to his city, and sent his son to all the other cities and districts, appealing for aid and support, imploring them to hurry to the Holy War, while he set about fortifying Antioch and expelling its Christian population. On the 2nd of Shawwal [12 September] the Frankish armies descended on Baghras and turned their attack towards the territories of Antioch, whereupon those who were in the forts and strong places close to Antioch revolted against us and killed their garrisons, except for a few who were able to escape. The people of Artah did likewise, and called for re-inforcements from the Franks. During Shaban a comet appeared in the west. It rose for a space of about 20 days, and then disappeared.

The campaign was going well for the crusaders. Then, in the middle of September, there occurred one of those moments of individualism – or indiscipline – that bedevilled the Christian army. Tancred, the energetic young nephew of Bohemond, and Count Baldwin, brother of Godfrey of Bouillon, decided to strike out on their own. Their decision was accompanied by, perhaps even resulted from, an omen which Fulcher, who was attached to Baldwin's party, described: 'We saw a certain sign in the sky shining with a whitish brilliance, appearing in the shape of a sword with the point towards the east. We did not know what it promised for the future, but committed both the coming time and the present to the Lord.'

For both sides, it was in the nature of holy warfare for moments of doubt or decision to be marked in the heavens.

Tancred headed south to Tarsus, birthplace of St Paul, a city of Greeks and Armenians governed by the Turks. He routed the Turkish garrison and was getting ready to enter the city when Baldwin's raiding-party arrived at the gates. At once, the two leaders quarrelled over the city, unable to agree whether to share it or to plunder it, until Tancred with scowls and ill-will was forced to withdraw by Baldwin's superior rank and by his larger and stronger band. Baldwin placed a garrison in Tarsus. Then, made bold by this success, he struck out on further independent adventures: 'Trusting in the Lord and in his own strength, he collected a few soldiers and set out towards the Euphrates river, and there he seized many forts both by force and by cunning.'

Emperor Alexius, the man who had an historical claim on all this territory, had expected and feared just this kind of behaviour. He knew that the crusading princes were bold, impatient, ambitious men, greedy for wealth and power. There was a limit to their piety, and likely to be a limit also to the amount of pain, boredom and frustration they could sustain as mere lieutenants in the unwieldy mass of the large army. Much better to risk all in an act of daring, to take advantage of the moment to carve out one's own small principality, and to let the great work of Christendom go hang. In the four months from October 1097, Count Baldwin showed how easily a brave and resourceful leader might do this.

He set out for Edessa, beyond the Euphrates in Mesopotamia. This was an Armenian city ruled by a prince who held it in fief from the Byzantine emperor. The Armenians were hard put to hold their city against the encircling Turks, and since the ruler Thoros had no children to succeed him, he welcomed a strong and active Latin to help keep Islam at bay. Fulcher, who was travelling with Baldwin, saw the enthusiasm of the local population: 'When we passed by the villages of the Armenians, it was astonishing to see them running towards us with crosses and standards, kissing our feet and garments most humbly for love of God, because they heard that we would defend them from the Turks.'

Joyfully received in Edessa, Baldwin and his small band of between sixty and eighty knights took over the city. Within fifteen days Thoros was dead, and Baldwin was seated in the palace as ruler. How it came about was something of a mystery. Fulcher, by now Baldwin's chaplain, spoke of an uprising by the citizens against Thoros, but a city chronicler said darkly that Baldwin himself incited and supported the uprising, and then took the benefit from it. If that were the case, Emperor Alexius at least would not have been surprised.

While Baldwin was playing the saviour-prince, in pursuit of his own fortune, the main army of the crusaders went steadily through Cilicia. The people of this land were Armenians formally under Turkish rule. They had no love for their Muslim masters and, as Ibn al-Qalanisi testified, they opened their gates to the westerners and gladly supplied their wants as far as they could. To repay this hospitality, and the trust placed in their arms, the crusaders went 'thirsting and raging after the blood of Turks', as the old campaigner of the *Gesta* phrased it. This savagery had an effect, and the disorganized Turks melted before the fiery Christian wrath. Once again, sickness rather than the enemy slowed the advance. Raymond of St Gilles was so ill, he held up all the Provençals as his men carried him carefully on a litter-bed. Feeling him close to death, with his pulse scarcely moving, they laid him on the ground, and the priest gave him the last rites, but his loyal chaplain proclaimed that God would not allow him to die, and 'divine clemency, which preferred him as leader of the army, lifted him from death and restored him to health'.

By early October the crusaders were on the border of Syria, strung out in thin files that wound into the high wastes of the Anti-Taurus mountains. The *Gesta* complained of the rough and dangerous road:

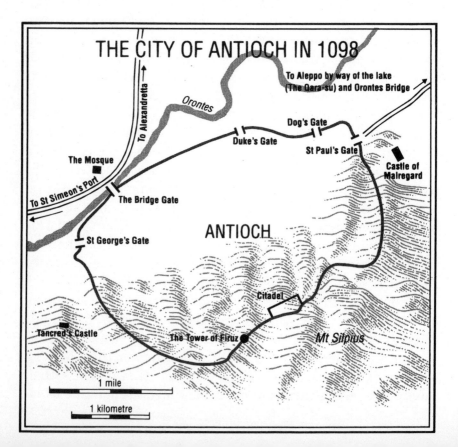

We began to cross a damnable mountain, which was so high and steep that two men could not pass on the path. Horses fell over the precipice, and pack-animals linked together pulled one another down. As for our knights, they stood about in a great state of gloom, wringing their hands because they were so frightened and miserable. They did not know what to do with themselves, they were so burdened and weighted with coats of mail and armour. They tried to sell shields and helmets and breastplates for a few pence or for whatever they could get. If there were no buyers, they threw their arms away and went on. When we had crossed that accursed mountain we came to a city called Marash, and so at last our knights marched more easily and came into the valley which contains the royal city of Antioch, capital of Syria.

The Turks and their allies had fallen back on Antioch, and there was much turmoil in the surrounding country as the invaders clashed with Muslim columns hurrying to the defence of the walls:

When we came near to the Iron Bridge over the River Orontes our scouts found innumerable Turks hurrying to the defence of Antioch. Our men dashed at these Turks at once, and the barbarians were thrown into confusion and fled, leaving many killed. Having defeated them, by God's grace we took many spoils, horses, camels, mules and asses laden with grain and wine. At length the main body of our army came up and camped on the bank of the river. The gallant Bohemond took 4,000 knights to guard the city gates, so that no one could go to and fro secretly in the night. Next day, by about noon on Wednesday, 21 October, a strict blockade was put on three gates of the city, for we could not besiege it from the other side where a high mountain stood in our way.

Bohemond and his Normans, as was usual, were eager to get into action, but as Raymond of Aguilers wrote, the general mood in the army was more cautious:

When we came near Antioch many of our princes did not wish to besiege it. Winter was close at hand, and our men were scattered and dispirited by the many storms. They said also that we ought to wait for re-inforcements rumoured to be coming from France, and thus they urged us to go into winter-quarters and await the spring. But other princes, with Count Raymond of St Gilles among them, said, 'We have come here inspired by God. Through His mercy we won Nicaea, a very strong city, and by the same clemency we have withstood all that the Turks could do against us. Our army is united and at peace one with another. Thus we should put our fate in the hands of the Lord. We ought not to fear kings, nor even the chief of kings, nor yet places nor times, when God has snatched us already from so many dangers.' Then we went up against Antioch and pitched our camp in the very eye of the enemy, so that his arrows might reach even into our tents.

Since July, it had been a long, hot, dusty, tedious road. The crusaders were done with marching for the moment. Pride, a soldier's sense of well-being, insisted that it was time for a fight.

In late October 1097 the siege of Antioch began. The city was only loosely invested because the precipitous mountain country rising tumultuously from the foot of the eastern wall made it impossible to close off that side. There were gates north and south, and three gates faced west into the river-plain of the Orontes. Here the western army camped in the meadows, commanding in particular the bridge over the river which carried the main road to the coast, fourteen miles away. Antioch was strategically placed in the narrow plain between mountains and sea, on the only practical western route into Palestine. The city was strongly defended, a compact place on a steep site, with massive, well-built walls, and both sides recognized that the fortunes of war could be made or broken here.

A medieval siege was often a curious undertaking, hardly ever strictly maintained, and with many exchanges and truces between attackers and defenders. The Arab historian Ibn al-Athir wrote of the Muslim preparations for the siege:

> When Yaghi Siyan, ruler of Antioch, heard of the Frankish approach, he did not know how the Christians of his city would react. So he sent the Muslims outside the walls to

dig trenches, and the next day sent the Christians out alone to continue the task. But at the end of the day he refused to allow them back, saying, 'Antioch is yours, but you will have to leave it to me till I see what happens between us and the Franks.' 'But who will protect our wives and children?' they cried. And he answered, 'I shall look after them for you.' So they resigned themselves to their fate and lived in the Frankish camp for all the months of the siege.

This was an astute move. It diminished the number of mouths to be fed among people who could hardly be trusted to defend the walls. Yet it kept within the city hostages for their good behaviour. It also recognized that a governor had a duty to a local population, even if those folk were of a different religion. But partly as a consequence of this divided Christian allegiance, within and without the city, there was even more coming and going than usual. 'Oil, salt, and other necessary things,' wrote Ibn al-Qalanisi, 'became dear and unprocurable in Antioch, but so much was smuggled into the city that they became cheap again.'

The first reaction of the crusaders, as they settled into waiting, was one of relief. The author of the *Gesta* noted a satisfactory period of recuperation after the pains of the long march:

> Our Turkish enemies inside the city were too much afraid of us to try to attack us for nearly two weeks. Meanwhile we grew pretty familiar with the surrounding country and found there plenty of provisions, vineyards full of fruit and stores of corn, laden apple-trees and all sorts of good things to eat.
>
> Armenians and Syrians [Christians] living in the city came to our men in the camp daily, pretending to flee to us, but their wives were in the city. These men were spying on us and reporting everything we said to the besieged in the walls. So the Turks found out about us, and they began gradually to emerge and attack our pilgrims, on this flank and on that, and everywhere that they could lie in ambush, from the sea to the mountains.

Soon, in the opinion of the *Gesta*, this Turkish confidence slid into insolence, when a woman doing domestic tasks in the safety of Bohemond's camp was shot by a Turkish archer. The western princes began to reconsider their strategy. Intending to bottle up the defenders more than before, they built a fort on the high point they called Mount Malregard, overlooking the northern gate and the main inland road to Aleppo. Later, this fort was balanced by another at the southern end of the city, built on the ruins of a monastery and known as Tancred's castle since it was manned by his troops.

After a month or so of siege the western leaders saw nothing in their position to worry them unduly. By Christmas, food was becoming scarce and very expensive. Bohemond and Robert of Flanders took a large detachment of knights into the countryside, to scour the land for provisions. In the course of their search, these crusaders ran into a Muslim army led by Duqaq, amir of Damascus, on its way to relieve Antioch. The Christians put this army to flight, but, returning in triumph, though still without food, discovered that the garrison of Antioch, taking advantage of the absence of 'some very valiant knights' had gone on the attack:

> Those wretched barbarians made a sudden, crafty attack on us, killing many soldiers who were off their guard. On that sad day the bishop of Le Puy lost his seneschal who was holding his banner. Had it not been for the river dividing us, they would have done great harm to our people. Then the gallant Bohemond arrived back from the region of the Saracens, where our men had been ransacking the whole countryside in their search for supplies. Some had found a few things but others were still empty-handed. Approaching our camp, Bohemond saw many fugitives running away, and he shouted, 'Miserable wretches! Scum of all Christendom! Why are you fleeing so fast? Stop and join forces, instead of scattering like stupid sheep. Halt, or the enemy will kill you. They're on the watch for ninnies like you, fools with no leader ripe for capture or death!' So Bohemond hurried back to the camp with his men, who were for the most part empty-handed.

This skirmish, coming on top of the fruitless search for supplies, was a bad set-back for the crusaders, and the chronicler

Raymond gave a fuller, grim account of those moments of blood, muddle and terror:

> The Turks formed a line and began to rush against our men at the bridge by a lower path. Meanwhile, our knights went chasing after a certain horse whose master had been over- thrown. When our people saw this, they thought the knights were in flight and at once showed their backs to the enemy. Then, even if our Frankish knights wished to fight for our people, they were caught up in the crowd of fleeing foot- soldiers. Arms and legs and manes and tails of horses were all entangled, men were thrown from the saddle, and knights backed away in fear for the safety of themselves and the foot-soldiers. The Turks, without delay or pity, pur- sued and slaughtered the living and despoiled the bodies of the dead. Also, in their shameful flight, our men plunged into the river, where they were easily assaulted with stones and arrows or carried under the water. In this encounter, the enemy killed about fifteen of our knights and about twenty foot-soldiers. The standard-bearer of the bishop was killed, and his banner was captured.

In the warfare of the time the loss of a standard was a dire event, reflecting badly on both the competence and the courage of the warriors. For this reason, for the deep misery of this Christmastide, and despite the success against Duqaq's army of relief, the crusaders were dejected: 'A strange result of this achievement was that after the enemy had been put to flight the courage of our men decreased, so that they did not dare to pursue those whom they saw running headlong.'

The consequences of scarcity and the set-back in battle were an army on the edge of famine and also an army suffering something worse than famine – a breakdown in military spirit and morale:

> The Armenians and Syrians, seeing that our men had come back with hardly any supplies, consulted together and went over certain mountain paths which they knew, enquiring everywhere and buying whatever provisions they could bring to our camp for sale. But even so there was a terrible famine. A single ass-load was sold for eight *perpre*, which is a

hundred and twenty shillings in our money. Many of our people died, not having the means to buy at so dear a rate.

In this great wretchedness and misery, William the Carpenter and Peter the Hermit fled secretly away. Tancred went after them and caught them and brought them back in disgrace. Then that said William lay all night, like a lump of evil rubbish, on the floor of Bohemond's tent. At dawn, he stood before Bohemond, red with shame, and Bohemond said to him, 'You disgrace to the Frankish army, you villainous blot on the people of Gaul! You loathsome man, you shame of the earth, why did you run away so vilely? Did you want to betray our Christian knights, just as you betrayed those others in Spain?' William was silent and nothing came from his mouth. But almost all his Frankish compatriots begged Bohemond to save him from worse punishment. Then my lord Bohemond calmly nodded, and said, 'Freely I grant this for the love I bear you all, provided this man will swear, heart and mind, never to turn aside, for good or ill, from the road to Jerusalem. And Tancred shall swear neither to permit nor to do harm to him.' Tancred agreed, and Bohemond sent the Carpenter away forthwith. But later, in greatest villainy, he sneaked off from us, for he was ashamed. This poverty and wretchedness was sent by God because of our sins.

This act of generosity by Bohemond, an unrelenting and usually unforgiving commander, was perhaps explained by Raymond of Aguilers, a Provençal deeply suspicious of the Norman soldier. According to Raymond, Bohemond was himself preparing a departure from the crusade that would be a kind of betrayal in its own way:

And so the poor began to leave and also many of the rich who feared poverty. Those who stayed for love or valour allowed their horses to waste away, because there was little straw and fodder was so dear that seven or eight shillings were not enought for a night's feed. Then another calamity fell on the army. Bohemond, who had distinguished himself in Spain, said he would leave. He said he had come for honour, but now he saw his men and horses dying for want. He also said he was not a rich man and his private means were not enough for so long a siege. We found out afterwards that he said all this because he was plotting to become the ruler of Antioch.

As so often in times of trouble, the pious Raymond saw God's displeasure manifest in portents and heavenly disturbance:

> There was a great earthquake on the third day before the Calends of January, and we saw a very marvellous sign in the sky. In the first watch of the night the sky in the north was so red it might have been the dawn. In this way God chastised his army, yet the minds of some were so blind and abandoned that they did not turn from luxury or robbery. At this time the bishop of Le Puy ordered a fast of three days and urged men to prayer and alms, and made a procession through the camp. And he commanded the priests to devote themselves to the mass and to prayers, and the clerics to sing psalms.

The priests put the crusaders in mind of their spiritual responsibility, while most of the leaders were working hard to stem the malaise and feelings of disaffection within the army. They had their suspicions about Bohemond and thought they had discovered signs of habitual Greek treachery:

> There was with our army a representative of the emperor, a certain member of his household named Tatikios, a man with a mangled nose and twisted in virtue. I had almost forgotten him, because he deserves to be lost to oblivion. This man was daily whispering in the ears of the princes, proposing plans and assaults and stratagems. Also, something else was happening. All the princes except Count Raymond promised the city to Bohemond, once it were taken, and they all swore an agreement to keep the siege going for seven years, if it took that long to capture Antioch.
> At this time, there was also a rumour that an army of the emperor was coming, made up of Slavs, Patzinaks, Cumans and those people called Turcopuli who are of Turkish father and Christian mother, the people who had hurt us on the march and were now afraid to meet us. But all this was invented by that twisted Tatikios, in order to be able to get away. Then this Greek, a master of betrayal and perjury, slipped off in flight, but first having granted Bohemond two or three other cities. With everlasting shame

on himself and his people, he abandoned his tents and his servants, feigned a journey to the army of the emperor, and fled cursed by God.

Anna Comnena ascribed the flight of Tatikios not to Greek treachery but to the plotting of Bohemond. He knew that Antioch, if it fell, should be handed over to the emperor's representative, so he made sure that, when the time came, there would be no representative available to claim Antioch from its Latin conqueror. All this was an example of the usual prejudice – Latins blaming Greek double-dealing, and Greeks blaming Latin greed and self-interest.

After three months of frustration and winter misery, Antioch began to hope for relief. Rudwan, amir of Aleppo, approached over the mountains at the beginning of February 1098 with a fair-sized Muslim army. 'The Turks were menacing us on the one hand,' said the *Gesta*, 'and hunger tormented us on the other, and there was no one to help us or to bring aid. The ordinary soldiers, and those who were very poor, fled to Cyprus or Roum or into the mountains. We dared not go down to the sea-coast for fear of those Turkish brutes, and there was no road open to us anywhere.' Pent up like wild animals in a cage, the crusaders welcomed the angry release of bitterness and warlike energy.

No one was more charged with purpose and ready for the fight than Bohemond. He, more than any, had the incentive to take Antioch, since he expected to keep it. When the battle came, the *Gesta* gave him the glory of the engagement, though the report by the cool Raymond, perhaps out of pique or loyalty to the Provençals, refrained from mentioning him. The crusaders divided their army, leaving the foot-soldiers entrenched before the city, while the knights hurried out to pick their ground. Finding a strip of level land between the River Orontes and a marsh, they made a stand there, knowing that the larger Muslim army could not be fully deployed on the narrow neck of land.

Then our men drew up in six lines. Five of them charged the enemy at once, while Bohemond held his troop a little in reserve. Battle was joined, and fought hand-to-hand. The din arose to heaven, and a storm of missiles darkened the sky. The main body of the Turks, kept in the rear, then attacked so fiercely that our men were forced to give ground. When Bohemond, a commander of the greatest experience, saw this, he groaned and gave orders to his constable, saying, 'Charge with fury and fight bravely for God and the Holy Sepulchre, for you know in truth that this is not a war of the flesh but of the Holy Spirit.' Protected on all sides by the sign of the Cross, Bohemond led the charge like a lion starved for three or four days that comes roaring from its cave thirsty for the blood of cattle. It falls upon the flocks, tearing sheep as they flee here and there. Bohemond's attack was so fierce that the points of his banner went flying even over the heads of the Turks.

The other troops, seeing the bold banner carried so bravely, stopped their retreat at once. Then all our men together rushed the amazed Turks and put them to flight, pursuing and massacring them right up to the Orontes bridge. The Turks fled to their fort, looted it, set fire to it, and ran away. Then the Armenians and the Syrians, seeing this complete defeat of the Turks, came creeping forth and laid ambushes in the wild passes, killing or taking many of the enemy.

Thus, by the will of God, the enemy was overcome. Our men captured many horses and other needful things, and they brought back a hundred Turkish heads to the city gates, to show to the ambassadors of the amir of Cairo [the Fatimid opponents of the Turks] who were camped there.

Once again, the Turks had been beaten by the Christian knights in open battle, but Antioch was no closer to surrender. The garrison still commanded the very strong walls and could sally out at will to harass and surprise the crusaders, even after three and a half months of siege. The princes found it necessary to contain these raids by building another fort dominating the Orontes bridge and the Bridge Gate of the city. Builders and materials for this task were waiting at Suwaidiyah on the coast, where they had been delivered by Genoese and English ships at various times since November, but the crusaders had been too afraid to attempt the fourteen-mile journey to the place they called St Simeon's Port. Now, under

MACHINES FOR THROWING DARTS AND STONES WERE WIDELY
USED WHEN ATTACKING FORTIFIED LOCATIONS

the compulsion of the moment, Bohemond offered to take an escort of knights to give safe-conduct from the port. On his return, on 6 March 1098, Bohemond arrived back just in time to help drive off another Turkish attack. Once again, there was a small, angry, bloody encounter that stained the river red, but proved nothing beyond the ferocity and unwarranted heartlessness of this kind of warfare:

> Next day, at dawn, Turks came from the city and collected all the stinking corpses of their dead and buried them at the mosque between the gate and the bridge. They also buried clothes and gold bezants and weapons and other instruments whose names we do not know. When our men heard that the Turks had buried their dead, they came quickly to that anteroom of the devil and ordered the bodies to be dug up and dragged from the graves and the tombs destroyed. They threw all the corpses into a pit and cut off the heads which they brought to our tents, to be counted exactly, except those they loaded on four horses belonging to the amir of Cairo and sent to the coast.
>
> When the Turks saw this, they grieved almost to death, lamenting every day and weeping and howling. On the third day, we came with great satisfaction to build the fort already mentioned, with stones we had taken from the tombs of the Turks. When the fort was finished, we began to press hard from every side on our woebegone enemy. Now we could go safely wherever we liked, to the gate and the mountains, praising and glorifying our Lord God.

Winter was over, and improving, sunny weather put men in a better mood. The tactical reassessment, and the firmer grip on the gates, had curtailed the Turkish freedom to attack. Now three crusader forts, blocking the skyline to north and south and west, effectively shut in the garrison. Pasture was becoming available for the horses, and a drop in the price of provisions slightly relieved the chronic shortage of money that had made itself known in so many desperate letters home. Poverty had caused as many to abandon the crusade as had sickness, wounds and disgust. Some of the influential men had even improved their finances greatly, though it is not clear how this happened. At the end of March, in a cheerful letter to his wife, Stephen of Blois wrote: 'This messenger left me before Antioch in good health and unharmed and, through God's grace, in the greatest prosperity. You may know for certain, my beloved, that I now have twice as much of gold, silver and other riches as your love assigned me at the time I parted from you.'

Despite this evident good cheer, there were still problems for the crusaders, and one of the most pressing was the question of authority and leadership. This was recognized by the chronicler Raymond when he described the construction and the manning of the new fort:

> We consulted at this time as to which of the princes could go to garrison the fortress. Truly, a matter of common responsibility is often neglected, since each thinks that another will look after it. And while some of the princes, as if for a price, sought the privilege of guarding it, Count Raymond took on the custody against the will of his men, both to avoid the charge of sloth and avarice, and to show the path of energy and valour to the lazy. For during the past summer he had been severely ill for a long time, and he had been so weak for the winter that men thought him neither ready to fight nor to pay. So there was a reflection on his courage, and he suffered such hatred that he was almost cut off from his own people.

As the richest lord and the leader of the largest group of crusaders, Raymond of St Gilles had expected to wield authority in the army. When he could not do so there was a gap at the top into which a poor but ambitious and forceful general like Bohemond tried to move. Bohemond, however, was an unloved Norman, with no rank and too much sly ambition. Perhaps it was an attempt to rein him in that explains a curious passage in Stephen's letter to his wife, when he boasts that the 'common consent of the whole army' had appointed him 'their lord and director and governor of all their acts up to the present time'. No one knows in what sense Stephen was 'lord and director' of the army. He was a high-ranking prince, an affectionate husband, and a likeable fellow, but the future proved him to be a poor solider and no leader. He was a frail staff for the army to lean on.

Still the siege went on. At last, as the summer heat was beginning to rebound from the walls, it took an act of betrayal to accomplish what the crusaders could not do. For some time Bohemond had been secretly sending messages to one of the defenders, a certain Firuz, whom some spoke of as a Muslim and others as a Christian renegade. Ibn al-Athir said Firuz was 'an armourer whom the Franks bribed with a fortune in money and lands'. The *Gesta*, which as usual applauded the cunning and enterprise of Bohemond, told the story in this way:

> There was a certain amir of Turkish race called Firuz to whom Bohemond sent messengers, to see if out of friendship he would receive him into the city. He promised to have Firuz christened and to give him riches and great honour. Firuz took this temptation, saying, 'I am custodian of those three towers, which I freely promise to Bohemond whenever he pleases.' Then Bohemond went coolly to the princes looking pleased with himself, and said jokingly, 'Most wise lords, all of us here, both great and small, are in dire poverty and misery, battered in fortune. Would it be a good and proper plan to set one of us above the others, and let him keep the city, if he can bring about its downfall?' But the princes indignantly refused, saying, 'This city shall not be granted to anyone. We all have had equal toil, so we shall share it alike, with equal honour.' Then Bohemond looked less pleased with himself, and went straight off.

So the matter rested for a little while until word came of the approach of another large and powerful army. Then the princes reconsidered, thinking that Bohemond might deserve the city if he could bring an end to this miserably protracted stalemate. They agreed to his plan, with the proviso that Antioch should revert to the Greek emperor 'if he comes to our aid and fulfils all the obligations that he vowed'.

Messengers were again sent to Firuz, with promises of riches heaped on riches, and a stratagem was agreed. Bohemond confided the plan to the princes and to the bishop of Le Puy and told them, 'God willing, this night Antioch shall be betrayed to us.'

All the preparations were ready. Our knights went by the plain and the foot-soldiers through the mountains, marching all night till towards dawn they approached the towers guarded by Firuz. Then the men found a ladder that was already lashed firmly to the wall, and nearly sixty of them went up into the towers where Firuz was waiting for them. But when Firuz saw them he was afraid because they were so few, and he cried out in Greek, 'Why so few Franks? Where is the hero Bohemond? Where is that unconquerable general?' At once, a Norman from southern Italy ran back down the ladder, shouting to Bohemond, 'What is the sense, sir, in standing there? What are you here for? Look, we have taken three towers already.' Then Bohemond leapt into action, and many others gladly followed him up the ladder.

When they saw this, those above called out cheerfully, 'God's will!' and we roared back the same. Now an amazing number of our men were on the walls, killing all they could find, and the brother of Firuz was amongst them. But then the ladder broke, and for a moment we were in grief and despair. But those below began fumbling and poking in the dark and found a little postern gate. All rushed at it, and broke it down, and entered.

The cries of countless people arose, making a terrible uproar in the city. Bohemond wasted no time but unfurled his glorious banner and ordered it to be carried to a hill opposite the citadel. All the city was screaming at once. As the sun came up, our men in their tents beyond the walls heard this overpowering noise. They ran out and saw Bohemond's standard flying on the hill. In triumph they beat down the gates, killing all the Turks and Saracens they could find, except for those who fled to the citadel. Some slipped through the gates and saved themselves by flight. Yaghi Siyan, the governor of the city, who was much afraid of the Franks, fled headlong with many companions into the country around Tancred's fort, not far from the walls, but their horses were tired and they stopped to rest, hiding in a village house. When the Syrians and Armenians of those hills caught the fugitive and knew who he was, they cut off his head at once and took it to Bohemond, as the price of their own safety. The governor's belt and scabbard alone were worth sixty bezants.

This happened on a Thursday, the third of June. All the streets of the city on every side were full of corpses, so that no one could endure to be there because of the stench. Nor could one walk in the paths and alleyways except over the bodies of the dead.

The accounts of the fall of Antioch given by the Arabic historians agreed on most points with the reports of the westerners. Firuz, the cuirass-maker, was reviled as a traitor, but for Yaghi Siyan, the governor, there was some sympathy. True, he had opened the gates and fled in panic, but he had repented and his death had a certain sad nobility:

> As for Yaghi Siyan, when the sun was up he recovered himself and halted his flight. He asked his companions where he was, and hearing that he was four parasangs from the city he repented that he had run away instead of fighting to the death. He began to groan and weep because he had deserted household and children. Overcome by grief he fell fainting from his horse. His companions tried to lift him back into the saddle, but they could not make him balance there, so they left him for dead and escaped. He was at his last gasp when an Armenian shepherd found him and killed him, and took his head to the Franks at Antioch.

The governor was a tragic figure, not a fool or a criminal, and indeed in the opinion of Ibn al-Athir he was a good man. 'Yaghi Siyan,' the historian wrote, 'showed courage and wisdom and judgment.' His defence of his city had been resolute, effective but also humane. 'If all the Franks who died at Antioch had survived, they would have overrun all the lands of Islam. He protected the families of the Christians in the city and would not allow a hair of their heads to be touched.

The Christian priest Raymond of Aguilers also thought that the fall of Antioch warranted something more dignified and sorrowful than the triumphal account in the *Gesta*. Raymond had less to say about Bohemond and his notorious duplicity, and more feeling for the fate of the unfortunate Muslim defenders:

As the day dawned, our standards appeared on the southern hill of the city. When the enemy saw our men on the mountain above them, some fled through the gates, others threw themselves headlong from the walls. No one resisted. In truth, the Lord had confounded them. Then after a long time a joyous spectacle appeared to us, with those who had withstood us for so many months now completely trapped. Our joy over the defeated enemy was great, but we grieved for the more than thirty horses that had their necks broken in the streets.

It was impossible to say how great were the spoils captured in Antioch. You may believe as much as you wish, and then add to it. Nor can we say how many Turks and Saracens were killed. Furthermore, it is cruel to exult in the many and various deaths that they had to suffer.

The siege of Antioch, which ate like a cancer into the resolve and the resources of the crusade, lasted from 21 October 1097 to 3 June 1098.

7

A WORLD OF QUARRELS

All was in the hands of God, life and death. 'He permitted it,' wrote Fulcher of Chartres, 'and the people deserved it, because so many times they destroyed cheaply all things of God. He permitted the Christians to be killed by the Turks, so that the Christians would have the assurance of salvation, and the Turks would have the perdition of their souls.'

For those touched by the spirit of God, departure from this life was no more than a welcome valediction, as it was said in the Epistle to the Romans: 'Whom He called, them He also justified; and whom He justified, them He also gloried.'

'What then?' Fulcher went on. 'There were some of our men who left the siege of Antioch because it brought so much anguish. Others left out of poverty, others for cowardice, others for fear of death, first the poor and then the rich. Stephen, Count of Blois, withdrew from the siege and eventually returned to France by sea. Therefore all of us grieved, for he was a noble man and valiant in arms. On the day after his departure the city of Antioch fell to us. If he had persevered, he would have rejoiced in the victory with us. This act disgraced him. For a good beginning serves no one unless it is well consummated.'

In this painful world of change, what chance was there for the success of the crusade when Stephen, the man chosen to be 'lord and director' of the whole army, deserted a day before victory? Lives were thrown up and down, as if in the hands of an inept juggler. Within three days of entering Antioch the crusaders were themselves under siege in the place they had spent seven months trying to conquer. Kerbuqa, amir of Mosul, had arrived with a strong force that seemed, for once, to transcend local Muslim rivalries. If this army had not lost two weeks failing to dislodge Baldwin from Edessa, it might have arrived in time to save Antioch for the Muslims.

As it was, in one day Kerbuqa turned jubilation into fear. Raymond of Aguilers wrote:

> While our men were busy counting their spoils, they had left off the attack on the upper fortress where some Muslims had fled for safety. We were watching the pagan dancing girls and feasting in splendour, not at all mindful of God who had blessed us, when suddenly, on the third day, we ourselves were under siege. And this was more dangerous for us, because the upper fortress of the citadel was still in enemy hands. So under the stress of fear we renewed the attack on the citadel.

With a fresh enemy without, and the rump of a defeated enemy still within the city, the crusaders were in great danger. Stores of food in the city were very low. Streets blocked with corpses bred disease. To man the full extent of the walls stretched the western army to the limit, and some of the citizens, particularly the Syrians, liked the Franks no better than the Turks and could not be trusted. On the other hand, the massive walls were undamaged, giving good shelter to the crusaders and their followers. And Kerbuqa, through poor generalship, failed to press home his advantage. The author of the *Gesta*, always ready to deride the enemy, thought that over-confidence caused Kerbuqa to throw the chance away:

> The Turks made mock of the Frankish soldiers and brought Kerbuqa a poor rusty sword, a thoroughly bad bow and a spear that was quite useless, all of which they had grabbed from the poor pilgrims. Then they said, 'Look at the

SCENES FROM THE SIEGE OF ANTIOCH

weapons the Franks have brought to fight us!' Kerbuqa chuckled and replied, 'Are these the warlike arms with which the Christians expect to drive us back beyond the borders of Khorasan? Are these the people who drove our Muslims out of Roum, and took the royal city of Antioch, the famous capital of all Syria?'

After a leisurely preparation Kerbuqa attacked Antioch, driving the knight outriders back within the walls, killing many as they tried to cram through the narrow gates, and inducing such a panic that once more some respectable knights preferred running to fighting:

William of Grandmesnil, his brother Aubrey, Guy Trousseau, and Lambert the Poor were all so scared by the previous day's battle that they slipped over the wall secretly in the night and fled on foot to the sea, fleeing so fast that both their hands and their feet were worn away to the bone. And many others, whose names I do not know, fled with them. When they came to the ships in St Simeon's Port, they cried out to the sailors, 'You poor devils, it's time to clear out. All our men are dead, and we barely escaped ourselves from the Turks besieging the city.' When the sailors heard this, they rushed in terror to their ships and put to sea. Then the Turks arrived and killed everyone they could catch. They burnt the ships still jammed in the mouth of the river and took their cargoes.

In the face of this reversal of fortune, the crusaders in Antioch had one steady hope. It was known that Emperor Alexius was bringing a large Byzantine army to help the Franks, though this army was making slow progress somewhere in the middle of Anatolia. In a short time, however, even that hope was denied to the crusaders:

> When we were shut up in the city, lacking help to save us, we waited each day for that coward Stephen, Count of Blois, to return with aid. But hearing that we were surround by Turks, he went secretly into a nearby mountain, and when he saw more enemy tents than he could number he ran away with his troops. Then he went to see the emperor at Philomelium and asked for a private audience, and said, 'I tell you truly that Antioch has fallen to our men, but now we ourselves are all closely besieged, and by this time all will have been killed by the Turks. Go back, as fast as you can, lest the enemy catch you also.'

This message brought by Stephen was confirmed by other deserters, and when William of Grandmesnil said the same thing, he was believed because he was married to Bohemond's sister. Alexius was a cautious man and the reports that he was receiving fell in well with the Byzantine view of the western warriors. They were violent and impetuous, but less successful when they met a steady, planned resistance. Anna Comnena voiced the Greek prejudice:

> The truth is that the Franks combine an independent spirit and imprudence, not to mention an absolute refusal to cultivate a disciplined art of war. When battle is imminent, inspired by passion, they are irresistible, provided that the opposition everywhere gives ground. But if their foes meet them in a systematic manner, all their boldness vanishes. Generally speaking, Franks are indomitable in the opening cavalry charge, but afterwards it is actually very easy to beat them.

On this view, Emperor Alexius expected the crusaders to fail under adversity, and since the safety of his whole empire rested on his decisions, the emperor abandoned Antioch, which he could not have reached for two weeks or more. He withdrew his army to prepare for an expected onslaught from victorious Turks. It was, to the crusaders, only another Greek betrayal. Now, without hope of military relief, they were ready to give way to despair:

> There was such famine in the city that a horse's head with-out the tongue was sold for two or three *solidi*, the guts of a goat for five, and a hen for eight or nine. And what shall I say about bread? Even five *solidi* could not buy enough for one man's hunger. These prices were not astonishing, for our men had much gold and silver and other spoils from the sack of the city, and they did not care what they paid for food. But such was the shortage of things to eat that unripe figs were plucked and cooked and sold. Leaves and withered plants were stewed. Hides of cattle and horses, skins and bones and other discarded bits were boiled and sold at a high price. Many of the knights drank the blood of their own chargers, though they could not yet bear to kill these horses. Another very serious calamity was the con-stant desertion of our men to the Turks who, learning of our misery and weakness, threatened us most violently.

In this emergency, Bohemond was given command of the army. Count Raymond and Adhemar of Le Puy were ill, Stephen of Blois had fled, and the other princes had trouble maintaining their own men. In any case, the ambitious Norman was the best soldier and he soon proved his ability by taking some vigorous if extreme steps. Parts of the conquered city were abandoned. Whole streets were burnt and razed, to clear space and open up lines of defence. A rough but impressive interior wall was built, more easily defended than the exten-sive outer fortifications. All this was something, but it was not enough. The task of the crusade was a work for God. Yet He, like certain princes and knights, seemed to be abandoning the crusaders. Who could understand this? In their grief and fear the crusaders railed against Him:

> You have thrown the whole Christian world into the ditch of utter desperation and unbelief, and given to the most evil of men an incontestable boldness against Your servants for all eternity. No man in future will dare to trust in You,

seeing that those who thought themselves Your servants, more so than any other mortals, are being overwhelmed in hideous ruin. Say, therefore, most pitiful Lord, how shall they have the face to call upon You henceforward, when Your own special servants can expect no better than this?

Then, at the blackest hour, it seemed as if the Lord had heard the crusaders' complaint and relented. A certain Provençal peasant named Peter Bartholomew, a young fellow known for riotous living, had for some months been persuading himself and a few of the idlers of the army that the Apostle Andrew had appeared to him in several visions. The Apostle had revealed that the Holy Lance, which had pierced the side of Christ on the Cross, was buried in Antioch. It was in the Church of St Peter, which the crusaders had just restored to Christianity after some time as a Muslim mosque.

For many weeks, despite the commands from St Andrew, Peter felt unable to bring himself and his revelation to the notice of the leaders. Then, on 10 June 1098, after a brush with the Turks that left Peter sitting on a rock bruised and winded, the Apostle appeared in such a hectoring temper that Peter took his story to Raymond of St Gilles and to the pope's legate, Adhemar of Le Puy. Bishop Adhemar, a level-headed and experienced churchman who might have remembered that a Holy Lance was among the many resplendent treasures already on display in Constantinople, was not inclined to believe Peter Bartholomew. He knew something of the man's reputation, and he felt the natural suspicion of senior clergy for the wilder fictions of ignorant peasants. Moreover, St Andrew, in his visionary lectures to Peter, had been less than complimentary about Adhemar's own part in the crusade. On the other hand, Raymond of St Gilles had the credulity so often shown by rich, pious laymen. He needed some talisman to bolster his fading authority, and he was shrewd enough to know how such a spiritual event, if it were believed, would steel the arm of Christ's warriors. Count Raymond wished to believe and he was easily convinced by Peter's story. He arranged for a search to be made in five days, during which time Peter was given over to St Gilles's own chaplain, who was the chronicler Raymond of Aguilers.

The very night after this decision was taken, a priest called Stephen, in mortal fear of the Turks and weeping in the expectation of his own death, had a vision of Christ in the Church of the Blessed Mary. Christ, in this vision, had a simple message for Bishop Adhemar. 'Then let the bishop speak to the people as follows. "The Lord says this, *Return to me, and I will return to you.*" And when our people enter battle let them say, "The enemy are assembled and glory in their own bravery. There is no other who will fight for us except You, O Lord. You shall destroy their might and scatter them." And say this also to the people, "If you do whatever I command you, even for five days, I will have mercy on you."'

This message, conveyed through a priest, was one that the bishop of Le Puy could well understand and accept. He received it in true faith and humbly submitted, for at the same time it seemed that the heavens also gave evidence. In the night there was a comet, which some saw as a fire from the west engulfing the Turks, and others as a star that split in three and fell on the enemy camp. Amid this abundance of signs, Bishop Adhemar tried to put heart into the crusade, drawing from the leaders an oath that none would leave Antioch without the consent of the others. This was cheering news to the ordinary knights and the men-at-arms who had seen their superiors leaking quietly away. A new stern enthusiasm gripped the army, and the moment for the search of the Lance was awaited with excitement and high anxiety, as Raymond of Aguilers, who was one of the search-party, related:

> On that day, after all preparations and after everyone had been cleared from St Peter's Church, twelve men, together with that man Peter who had spoken of the Lance, began to dig. After we had dug from morning to evening and found nothing, some began to despair. Count Raymond left, because he had to guard the fort. But in the place of him and others who were tired, fresh limbs continued to dig sturdily. Then, when the youth Peter Bartholomew saw that we were worn out, he disrobed and shook off his shoes and jumped into the pit in his shirt, earnestly entreating us to pray to God to give us His Lance for the comfort and victory of His people. At length, the Lord was minded in His

mercy to show us the Holy Lance. And I, who have written this, kissed it as the point alone appeared above the ground. What great joy and exultation then filled the city I cannot describe. The Lance was found on the 18th day before the Calends of July [15 June 1098].'

The occasion was obviously fraudulent. The Arab historians were indignant about this gross superstition, seeing it for what it was. Ibn al-Athir wrote:

There was a holy man, a man of low cunning, who proclaimed that the Messiah had a lance buried in the Qusyan, a great building in Antioch: 'And if you find it you will be victorious and if you fail you will surely die.' Before saying this he had buried a lance in a certain spot and concealed it. After they had all fasted and repented for three days, he led them on the fourth to the spot with soldiers and workmen, who dug everywhere and found the lance, as he had promised. Whereupon he cried, 'Rejoice! For victory is secure.'

Nor were many crusaders completely convinced. Much later, when events had turned sour once more, Peter Bartholomew was tried and suffered for his deception – but for the moment, what did it matter? Raymond of St Gilles had his holy talisman, and the fighting spirit of the army was rejuvenated. Among men of steadfast belief (and much superstition), miracles were accepted as nothing more than providential acts of radiant and divine good sense. No thoughtful contemporary in this age, neither Christian nor Muslim, doubted the power of religion to raise men above their sorry circumstance and give them the hearts of lions. The author of the *Gesta*, that tough unsentimental Norman campaigner, knew this better than most, because he had seen beaten and war-weary soldiers draw deeply at this spring of hope and suddenly grow strong. In one of the little fictions with which he embellished his otherwise forthright narrative he had a telling scene (completely invented) between the Turkish general Kerbuqa and his mother. Kerbuqa is scoffing at the power of the Christians to resist him, but his mother warns him against such complacency:

CRUSADERS PURSUING SELJUKS
From the Abbey St Denys

'O sweetest son,' said his mother, 'the Christians alone cannot fight with you – I know that they are unworthy to meet
you in battle – but their god fights for them every day, and
keeps them day and night under his protection. He watches
over them as a shepherd over his flock, and suffers no
people to hurt or vex them. Even before they are ready to
join battle, their mighty and powerful god, with his saints,
has already conquered all their enemies. How much more
will he do to you, who are his own enemy?'

This was conventional piety, but it contained elements of
hidden truth. The woeful besieged men in Antioch were puri-
fying themselves for a renewed effort. The chronicler
Raymond, an enthusiast for the Lord, was amazed by the
change of heart:

O, how blessed is the people whose Lord is God! How
changed the army from sadness to eagerness! Indeed, during

the past days princes and nobles went about the streets calling upon the aid of God at the churches. The common people walked with bare feet, weeping and striking their breasts. They had been so sad that father did not greet son, nor brother greet brother, nor did they glance back at each other. But now you could see them going forth like swift horses, rattling their arms, brandishing their spears, showing their joy in every word and deed. Why do I grieve about many matters? Now they were given the power to go forth.

With the Holy Lance held aloft in their battle-ranks nothing could frighten them, and hearing of strains among the Muslim alliance Bohemond had decided on a characteristic bold thrust. He would attack the Turkish camp and take the battle to them, but first, on 27 June, he sent Peter the Hermit as an envoy to Kerbuqa. Peter the Hermit was a suitable hostage to fortune. Because of his history in the people's crusade, he was known to the Turks, but his crusading life had been such an inglorious muddle that few would miss him if the Turks kept him captive. Peter, however, did return from his embassy, with the bleak message that Kerbuqa refused to call off the siege. On the contrary, he expected unconditional surrender from the crusaders. Next morning, on Monday, 28 June, Bohemond moved his army out of Antioch:

At last, after three days spent in fasting and in solemn procession from church to church, our men confessed their sins and received absolution. They took the Body and Blood of Christ in communion, and gave alms and arranged for masses to be said. Then six lines of battle were drawn up from those in the city. In the vanguard were Hugh the Great, with the French troops, and the Count of Flanders; in the second line, Duke Godfrey and his men; in the third, Robert of Normandy and his knights; in the fourth, the bishop of Le Puy, bearing the Lance of Our Saviour, and with him were both his own men and those of Count Raymond, who stayed behind on the hill to guard the citadel. In the fifth line was Tancred with his men, and in the sixth Bohemond with his militia. So we closed our ranks and protected by the sign of the Cross we marched out by the gate that is over against the mosque.

Kerbuqa, so it was said, was playing chess in his tent when he heard of the Christian advance. According to Raymond of Aguilers:

> This message disturbed him because it seemed beyond expectation. He called to him a certain noble Turk, known to us for his prowess, who had fled from Antioch. 'What is this?' said Kerbuqa. 'Did you not say that the Franks were few and would not fight?' But the noble replied, 'I said they would fight but not attack. Let me look on them and I'll tell you if they may be easily overcome.' By now, the third line of men was advancing. When he saw this, the noble turned to Kerbuqa and said, 'These men may be killed, but they cannot be put to flight.' 'Can they not be driven back at all?' said Kerbuqa. 'They will not yield a footstep,' was the reply, 'even if the whole of the pagan army attacks them.'

This news dispirited the Turkish commanders, and already their courage was beginning to falter in the face of the steady crusader advance. The author of the *Gesta* sensed the dejection and fear of defeat in the enemy:

> When all our men were outside the city, and Kerbuqa saw the great force of the Franks, he was much afraid and told the general of the Turks that if he saw a fire lit in the vanguard he should retreat at once, for he would know that the Turks had lost the battle. Then without delay Kerbuqa withdrew a little towards the mountain, and we followed him. Other enemy forces were drawn up between the river and the mountain two miles away, and these troops began to circle on each wing, trying to surround our men, throwing darts, shooting arrows, and wounding many.
>
> But the Turks stretching towards the sea, seeing that they could no longer withstand us, set fire to the grass, so that those in the camp might see the sign and flee. When they saw the signal, they snatched up their property and valuables and fled. Then we called upon the true and living God and charged against them, joining battle in the name of Jesus Christ and the Holy Sepulchre. And with God's help we defeated them. The Turks ran in terror and we pursued them, more eager for the chase than for plunder, as far as

the Orontes bridge in one direction, and Tancred's castle in the other. The enemy abandoned their camp, leaving their pavilions, with gold and silver and rich furnishings, as well as sheep, oxen, horses, mules, camels, asses, and also corn, wine, flour, and many other things that we badly needed.

The Armenians and Syrians who lived in those parts, hearing that we had overcome the Turks, rushed into the mountains to cut off their retreat, and killed all the fugitives they could catch. We returned to the city with great rejoicing, praising and blessing God who had given victory to His people.

The victory, so sudden and comprehensive, left the Muslims aghast. The report by Ibn al-Athir was an angry and contemptuous condemnation of Kerbuqa: 'When all the Franks had come out and not one was left in Antioch, they began to attack strongly, and then the men of Islam turned and fled. This was Kerbuqa's fault, first because he treated fellow-Muslims with scorn, and second because he stopped them killing the Franks. The Muslims were completely routed without striking a single blow or firing a single arrow.'

This account gave scant credit to Bohemond's daring generalship, or to the fervour and courage of the crusaders, but it stated baldly the facts of a defeat that Muslims had reason to weep over.

In a startling moment it was all over. Kerbuqa and his army vanished from sight into the mountains, and with them went the last hope of a strong, organized resistance by the Seljuk Turks and their allies of the Baghdad caliphate. On a hot sweaty day in late June, with stained armour unlaced to catch the breeze from the sea, the crusaders, who had been fearing the annihilation of defeat, suddenly contemplated the troubles of victory. They now had a degree of freedom that was puzzling, if not almost unwelcome. To begin with, they were exhausted, and it was difficult to make sound judgments in their condition. For eight months they had endured the hard discipline of the siege, followed by the fall of the city that had brought the even harder pain and privation of the counter-siege. In the last days of the resistance in Antioch, bodies shrunk by famine and pinched by disease had been pushed to the edge of hysteria by the powerful religious enthusiasm over the Holy Lance. Then Bohemond had gambled everything on one desperate sally against the entrenched and well-positioned Turks.

The gamble had succeeded but fundamental questions were still unresolved. No one wished to face these questions. Everyone from the princes (several of whom were ill) to the lowest foot-soldiers wanted rest and recreation. The first formal task was to fulfil the oath to Emperor Alexius and offer him the captured city of Antioch. 'Without delay,' said the *Gesta*, 'all our leaders sent the high-born noble Hugh the Great to the emperor at Constantinople, asking him to come and take over the city and fulfil the agreements he had made with our princes. Hugh went away and never came back.' Hugh, the brother of the French king, was another noble deserter who was not missed. His absence only simplified the problem of command, which was difficult enough as it was.

Next, the leaders convened a council to decide how best to go on. 'In this council, they decided that they dare not yet enter further into the lands of the pagans, because of the summer drought and lack of water. And so they agreed to wait until the beginning of November. Then our leaders separated, each to a territory that pleased him, until it would be time to resume the march. And the princes had the trumpets sounded throughout the city to announce that they would gladly take on any poor man who wished to continue the march but lacked the money to do so.'

Coffers and treasure-chests needed to be replenished. A freebooting diversion into the Muslim countryside seemed like an agreeable and profitable way to pass the hot season before the serious task of the crusade was taken up once more. Individual dreams of sunny fiefdoms and principalities, never wholly forgotten by the leaders, could be indulged again. As Baldwin had shown in Edessa, these dreams were not beyond hope. Also, the scattering of the princes would lessen the quarrels and rivalries so evident in Antioch, in particular the contest between Bohemond and Raymond of St Gilles. Bohemond insisted that the city belonged to him – the other leaders had promised it to him (always leaving aside the prior claim of the emperor), and his skill and daring had been decisive in the fight for the city. However, Count Raymond feared Bohemond. If he gave way to him now, he would have to give way to him always, and this he could not do, for he suspected that the Norman soldier had no deep commitment to the fight for God and for the relief of the Holy Places. Anger and suspicion between these two leaders spilled over on to their followers and supporters, as the chronicler Raymond complained:

> After the victory, our princes received the fortress of the city. But Bohemond, who was already planning an injustice, took the highest towers. Next he violently drove from the citadel the men of Duke Godfrey, those of the Count of Flanders and of Count Raymond also. He said he had given an oath to the Turk who had surrendered it that he alone would hold it. Having done this, he tried to take the forts and the gates which others had guarded in the siege. All gave in to him, except Count Raymond who, although he was ill, refused to hand over the important bridge gate for prayers, promises or threats.
>
> But all this time discord was not only disturbing our princes but it also destroyed the harmony among our people. There were few men who did not fight and argue over thefts and plunder. Nor was there any judge in the city willing to settle these disputes, but each man had to bear such injustice as fell upon him. Moreover, Count Raymond and Bishop Adhemar were both very ill and unable to protect their men from wrong. But why did we delay putting these matters right? It was for the sake of ease and riches, against the command of God, that our men set back their necessary journey until November, although the cities of the Saracens were so terrified by the defeat and flight of the Turks that, if our Franks had ridden forth, not a single city, not even Jerusalem, would have dared to throw a stone at them.

On 1 August 1098, the quarrels in the city were made worse when the pope's legate, Bishop Adhemar of Le Puy, died, most likely from typhoid. As the pope's representative in a religious cause, Adhemar was the one leader in the army with uncontested authority. Without personal ambition, he had shown himself to be a man of excellent character, intelligent, shrewd, tactful, kindly and brave. A good tactician and unafraid in battle, he had carried the Holy Lance, for the army to keep in sight and remember. In his life and conduct, Bishop Adhemar tried hard to embody whatever Christian idealism existed on the crusade, advancing the claims of Christian charity and lessening the evils of Christian warfare. He was much loved by the poor pilgrims and the ordinary soldiers and they mourned for him:

> By God's will, the bishop of Le Puy departed from this world and, resting in peace, fell asleep in the Lord on the Feast of St Peter Ad Vincula. Then there was grief and sorrow and great mourning in the whole army of Christ, for the bishop was a helper of the poor and a counsellor of

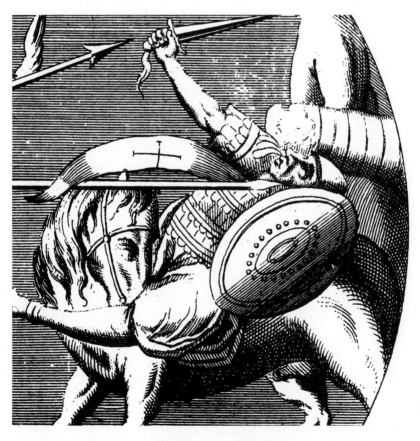

DEATH OF A SARACEN

the rich. He used to keep the clergy in order and preach to the knights, warning them, 'None of you can be saved unless you respect the poor and give them aid. They will not survive without you, but you cannot be saved without them. They ought every day to pray God to show mercy to you for your manifest sins, with which you daily offend Him. And therefore I beseech you, for love of the Lord, be kind to the poor and help them.'

Although Bishop Adhemar had been numbered among the Provençals, and his name bracketed with their leader Raymond of St Gilles, his death was felt just as keenly by the rest of the army, by the Normans and the followers of Bohemond, who himself promised to carry the bishop's body to Jerusalem. But the common grief over the legate was the last act of unity in the army. Soon Peter Bartholomew was reporting new visions from the Apostle Andrew. These visions made some troublesome accusations which seemed to show Bishop Adhemar in a bad light, but in doing so they only reinforced suspicions that had already begun to form about Peter and the dubious discovery of the Lance. Count Rayamond, who had accepted the Lance so wholeheartedly and used it to raise his own prestige, could not now abandon Peter. He tried to temporize, but Bohemond hinted around the city that the episode of the Lance was not all that it had seemed. For Bohemond, this dissension was only another stick with which to beat Raymond, but within the town it became another reason for factional jealousy and riot. 'Thus through discord and seditions of this kind,' Raymond of Aguilers lamented, 'the goods of the poor were wiped out.'

It was time to get away from the city. There was too much death in the streets, both from the typhoid epidemic that carried off the bishop and from the feuds of Christian in-fighting. Already, in mid-July, the minor Limousin lord Raymond Pilet had taken a small force east of the Orontes and occupied the Syrian town of Tell-Mannas. He pressed on with some untrained bands of local Christians to attack Maarat an-Numan but overreached himself. The amir of Aleppo forced him back to Tell-Mannas where Pilet dug in and stayed. Soon, with nosegays held to the face to ward off the evil fluxes of the city, other princes were leading out their own expeditions. Godfrey of Bouillon, envious of his brother Baldwin's success in Edessa, went north to join Baldwin and received from him, in an act of fraternal piety, two small towns. Robert of Normandy went to the Mediterranean port of Latakieh, which was already in crusader hands and had been begging for a larger garrison, but he was so grasping and greedy that the towns-folk very quickly drove him out and willingly put themselves under a Byzantine governor from Cyprus. Bohemond went west over the mountains into Cilicia, to receive homage from the Armenian towns that Tancred had garrisoned on the march of the previous year. Bohemond was determined to hold on to Antioch, and he planned to make it the capital of a strate-gic principality dominating the coastal routes in the northeast corner of the Mediterranean.

In September, the princes were drifting back to Antioch. The worst of the epidemic was over, but the city was still ruinous, overcrowded, sickly, and very short of food. A year of fighting had destroyed farming and crops for many miles around the city. Count Raymond and Duke Godfrey took a large foraging party into Muslim territory to search for supplies.

By now, relations between Christians and Muslims had changed. The opposition between them was no longer absolute. The events of the last year, both politically and militarily, had shown that neither side was strong enough to enforce its will completely. When Godfrey set out into Muslim territory, he went at the invitation of Omar, amir of Azaz, who was in dispute with his overlord Rudwan, amir of Aleppo. One of Omar's officers was in love with a Frankish lady, the widow of a knight from Lorraine, and this officer had suggested the appeal to Godfrey who was, after all, the duke of Lorraine. Godfrey gladly accepted the invitation. He and Raymond marched boldly to Azaz, forcing Rudwan to fall back on Aleppo. Then Godfrey reinstated Omar in the city, but only as a vassal of Godfrey. And Omar willingly paid homage to his new Christian master.

The black and white world of Christendom and Islam had become a shifting grey of temporary alliances, shamefaced agreements, calculations of advantage, cities held by Muslims

on behalf of Christians, and Christians relying on the tacit support of Muslim rulers. There was no true understanding or
meeting of minds, just a cool expediency that could break, at
a moment's notice, into the old savagery of blood and iron.

On the Feast of All Saints, 1 November 1098, the leaders
convened as they had promised at St Peter's Church in
Antioch, 'to see how they should continue their journey to the
Holy Sepulchre, for, said they, "The appointed day is at hand,
and it is no time for further quarrels."' Count Rayamond
hurried back from al-Bara. Bohemond was a little late, having
been taken ill in Cilicia, and Duke Godfrey, fresh from a
skirmish with Turks, arrived with the severed heads of the
enemy. Again, nothing could be agreed. Bohemond still
demanded the city, since it was clear that Emperor Alexius
was not coming to claim it. Count Raymond was unwilling to
let Bohemond have his way. The other princes were vacillat-
ing between the two. In the meantime the march on Jerusalem
was forgotten, and the affairs of the poor soldiers and pilgrims
were neglected. Starving and poverty-stricken, the ordinary
folk at last decided to enter the argument:

> When the people saw all this discord, they began to mutter
> openly, 'Since the princes are unwilling to lead us to
> Jerusalem, let us choose some brave knight whom we can
> serve loyally and safely, and he will take us to Jerusalem.
> Alas, is it not enough for our leaders that we have been
> stuck here for a year, and a myriad armed men have been
> wasted? Let those who want the emperor's gold keep it, and
> likewise those who covet the wealth of Antioch. But let us
> take up our march with Christ as leader, for whose sake we
> have come this far. If this dispute over Antioch goes on any
> longer, let us tear down the walls ourselves, destroy the city,
> and then our princes will have no more than they had before
> they reached here. Otherwise, let us return to our homes
> before we are utterly undone by hunger and disease.'

With the army on the edge of rebellion, a compromise was
botched together. Bohemond and Raymond both uneasily
promised to complete the journey to Jerusalem, though the
status of Antioch was still left undecided. Bohemond retained
the citadel and most of the town, while Count Raymond kept

control of the important bridge gate and the palace of Yaghi Siyan.

Although no new date was set for the departure to Jerusalem, Count Raymond thought it safest to keep his army occupied. In late summer he had begun to test the strength of the Muslim garrisons in Syria, and in November he went east to attack Maarat an-Numan, on the excuse that this move was necessary to protect the left flank of the advance into the Holy Land. At Maarat an-Numan, the author of the *Gesta*, who by this time had transferred himself from Bohemond's to Count Raymond's men, witnessed a violent, brutish encounter:

> On 28 November, Count Raymond reached the city of Maarat, in which there were many Saracens, Turks, Arabs and other pagans. He attacked it the next day. Bohemond and his army arrived soon after, and they joined forces on a Sunday. On Monday we attacked very bravely on all sides, with scaling-ladders up against the wall, but we could not come to grips with or do harm to the pagans. Then Count Raymond caused a wooden siege-tower to be built, strong and lofty and running on four wheels. On the top storey, among many knights, Everard the Huntsman blew loud blasts on his horn, and armed knights pushed the tower against the city wall. When the enemy saw this, at once they made an engine to throw great stones at our siege-tower, and they hurled Greek fire at it, hoping to burn it, though Almighty God did not let this happen. Back and forth the fight went till evening. And behind the siege-tower stood the priests and clerks in their vestments, praying God to defend his people, to exalt Christendom and cast down idolatry.

After ten days of vicious but inconclusive fighting, the crusaders captured a small section of the wall while a company of sappers, under shelter of the siege-tower, undermined the foundations:

> When the Saracens saw that our men had undermined the wall, they panicked and fled into the city. This was on Saturday, 11 December, at the hour of vespers, when the sun was setting.

Then Bohemond sent interpreters to the Saracens, promising safety to those who would take wives and children and goods into a palace that lay above the gate. Our men all entered the city and seized whatever loot they could find, and when it was dawn they killed everyone they met, man or woman. There were Saracen corpses in every corner of the city, and we could not go through the streets without treading on dead bodies. Then Bohemond went into the palace where the enemy, at his invitation, had taken refuge, and he stripped them of all their wealth and belongings. Some of them he had killed and others taken to Antioch to be sold as slaves.

Then for one month and four days we stayed in Maarat an-Numan. While we were there some of our men were still desperate for both food and plunder, since there was nothing to be had outside the city. So they ripped up the bodies of the dead, hoping to find bezants hidden in the entrails, and others cut the dead flesh into slices and cooked and ate them.

There were uses in terror, and the horror at Maarat an-Numan had an affect on the Muslims. The historian Ibn al-Athir wrote with despair, and some exaggeration, of three days of uninterrupted slaughter in which 100,000 townspeople were killed. Raymond of Aguilers, a priest and not a soldier, felt the Christian disgrace of the bestiality, but put it down to the frustration and misery of the crusaders 'to whom life was not very dear, and for whom long fasting had led to contempt for self'.

Whatever the effect on Muslims, the capture of Maarat did nothing to stop the quarrels of the leaders. Bohemond and Count Raymond had joined forces in the attack, but Raymond's men had secured the victory only to see the best fruits of war snatched from them by Bohemond's trickery and treachery. The weary rivalry over Antioch continued, and this was now made worse by further disagreements over Maarat an-Numan. Once more the army was neglected, starving and angry, as the chronicler Rayamond related:

Again, the knights and people began to ask when it would please the princes to press on to Jerusalem, for our journey was far from finished. It was now Christmastide, but Bohemond wanted to delay the start until Easter. So many despaired. Now there were few horses in the army, and Duke Godfrey was absent, and many knights preferred to join Count Baldwin in Edessa. Therefore many of our people turned for home.

Then news came to the poor who had remained in Maarat that Count Raymond wished to leave many knights and foot-soldiers to hold the town on his behalf. But the people cried out, 'First quarrels about Antioch, now quarrels about Maarat! Will the princes squabble over every place that God shall give us, while the army of the Lord suffers? To hell with this city! Let us destroy the walls and leave it.'

So the sick and the weak arose from their beds and armed with clubs and picks and levers went at the walls. The bishop of al-Bara and other friends of Count Raymond hurried about trying to prevent them. But the people waited until the important men had passed, then they attacked the walls again. And those who could not work by day, took up the task at night. This they did no matter how weak or ill they might be.

These men were desperate, for the army was so hungry that we greedily ate the already fetid bodies of the Saracens thrown into the swamp two or more weeks before. These events frightened us, as well as others, and many of our people wandered away, despairing of help. But the Turks and Saracens said, 'Who can resist such an obstinate and cruel people, who after a year of famine, war and danger now live on human flesh?' So the pagans saw the cruel practices that existed among us, and God put fear into their hearts, but we did not know it.

At last, the army of the poor and the hungry and the dispossessed forced a decision on Raymond of St Gilles. He stopped looking over his shoulder, to see what his jealous rival Bohemond was doing, and assumed the Christian leadership that was perhaps his due, on account of his very great wealth, his religious idealism (tainted though it was with a familiar lust for power and possessions), and his at least moderate commitment to Christendom. Already he had distributed large sums of money to some of the other princes, partly as bribes, but also as a recognition that even rich lords were unable to bear the expenses of the crusade. He gave 10,000 *solidi* each to Duke Godfrey and to Robert of Normandy, 6,000 to the Count of Flanders, 5,000 to Tancred, and lesser sums to lesser figures. To Bohemond he gave nothing. In the eyes of the whole army, except for Bohemond and his close followers, Raymond of St Gilles, Count of Toulouse, had secured his position as chief Christian prince of the crusade.

On 13 January 1099, Count Raymond set fire to Maarat an-Numan, so that there should be no turning back. 'Invoking the compassion of God and the protection of the saints', he led his army on the long-delayed road to Jerusalem, going barefoot, as befitted a pilgrim of Christ.

8

THE HOLY CITY

The suspicion was shameful for Islam, but Ibn al-Athir thought it the duty of an historian to record it: 'Some say that when the Fatimid rulers of Egypt saw the conquests of the Seljuk Turks, they took fright and asked the Franks to march into Syria, to make a zone of safety between the Fatimids and these Turks. Allah alone knows the truth.'

Nothing helped the campaign of the crusaders quite so much as the Muslim rivalries of the Middle East. An understanding of the ethnic, dynastic and theological divisions that split the Muslim world was beyond the crusaders, who persisted in calling the Muslims – the most austerely rigorous of all monotheists – 'pagans' and 'idolaters', but it was an easy matter for the Christian leaders to see the dissensions and hatreds among the governors, generals and petty rulers of these ancient lands. Greed, personal ambition and the scramble for territory were not new to the crusaders, and they recognized these forces at work among the enemy. The hold of religion only went so far. Sharing the common failings of humanity, both Christians and Muslims were prepared to compromise the ends of faith for the advantage of the moment.

So every setback for the Turks brought joy to the Fatimids in Cairo. The powerful vizier al-Afdal, who effectively ruled in Cairo during the boyhood of Caliph al-Mustali, was an Armenian soldier and he watched with pleasure the gradual retreat of the Turks before the Christian army in his homeland of Anatolia and Cilicia. He had already made diplomatic overtures to Emperor Alexius, which had been sympathetically considered by that subtle ruler. So it was well in accordance with Fatimid policy for al-Afdal to send an embassy to the crusaders at Antioch, before the fall of the city, suggesting a partition of Syria and Palestine between the crusaders and the Fatimids. This would cut out the Turks and allow enough land to satisfy the territorial ambition of each partner to this agreement. The crusaders would take the lands north of Beirut and the Dog River, while the southern part, including Palestine and Jerusalem, would belong to Cairo. Here al-Afdal miscalculated. He did not understand the nature of the crusade, nor the way Jerusalem burned in Christian consciousness.

No agreement was made with the crusaders, but in June 1098, after Antioch fell and when Kerbuqa and his allies were completely vanquished, al-Afdal seized this moment of Turkish defeat to attack Jerusalem, which was then held by two Turcoman chieftains on behalf of the amir of Damascus. After a siege of forty days the Fatimid army took the city and set about the repair of the badly damaged walls, while the Turks were permitted a graceful retreat to Damascus. For some months al-Afdal listened to the chorus of Shia applause, that the city holy to the Prophet Mohammed was freed from the soiled hands of Sunni heretics. Nor did there seem to be any danger from the crusaders, still stalled by their own obstinate aims in Antioch and Maarat an-Numan. Then in January 1099 came the dreadful news. The Christian army had begun the march towards Jerusalem, and al-Afdal had done most to destroy the opposition that stood in the way.

For it soon became clear that when Raymond of St Gilles set out barefoot from Maarat he was embarking on a road made plain and easy by the jealousy among his enemies. Local Muslim rulers outbid each other to accommodate the crusaders, as the *Gesta* happily related:

The amir of Shaizar had sent many messengers to Count Raymond, because he wanted a treaty of peace, and he swore to pay an indemnity and to be kind to the Christian pilgrims, so that while they were within his lands they would not suffer the least offence, and he said he would gladly sell them horses and supplies. So our men camped near Shaizar, on the River Orontes. Next day, two Turkish guides showed them the ford over the river and led them to a place where they could find booty. So we came to a fortress in a valley, and we seized there more than five thousand animals and plenty of grain and other goods, which were a great refreshment to the whole army of Christ. The fortress surrendered to Count Raymond, and gave him horses and pure gold, and the pagans swore by their law that they would do no harm to the pilgrims. We stayed there for five days, and then went on our way rejoicing and took up quarters in an Arab fort, for its lord came out and made an agreement with us.

The march south became an almost regal progress. The inhabitants of the countryside fled into the mountains or retreated into towns and forts. The lords of the towns did not dare risk an armed encounter with the crusaders, so they emerged humbly from behind their walls and abased themselves and made the best agreement they could. In this way the Christian army journeyed peacefully over the Ansarieh mountains and through the fertile valley of Sem. Occasionally, the people of a region would try to make a stand. In the rich Bukaya plain, farmers and peasants took refuge on the high hillside, in the dominating but disused fort of Hisn al-Akrad, the site forty years later for the Krak des Chevaliers, the most brutally imposing of all crusader castles. On 28 January the crusaders attacked the old but still substantial walls. Defence was hopeless against this seasoned army. To distract the attackers, the farmers drove out their animals, causing a wild chase by the crusaders, who were keener on horses and cattle than on the siege of castles. Then in the night the Muslims slipped quietly away. 'Our men entered and found plenty of grain, oil, wine, flour and other things that we needed, so we celebrated the feast of Candlemas there with great devotion.'

Seeing all this bounty falling into the lap of the army, the chronicler Raymond reported with satisfaction that 'the poor daily grew better and the knights were comforted; day by day the army of Christ seemed to be multiplying, and the further we went the greater benefits God provided for us.'

The outlook seemed cheerful indeed, but as so often, the danger to the crusaders lay not with the Muslims, but in their own turbulent conflicts and in the insatiable need of the leaders for money and possessions to support the very great expense of the campaign. Tancred, who had taken over from his absent uncle Bohemond (the cloak of military prudence), urged a quick dash to Jerusalem through the demoralized countryside, before Amir Duqaq of Damascus could re-organize and give spirit to the Muslim resistance. Count Raymond, on the other hand, was tempted by the wealth of the Mediterranean ports. He saw the lure of easy riches and was reluctant to forgo the chance to make a principality for himself on that prosperous coast.

While the crusaders were resting with ample supplies at Hisn al-Akrad, Muslim envoys still came to offer help and allegiance. The large empty vaults of the old fort were filled with whispers of secret deals and strange promises. The ruler of Hama, a very minor lord, offered what little he could and was dismissed, but the amir of Tripoli, whose envoys were next to arrive, made Count Raymond pause. Jalal al-Mulk, of the famous and learned Banu Ammar family, had successfully kept a balance between Fatimids and Turks, and in this way he had preserved Tripoli as one of the richest, grandest and safest cities of the region. He had no intention of fighting the crusaders, but in trying to tempt them towards a peace treaty he made the mistake of inviting a delegation to visit Tripoli.

An embassy sent by Count Raymond came and saw one of the jewels of the Mediterranean. In the port, the merchant ships rubbed against each other at the quays, and every cargo loaded or unloaded left a small accretion of wealth to the city. This prosperity was easy to see in wide, palm-lined streets, in noble houses, in the vast dignity of the Dar al-Ilm, a public building containing a library of some 100,000 volumes, as many manuscripts perhaps as Rome, Paris and London could put together between them. The city sat in a garden of green, surrounded by orchards and olive-groves and fields of sugar-cane. Nothing was more likely to raise the envy and greed of the crusaders, as the chronicler Raymond ruefully admitted:

> When our knights who had been sent as envoys to Tripoli saw the royal wealth of that most rich kingdom, and that great populous city, they persuaded Count Raymond to besiege Arqa, a place very strongly fortified and hardly assailable by human might. By this means they hoped to wring from the amir of Tripoli, after a few days of siege of this town that belonged to him, as much gold and silver as the Count could desire. So at the wish of these envoys we besieged this fortress, where our brave men endured such troubles as they had never seen before. Here, most bitter to tell, we lost so many fine knights.

It was another weary siege, this time quite unnecessary. On 14 February, in a mood of high confidence, the crusader army settled before Arqa, about fifteen miles from Tripoli. Elsewhere, the course of events was still running well for the crusaders. Two energetic knights, Raymond Pilet and Raymond of Turenne, had taken a raiding-party to attack the city of Tortosa, to the north of Tripoli. The citizens fled without a fight, leaving the crusaders with a well-placed harbour safe for Christian ships. At once, the governor of Marqiye, a little further up the coast, capitulated and threw open his town. Also in February, Duke Godfrey, Robert of Flanders and Bohemond had at last set out from Antioch. Bohemond went no further than Latakieh. Then he returned to Antioch, determined to hold it, for he had decided that there could be no gains in the future which could compensate him if he were to lose the city won at the cost of so much blood and suffering. Godfrey and Count Robert, however, were anxious to press on. They captured Jabala and were resting there when news came that the siege of Arqa was going badly.

The chill air of February, blowing off the mountains, had given way to a warmth that brought out the blossom of late March, and still the Muslims of Arqa held out. They resisted grimly because they knew that a single breach of their walls would signal their end. They were likely to be massacred without compunction, as the people of Antioch and Maarat an-Numan had been killed before them. In the face of this determination, crusader confidence soon drained away. The defences were compact, strong and well organized. As the days passed, despondency grew in the army of besiegers. There was a strong feeling that this siege had been undertaken at the wrong time for the wrong reasons, and that God would not help the Christian army because the actions of the crusaders were 'contrary to justice', as Raymond of Aguilers expressed it. 'In all our battles and assaults,' he went on, 'our men have been prompt and ready for the fight. But in this siege it was wonderful that they were found so sluggish and useless. The fervent soldiers who wished to do great things were either killed, wounded, or their efforts came to nothing.'

In their depressed state, the crusaders rekindled old quarrels, blowing embers of ancient doubts and hatreds once more into livid flame, and one of the old sores still chafing in the army, from the leaders to the least pilgrim, was the question of the authenticity of the Holy Lance. In the camp, Peter Bartholomew had begun his ranting again, speaking of visions and divine commands. His critical, nagging voice was tedious to many, particularly at this time of disappointment and low energy. Bohemond and the Normans had always distrusted him, looking on Peter and his Lance merely as adjuncts to Count Raymond's plotting. Now, in the absence of Bohemond, a priest called Arnulf, chaplain to Robert of Normandy, became the chief doubter. Rancorous words were hurled between the parties until Peter agreed, under pressure of hostile gossip, to put his truthfulness to the test of a trial by ordeal.

On Good Friday, 8 April, on the anniversary of the day when Christ on the cross was wounded by the Lance, a large fire of dry olive-wood was prepared, thirty feet long and four feet high, with a narrow passage left clear through the middle. A vast multitude of the army assembled. Even a churchman as sophisticated as Abbot Guibert of Nogent found in this macabre theatre, in this scene of hell-fire and scorched flesh played out before the excited and unforgiving beast of the crowd, some reflection of the Lord's will:

The crowd, eager for any novelty, heaped more stuff upon the fire, and what with the wind hurling the flames about a very narrow path was left between the piles of burning wood. Peter, as was right, first prayed piteously to the merciful God, who is the Truth, and apart from whose Will he knew himself to have done nothing wrong. Then he flew as fast as he could along the path between the raging flames, and came back the same way.

When he came out of the fire, as I have said, he was welcomed by an infinite crowd of people. And seeing that he had emerged little hurt, they wished to keep something of him for relics, either from his clothes or from his body, so they clutched at him and pulled him about and hacked him, trampling and dragging him here and there, till the poor helpless fellow gave up the ghost.

Now that the man was dead, the slippery and inconstant crowd began to waver again in far more hopeless doubt. Some men interpreted the ordeal one way, and some another way. Then they began to quarrel with each other, and some upbraided others for killing this man for nothing.

The abbot was among the believers, and he was sympathetic to Peter Bartholomew. Writing later, the young Norman knight Raoul of Caen put the contrary point of view in two sharp sentences:

> Branches were set on fire in a double row, and Peter, dressed in a shirt and breeches but otherwise naked, going through the midst of the fire, fell burned at the other end and died on the following day. The people, having seen what was done, confessed that they had been deceived by his words and trickery, and they testified that Peter was a disciple of Simon, the Magician.

The trial of Peter and the Lance was one piece of evidence of discord among the crusaders. There were many other outbursts of passion and disagreement. 'So many and such great disputes,' wrote Raymond of Aguilers, 'arose between the leaders of our army that almost the whole army was divided.' In March, there had been a rumour of the advance of a large Muslim army led by the caliph of Baghdad himself. This was false, but it had made Count Raymond send quickly for help from Duke Godfrey and Robert of Flanders who were still at Jabala. When they arrived they caused more trouble. Count Raymond found that he was no longer the undisputed Christian leader, and the old fractious contest for supremacy began again, with Tancred now assuming the sceptical and troublesome part once held by his uncle Bohemond.

For three months the pointless siege of Arqa dragged on, despite repeated attempts by various Muslim princes to come to an agreement with the Christians. From Tripoli, Jalal al-Mulk still sued for peace; al-Afdal, in Cairo, was offering free access for Christian pilgrims to the Holy Places if the crusaders would not attack the Fatimid lands – but Count Raymond turned all envoys away. He would listen to sense from neither Muslim nor Christian. He was determined to take Arqa, until the weariness and frustration of his men in the long hopeless continuation of the siege forced, in early May, a change of mind, which the *Gesta* noted with underlying scornful irony:

> The amir of Tripoli sent frequent messengers to our leaders, asking them to raise the siege and make a treaty with him. When Duke Godfrey and Raymond of St Gilles and Robert the Norman and the Count of Flanders considered this, and saw that the produce of the season had begun to come in, for we were eating spring beans in the middle of March and corn in the middle of April, they took counsel together and decided that it would be a very good thing to finish the journey to Jerusalem while the harvest was being gathered in.
>
> Therefore we left Arqa and came to Tripoli on Friday, 13 May, and we stayed there for three days. The amir of Tripoli finally agreed to free some three hundred pilgrims he had captured, and he gave us 15,000 bezants and fifteen very valuable horses. He also sold us horses, asses and provisions, so that the whole army of Christ was well supplied. The treaty we made with him also said that if we could defeat the amir of Cairo, and take Jerusalem, then the amir of Tripoli would be christened and hold his land from our leaders. That was the lawful agreement.

On 16 May the crusaders left Tripoli and went south on a

safe route shown to them by Muslim guides. On the 19th, without any opposition, they crossed the Nahr al-Kalb, the Dog River, near Beirut. Here they entered Fatimid territory, and in doing this they showed that they were ready to fight for Jerusalem, though the prospect of a battle for the city was sad and painful for Cairo. Jerusalem, in the mind of Muslims, was not a place to fight over. It was a holy place to which one submitted in all humility. For this reason, in February 638, when Caliph Omar annexed Jerusalem for Islam, he came not as a conqueror but as a single suppliant, riding on a white camel, with one servant.

Very little now stood in the way of the crusaders. Al-Afdal had withdrawn the Fatimid soldiers in Palestine for the defence of Jerusalem, and without Egyptian support local governors did not dare oppose the Christian army. From Beirut to Sidon to Tyre to Acre a silent and frightened population watched the foreigners march by. Even nature seemed to conspire to help the crusaders, to the wonder of Raymond of Aguilers:

> Setting out from Acre at vespers, we pitched camp by the swamps near Caesarea. While many were running here and there to put up the camp, a pigeon mortally wounded by a hawk fell in the middle of the soldiers. The bishop of Agde took it up and found that it carried a message, which we read thus: 'The amir of Acre to the lord of Caesarea. A canine breed, a foolish and troublesome and disorderly host, has passed me. If you love the Law, try with all others to do them hurt. You may easily to do this, if you wish. Send this message to other cities and forts.'

Then the chronicler knew that the Muslims were whistling in the wind, to keep up their spirits, and he thanked God 'that not even the birds would cross the air to harm us, and that He disclosed to us the secrets of our foes'. With easy minds the crusaders went on to Ramleh, on the road from the port of Jaffa to Jerusalem, and they thought they detected other marks of divine favour:

> When the Saracens who lived in Ramleh heard that we had crossed the river near by, they abandoned their defences

and left their arms and their grains and their crops, all of which we gathered. And when we came to the city next day we found that God was truly fighting for us. So we offered vows to St George, who was our guide. Then our leaders and all our men agreed that we should choose a bishop for this place, since this was the first church we had found in the land of Israel. In this way St George might entreat God on our behalf, and lead us faithfully through the country where He was no longer worshipped, even to the walls of Jerusalem, which were but fifteen miles away.

However, at Ramleh arguments broke out again. On the evidence of Fatimid weakness, some wanted to attack Cairo immediately, others feared another long summer siege in the dry country of Jerusalem. But the Holy City was on the horizon. After the long pain of the journey, now a hand reached out might grab it. The impatience and expectation of the army could not be reined back. On 6 June 1099 a dash for Jerusalem began:

We loaded our camels and oxen, and then all our baggage animals and horses, and turned our steps to Jerusalem. But because of a habit customary to us, to occupy forts and estates on the way by placing a personal standard there, many rose at midnight and galloped off without companions, to gain the villas and farms that are in the meadows of the Jordan. A few, however, to whom the command of God was more precious, walked with naked feet and sighed heavily for the contempt of the divine word.

On the morning of Tuesday, 7 June, the main body of the Christian army was on the hill by the mosque of the Prophet Samuel. By late afternoon the crusaders were camped at the foot of the walls of Jerusalem.

The Egyptian commander of the garrison, Iftikhar al-Daula, surveyed the besieging army from his post in the Tower of David and he was not greatly perturbed. Antioch had held out against the westerners until brought down by treachery, and Arqa had just withstood a siege of three months and emerged unharmed. The fortifications of his own city were excellent. In the past, Palestine had suffered several earthquakes, and as recently as 1033 much damage had been done to the region. The historian Yahya ibn Said spoke of destruction and many deaths in Jericho, Nablus and Jerusalem: 'A part of the mosque of Jerusalem collapsed, and so did a number of other religious buildings. Much also was ruined in the city of Acre and a great many died. The water drained from the harbour for a whole hour before it came surging back.' But after the Fatimid conquest of Palestine, one of the first cares of the administration in Cairo was to oversee the rebuilding and strengthening of city walls. The caliph in Egypt, wrote William of Tyre in his comprehensive twelfth-century history of the region, 'ordered each city to look to its walls and raise strong towers around it. This edict was enforced, and the governor in Jerusalem compelled the citizens to obey, and to restore the walls and towers to their former state.'

With the walls in good repair, the city was made ready for a siege. The early harvest was gathered in and there were large stores of food. The water cisterns were full and the wells were cleaned and checked. For fear of divided loyalty, local Christians were banished from the city. In the surrounding countryside, the wells and water-sources had been poisoned or drained. A siege in the arid hills under a June sun would be penance enough, but without water for men and animals it would be an almost unbearable hell. The garrison commanded by al-Daula was a little stretched, but it included a sufficient number of competent soldiers. Among these troops were fast Arab horsemen, capable of punitive raids and sudden counter-attacks, and many experienced Sudanese archers to shoot from the walls. Best of all, al-Afdal was already gathering a large army in Egypt to come to the relief of the city.

If the Muslims were not dismayed, neither were the crusaders when they arrived at the walls. 'Rejoicing and exulting,' wrote the author of the Gesta, 'we came to the city of Jerusalem and invested the walls very thoroughly. Robert of Normandy took the northern sector, next to the church of St Stephen the Protomartyr, and Robert of Flanders had the place beside him. Duke Godfrey and Tancred looked after the whole of the western side, and Raymond of St Gilles was in the south, on Mount Sion, near the church of Mary the Mother of God, where the Lord shared the Last Supper with His disciples.' No one covered the eastern side, for the steep fall into the valley of Kedron made it impossible to attack from that direction.

In fact, the balance of advantage was delicately poised. Neither attackers nor defenders had sufficient men to cover the full length of the walls. Time was on the side of the Muslims, with their adequate stores and with al-Afdal almost ready to march. The crusaders were worried by heat and lack of water, but sudden weaknesses were likely to appear in the thinly manned defences, where the crusaders could concentrate the full force of their attack. It was clear to the Christian leaders that they could not afford another long siege. They must break through with a quick assault. For this they needed siege-engines and catapults, which they did not have, and al-Daula had festooned the vulnerable places in the walls with bales of hay and cotton, to cushion the shock from stones and heavy missiles.

On 13 June, urged on by a hermit from the Mount of Olives, who upbraided them for lack of faith, the crusaders attacked with their usual impetuous boldness, overran the outer defences, but could not get a foothold on the wall for lack of scaling-ladders and siege-towers. The curtain-wall was destroyed but the strong inner fortification remained intact. After several hours of fighting the crusaders withdrew with many losses.

The first shock had failed and the Christian army had to settle for a period of attrition and preparation for a new assault. Now the crusaders began to suffer those pains of siege warfare already too well known to them from the bitter days at Antioch. In particular, the *Gesta* lamented the shortage of water:

> During this siege we could not buy bread for nearly ten days, until a messenger arrived from our ships. Also we suffered so badly from thirst that we had to take our horses and other animals six miles to water, going in fear and apprehension all the way. The pool of Siloam, at the foot of Mount Sion, served us well enough, but water was sold at a very great price in the army.

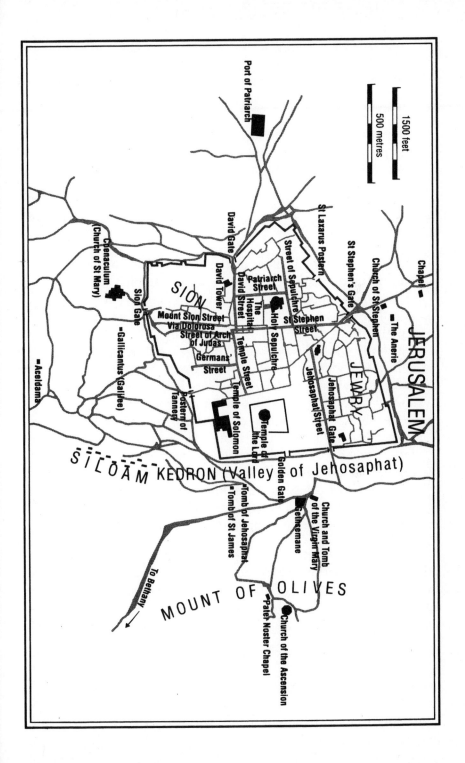

Indeed, we suffered so badly from thirst that we sewed skins of oxen and buffaloes, and used them to carry water these six miles. We drank the water from these leather sacks, though it stank, and what with this foul water and coarse barley bread we were distressed and afflicted every day. Saracens used to lie in wait for our men by every spring and pool, surprising us and cutting us to pieces. Then they would carry off our beasts to their caves and secret places.

This lack of water was a serious cause of weakness and disease, and Raymond of Aguilers gave another bleak picture of the parched army.

When the water did flow in the Pool of Siloam, so many hurried to drink there that men were trampled underfoot and animals slipped and drowned. The pool was filled with a jostling crowd and with the bodies of dead animals, but still the strong tried to force their way to the very crack from which the water flowed, while the weak and sickly were left with the muddy and contaminated dregs. Many sick people collapsed by the spring, with swollen tongues unable to utter a word, only able to hold out their imploring hands for water. In the fields, horses, mules, cattle, sheep, indeed most of the beasts, had no strength to move. They died of thirst and rotted where they fell, making a most sickening stench throughout the camp. A cup of foul water was sold for five or six valuable coins, and still thirst was not quenched. And as if this was not bad enough, the sun and the dust and the hot summer wind left man gasping.

Spirits were raised a little when Genoese and English ships outran the Egyptian blockade and docked at Jaffa, bringing much needed supplies of all kinds. After the failure of the first assault, the crusader leaders had decided at once to build wooden towers and siege-engines. Providentially, with the arrival of the ships, ropes and tackle and fastenings and iron-work became available for this task, although timber in the dry bare hills was in very short supply. Robert of Flanders and Tancred had to scout as far as the forests of Samaria before they could find sufficient trees to provide the planks and baulks of timber needed. These were loaded on to camels and driven to the camp by Muslim prisoners. The work of construction was entrusted to Gaston of Béarn and William Ricou who pressed into service as many captives as they could lay hold of, forcing them to work as if they were serfs:

> To make the machines, fifty or sixty men carried on their backs a great beam that could hardly have been dragged by four pairs of oxen. All worked with a single purpose, and no hands were idle. All worked without wages, except the craftsmen, who were paid out of a collection taken from the people. But Count Raymond was able to pay his own workmen out of his treasury. Surely the hand of the Lord was with us and aided those who were working!

It was slow labour. A hot late khamsin wind was blowing and tempers were on edge. There were further quarrels among the leaders. Tancred, with that naked self-interest that the army had come to expect from Norman chiefs, had raised his standard on the Church of the Nativity in Bethlehem, claiming the town as his fief. This cool appropriation of one of the holiest places in Christendom was an outrage not only to the other princes but also to the Church and the clergy. The wrangle went on unresolved. The miseries of the time and the lack of military success were leading to new waves of desertion. A company of men, going to renew baptism in the River Jordan, continued straight on to Jaffa and looked for a ship to take them home.

In the first week of July came the news that a large Egyptian army was marching towards Jerusalem. On the 6th, a priest reported to William of Monteil that he had seen the ghost of William's brother, the dead bishop of Le Puy, in a vision. Bishop Adhemar had berated the crusaders for their selfish divisions and promised the fall of Jerusalem within nine days, if the whole army would fast and walk in solemn barefoot procession around the city. On Friday, 8 July, the procession set out, led by priests holding crosses and relics of the saints, and accompanied by trumpets, drums and standard-bearers. The procession paused on the Mount of Olives to listen to a number of fiery, passionate sermons. Then the crusaders completed their circuit uplifted by faith, firm in mind and full of warlike anger against the Muslims, a mood that was reinforced by the jeers and insults from the enemy on the tops of the walls.

A few more days were needed to finish the construction of the siege-works and to move them into position. The attack was planned for the night of 13 July. Old men, women and children were pressed into the final work on the machines, shaping and sewing ox-hides and camel-skins and fastening them to exposed woodwork, to protect the timber from Greek fire. When the machines were moved out to the two focal points chosen for the assault – near Mount Sion in the south and at the east end of the northern wall – the Muslim garrison was taken by surprise and hastily tried to strengthen the section of wall opposite the siege-towers.

The balance of forces still seemed slightly in favour of the defenders, as Raymond of Aguilers acknowledged, though the crusaders had the advantage of choosing the place and timing of the attack:

> According to our estimate, there were 60,000 enemy soldiers in the city, not counting women and those unable to bear arms, and there were not many of those. At most, we had no more than 12,000 in arms, for we had many poor pilgrims and many sick. As I reckon it, there were only twelve or thirteen hundred knights left in our army, not more. But nothing great or small, undertaken in the name of the Lord, can fail.

Slowly the ungainly towers were wheeled into position, for they could only roll on level ground, and there were many gullies and outcrops of rock to be smoothed. Against the advance of these monstrous wooden sentinels the Muslims loosed volleys of stones and arrows. Through the dark hours the siege-towers crept within reach of the walls. The dawn flared with the streaked and sulphurous light of Greek fire. The assault had begun:

> Our men began to undermine the walls and forts. From the height of the towers, catapults and mangonels threw missiles like rain. And when our machines were close enough to the walls, they hurled not only stones and arrows but also burning wood and straw. The wood was dipped in pitch,

THE SIEGE OF JERUSALEM BY THE CRUSADERS

wax and sulphur, then straw and tow was bound to it, so
that the whole flaming mass held together when it fell and
continued to burn. No one was safe from such burning
missiles, not even in the lee of the walls. Thus the fight
went on from rising to setting sun, and it is hard to believe
that anything more glorious was ever done.

Night brought fear to both sides. The Saracens thought
the city might fall in the dark, for we had broken through
the outer works and filled the ditch, and it would be
possible to break an entrance through the wall very quickly.
But we feared that our wooden towers, so close to the
walls, might suddenly be set on fire. Thus both hopeful and
doubtful, the two sides spent a night of watchfulness
and sleepless caution. We laboured gladly for the glory of
God, they less willingly for the laws of Mohammed.

In the dawn, our men rushed eagerly to the walls and
dragged the machines forward. But the Saracens had made
many defensive engines of their own, and each one of ours
seemed to face now nine or ten of theirs. In this way they
repulsed our attacks. Yet this was the ninth day, the day on

which the vision of the good bishop had promised victory. But our machines were being shaken apart by the blows of many stones, and our men were faint with fatigue. I must not omit one incident. Two of their devil-women tried to bewitch one of our machines. But a stone struck and crushed them so that their lives were snuffed out and the evil spells averted.

By noon our men were greatly discouraged. They were falling down from weariness and at the end of their strength. Each one of us seemed to face a dozen of the enemy. The walls were high and strong, and the skill that the Saracens had shown in repairing and organizing their defences seemed too much for us to overcome.

Ibn al-Athir noted the burning of the southern siege-tower, with the death of everyone in it, but 'it had scarcely ceased to burn before a messenger arrived begging for help, for he brought the news that the Christians had broken in on the other side of the city'. In the north, the tower commanded by Duke Godfrey and his brother Eustace had forced a bridge on to the top of the wall. On Friday, 15 July, at about the hour of the Passion, as the *Gesta* related, 'one of our knights, Lethold of Tournai, struggled on to the wall. As soon as he reached it, all the defenders fled along the walls and down into the city. Our men went after them, killing them and cutting them down as far as the Temple of Solomon, where there was such a massacre that our men were wading up to their ankles in Muslim blood.'

At the southern wall, however, where the general al-Daula was himself in command, the defenders held out, as if the events to the north were of little account. Raymond of Aguilers wrote:

Strange to say, at this very time when the city was on the point of capture by the Franks, the Saracens were still fighting bravely on the other side, where Count Raymond was attacking as if the city would never fall. But now that our men had possession of walls and towers, things of wonder were to be seen. Some of our men – and this was more merciful – struck off the heads of the enemy at once. Other Muslims plunged from the walls pierced by arrows, yet others had to suffer the long torture of being cast into the flames. The streets were littered with heads, hands, feet and bits of bodies. We were slipping on the gory mess of dead humans and horses. But these were small matters compared to what happened at the Temple of Solomon, a place holy to all religious people. If I tell the truth, it will exceed your powers of belief. It is enough to say this much at least – in the Temple and the porch of Solomon, men rode in blood up to their knees and bridle-reins.

The white Fatimid flag of Iftikhar al-Daula still flew from the Tower of David, an extremely strong bastion whose foundation stones were bound together with lead, but the city was lost, as Ibn al-Athir recorded, and there was nothing to do but flee and lament:

> Jerusalem was taken from the north on the morning of 22 Shaban 492 [15 July 1099]. The population was put to the sword by the Franks, who pillaged for a week. A band of Muslims barricaded themselves in the Tower of David and fought on for several days. In return for surrendering, they were granted their lives, and the Franks honoured their word, allowing these men to leave by night for Ascalon. In the Masjid al-Aqsa [built on the edge of the Temple platform] the Franks slaughtered more than 70,000 people, among them a large number of Imams and Muslim scholars who had left their homelands to live in the pious seclusion of the Holy Place. The Franks stripped the Dome of the Rock of more than forty silver candelabra, each weighing 3,600 drams, and a great silver lamp weighing 44 Syrian pounds, as well as one hundred and fifty smaller silver candelabras and more than twenty gold ones. And they took a great deal more booty besides these.

Ibn al-Qalanisi gave a more cautious account, not being able to confirm the incredible numbers of the massacre set down by Ibn al-Athir. 'A great many people were killed,' was all he said. 'The Jews had gathered in their synagogue and the Franks burnt them alive. They also destroyed monuments of saints and the tomb of Abraham, may peace be upon him!'

The horrific extent of the slaughter was quite clear from Christian sources. As usual, the author of the *Gesta* went into the matter with brutal simplicity:

THE TOWER OF DAVID. IFTIKHAR AND HIS MEN MADE
THEIR LAST STAND HERE AND THE TOWER WAS FINALLY
OCCUPIED BY RAYMOND.

Our men killed whom they chose and saved whom they
chose. They rushed around the city, seizing gold and silver,
horses and mules, plundering every kind of goods from the
houses. Then they all came rejoicing and weeping for gladness to worship at the Holy Sepulchre of our Saviour Jesus,
and there they fulfilled their vows to Him. Next morning,
stealthily they climbed to the roof of the Temple and
attacked the Saracens sheltering there, both men and
women, slashing their heads from their bodies with their
swords. Then our leaders ordered that all the Saracen
corpses should be thrown outside the gates on account of
the fearful stench, for almost the whole city was full of
their dead bodies. The surviving Saracens dragged their
fallen comrades out through the gates and piled them in
mounds as big as houses. No one has ever seen or heard of
such a slaughter of pagans. They were burned on pyres like
pyramids, and none save God knows how many there were.

This sanctimonious slaughter, the conjunction between
plunder and righteousness, between massacre and religious

jubilation, was also noted by Fulcher of Chartres, who was not present at the fall of the city but had reports of it very soon afterwards:

> After this great slaughter, our men went into the houses of the citizens and seized whatever they found. The first to enter the house, whatever his position or rank, had the right to plunder it, and this was acknowledged by all the Franks. That house or even the palace was his, and he could take whatever he wanted. In this way many poor people became wealthy. Then all the clergy and laity went to the Sepulchre of the Lord and His most glorious Temple, singing a new canticle to the Lord in voices of exaltation, making offerings and supplications, and joyously visiting the Holy Places as they had so long desired to do.

The very fact of faith made the killing more certain. To overwrought minds and bodies, blood-lust was close in emotion to the high hysteria of religious exultation. For three years God had been calling the crusaders to relieve His city. For three years the Muslims had blocked their path. Now the enemy would pay, not just for their presumption in the places of the Lord, but also for the misery of the long campaign, for heat, disease, weariness, dirt, thirst, hunger, for the pain of wounds and the wasting of sickness, for the heartache of loneliness and separation from home, and for the death of so many friends and companions who were not forgotten. For all this, there was a high price to pay, and the Muslims in Jerusalem would have to pay it to the very last drop of their blood. Raymond of Aguilers, a priest who was by no means cruel or vicious, gave way to the feeling of the moment and celebrated a savage crusader glory:

> Now that the city was taken it was well worth all our previous labours and hardships to see the devotion of the pilgrims at the Holy Sepulchre. How they rejoiced and exulted and sang a new song to the Lord! A new day, new joy, new and perpetual gladness, the consummation of our effort and devotion drew forth from all new words and new music. This day, I say, will be famous in all future ages. This day, I say, marks the justification of all Christianity, the

humiliation of paganism, and the renewal of our faith. 'This
is the day that the Lord hath made, let us rejoice and be
glad in it.' For on this day the Lord revealed Himself to his
people and blessed them.

It was a blood sacrifice, a retreat to the dark places of the
heart.

At Christmas, more than five months after the fall of
Jerusalem, when Fulcher of Chartres came from Edessa to
visit the city, he was distressed and disgusted by the stink of
Muslim corpses still left rotting in the fields.

This age was no stranger to violence and cruelty, but some
cataclysm of the spirit had happened, which the crusaders
could barely understand. These men were not given to intro-
spection. The powerful, contrary emotions of horror and joy
had swamped their minds. William of Tyre, of the next generation of crusaders, in his history tried conscientiously to
arrive at an understanding of the moment from the memories
of the participants and from eye-witness reports. The first
impression was one of overwhelming shame and disgust:

> It was impossible to look upon the vast numbers of the
> slain without horror. Everywhere lay bits of human bodies,
> and the ground was soaked with the blood of the dead. And
> it was not only the spectacle of the headless bodies and
> mutilated limbs thrown in all directions that aroused horror
> in all who saw them. It was still more dreadful to gaze upon
> the victors themselves, covered in gore from head to foot,
> a sight that brought terror to everyone they met. It was
> reported that within the Temple precinct alone 10,000
> infidels were killed, in addition to the bodies that lay
> uncounted in the streets and squares of the city.
>
> Soldiers roamed the streets in search of any wretched
> survivors who might be hiding from death. When found,
> these were dragged into public view and slaughtered like
> sheep. Some of our men formed bands and broke into
> houses where they laid cruel hands on men, women and
> children, and whoever else was in the household. The vic-
> tims were either put to the sword, or thrown from some
> high place to perish miserably on the stones of the street.

At the same time, the crusaders felt a wild joy, not just the religious joy of a task completed for the sake of the Lord, but also the simple joy of possession, the pirate's joy, or of children who have luckily stumbled on a treasure-trove:

> The city was found to be full to overflowing with goods of all kinds. All the soldiers, from the least to the greatest, found an abundance of everything. In the houses were large amounts of gold and silver, valuable stones, and fine clothes. There were stores of grain, wine, oil, and plenty of water, for lack of which the army had suffered so much during the siege. Even our most needy pilgrims and brethren were satisfied with affectionate gifts from the more successful. By the second and third day of the occupation, an excellent public market was established for the sale and exchange of goods. Even the common people had all they needed in abundance. So days passed in joyous celebration, as the pilgrims refreshed themselves with the food and rest they so badly needed.

Unhappy Islam! The fall of Jerusalem was a heavy loss. How had it happened? Ibn al-Athir was quite clear on that point. 'Discord between the Muslim princes,' he wrote, 'enabled the Franks to overrun the land.'

–9–
'WHAT HAPPENS NOW?'

Muslims said that if Mecca was the body of the faith, then Medina was one wing and Jerusalem was the other. The implication was clear. For the progress of the whole faith both wings were needed.

After the fall of Jerusalem there was an expectation within Islam that the disaster would soon be reversed. Many voices were raised, fiercely reminding Muslim princes of their duty. The Iraqi poet al-Abiwardi wrote:

> Sons of Islam, behind you are battles in which heads
> rolled at your feet.
> Dare you sleep in the blessed shade of safety,
> where life is as soft as an orchard flower?
> Must the foreigners feed on our shame, while you
> are lost in pleasures, as if the world is at peace?
> When the points of the white swords are bloodied red,
> and the brown iron of the lances is stained with gore!
> This is war, and he who shuns the whirlpool to save
> his life shall grind his teeth in penitence.
> This is war, the infidel's sword is naked in his hand, and
> ready to be sheathed in necks and skulls again.

Nor were Muslims the only ones to hope for a return to Islam. For generations, apart for some years of madness under Caliph al-Hakim, the Jews of the land and the city had, on the whole, been treated with tolerance by the Muslim rulers of Palestine. Yet what had the Christians done? Among the first monstrous acts of their presence in Jerusalem they had shut Jews in a synagogue and burnt them alive. It was no wonder that the whole Jewish community, within Palestine and beyond, thought wistfully of a better time with better masters. In particular, they missed the temperate, sensible government of al-Afdal. The Fatimid vizier knew the vicissitudes of faith and fortune and had learnt a tolerant wisdom from them. He came from a family of Christian Armenian slaves who had converted to Islam and risen by ability in the service of the caliph. His administration of Jerusalem had been mild, and Jews had good reason to regret the fall of the Fatimids. An elderly Jew from the West, who had seen and approved Fatimid justice in Alexandria but had been prevented from completing his pilgrimage to Jerusalem by the fall of the city, wrote home in early 1100:

> I had come to hope that because of al-Afdal's justice and strength God would give the land into his hands, and then I could go to Jerusalem in safety and tranquillity. But the Franks arrived and killed everybody in the city, whether of Ishmael or of Israel, and the few who survived the slaughter were made prisoners. Now, all of us had anticipated that the vizier – may God bestow glory in his victories – would march against the Franks and chase them away. Yet time after time our hope failed. But to this very moment we continue to hope that God will deliver the vizier's enemies into his hands.

The preference among Jews for Islam over Christendom was perhaps not astonishing, but the Jewish community was not the only one to learn a grim lesson from the unthinking fanaticism of the crusaders. The sects of the eastern Christian Church – not only Orthodox Greeks but also Copts, Syrians, Jacobites and Armenians – had co-existed amicably enough with the Muslims, who had permitted them the autonomy of their own shrines and churches. At the beginning of the siege, al-Daula had banished all Christians from the city as a wise precaution against the possibility of treachery from within, but he had done them no further harm. When they returned, exulting in Christian victory, they saw the new harsh reality. There would be no further autonomy. All Christian sects were made subordinate to the new Latin patriarchy, and those who were not Latin were expelled from worship in the Church of the Holy Sepulchre. At once, the new patriarch, Arnulf, set to work torturing certain Syrian priests to discover where they had hidden the relic of the True Cross.

A Muslim counter-attack on Jerusalem was expected within a month at the most. Envoys arrived from Cairo accusing the crusaders of an unwarranted attack on the city and demanding that the westerners withdraw altogether from the Fatimid territory of Palestine. At the same time, the army of al-Afdal was steadily advancing. In the first week of August it had reached Ascalon, on the coast to the south of Jaffa. When the news came of this close threat, the crusader leaders were dispersed. Duke Godfrey, who had been elected ruler of Jerusalem, was trying to make good his claim to the city. Count Raymond, upset by Godfrey's actions, was foraging in the Jordan valley. Tancred and Count Eustace had gone to Nablus to receive its surrender.

Messengers set out hastily to summon all the Christian princes to gather with their forces at Ramleh, on the coastal plain, a few miles from Ascalon. Tancred and Eustace, coming south through the hills, captured some Muslim scouts and learnt that al-Afdal was waiting at Ascalon for reinforcements to be brought by the Egyptian fleet. Tancred, who as usual favoured boldness, wanted to mount a surprise attack as soon as possible. This was agreed, though Count Raymond and Robert of Normandy, embittered as they were against Godfrey, hung back as long as they could, until their own knights confirmed the Egyptian position.

By Wednesday, 10 August, all the leaders were at Ramleh with their troops, leaving Jerusalem almost empty of soldiers. The safety of the city was put into the hands of the Lord, and Peter the Hermit was instructed to lead the clergy, both Latin and Greek, in procession to the Church of the Holy Sepulchre 'to pray and give alms, so that God might grant His people victory'. From Ramleh, the crusader army marched on to the plain of Ashdod. The attack was planned for dawn on Friday, 12 August 1099. On the evening before, Patriarch Arnulf admonished the men, threatening to excommunicate all those who turned aside from the battle for the sake of plunder, but promising that 'thereafter they might return with great joy to take whatever the Lord should grant'. At daybreak on the 12th, a sudden charge took the Egyptian army by surprise. Al-Afdal was either badly informed or he had misread the crusaders' intentions, though Raymond of Aguilers claimed that it was chiefly arrogance that caused the enemy to be so unprepared: 'Truly, they were being daily informed by those who fled from Jerusalem of our small numbers and of the weakness of our people and horses. Besides, relying on their strength, they believed that they could drown us and our camp in their spit alone.'

In any case, it was another bloody occasion for slaughter, which the *Gesta* recalled with relish:

> Our men entered into a beautiful valley near the coast and drew up their lines of battle. Thus all was arranged, and they joined battle at once in the Name of our Lord Jesus Christ. The pagans stood before us. Each one had a flask around his neck, from which he could drink if he had to pursue us. But by God's grace this was not to be.
>
> The count of Normandy, seeing the golden apple on the top of the pole that held the amir's standard, rushed straight at the bearer and gave him a mortal wound. The count of Flanders attacked from the other side, and Tancred charged straight into the middle of the enemy camp. The pagans began to flee at once. The battle was terrible, but we gained an immediate victory. The enemies of God stood about blinded and bewildered. Some in their panic climbed trees, but our men killed them with arrows and spears and swords, and cast them to the ground. Others threw themselves flat, not daring to stand against us, so our men killed them as one slaughters beasts in a shambles.
>
> We captured the amir's standard, which Robert of Normandy redeemed for 20 marks of silver and gave to the

patriarch in honour of God and the Holy Sepulchre. The amir's sword was bought for 60 bezants. When the crews from the pagan ships saw the amir and all his men fleeing they set sail at once and made for the open sea. Then our men went back to the enemy camp and found innumerable spoils of gold and silver, great piles of riches, and all kinds of arms, implements and animals. They took what they wanted and burnt the rest.

Almost before the countryside was awake the battle was over. Farmers rubbing sleep from their eyes saw fleeing horsemen rearing like ghosts out of whirlwinds of dust, pursued by cries of victory that were as terrible to their ears as the howls of the dying. The Egyptian army was broken. Although the crusaders did not know it then, no further counter-attack would come from the Fatimids. Ibn al-Qalanisi briefly noted the finality of the defeat:

> The Egyptian army was thrown back towards Ascalon, and al-Afdal himself took refuge in the city. The swords of the Franks were given mastery over the Muslims, and death was handed out to foot-soldiers, volunteers and townsfolk. About 10,000 souls were slaughtered, and the camp was plundered. Then al-Afdal retreated to Egypt with his officers, and the Franks besieged Ascalon. The number of worthy citizens killed in the campaign – apart from the soldiers of the militia and the levies – amounted to 2,700 souls.

Whatever slim hope was left to the Muslims for the recapture of Jerusalem now rested with the Abbasid caliph in Baghdad. Within days of the fall of the city, the Jerusalem qadi Abu Saad al-Harawi led a group of refugees into Baghdad. It was Ramadan, the month of fasting, but al-Harawi wanted to shake the easy-going young Caliph al-Mustazhir out of the torpor with which the Abbasids had so ineffectively watched the spiral of Islamic defeat, from Nicaea to Antioch to Maarat to Jerusalem. The qadi made known his grief and anger, and he was heard with sympathy. These refugees, wrote Ibn al-Athir, 'told the caliph's ministers a story that wrung their hearts and brought tears to their eyes'. Nor was it only the ministers who were moved:

On Friday the refugees went to the Great Mosque and begged for help, weeping so that their listeners wept with them when they described the sufferings of the Muslims in that Holy City – the men killed, the women and children taken prisoner, the homes pillaged. Because of the terrible hardship these refugees had suffered, they were permitted to break the Ramadan fast.

What could the caliph do? Al-Mustazhir, the titular head of the Sunni branch of Islam, like others before and after him, was only a puppet in the hands of foreigners. The Turks ruled in Baghdad. The caliph, an artistic and talented young man, composed love-poems behind the extensive walls of his compound, which he himself had helped to design. He had no political authority, and no army beyond the many eunuchs of his personal guard. The man who governed in Baghdad was Barkyaruq, a Turkish prince who spoke only broken Arabic, and his attention was firmly taken up with the struggle for power within the Turkish ruling families. Al-Harawi never met Barkyaruq to put the case for Jerusalem. The Turkish sultan was away in Persia fighting his own brother. In October 1099, that brother, Mohammed, became the new master of Baghdad. But in January 1100, Barkyaruq was back in command. In another three months he was gone again. In this period of Muslim helplessness against the crusaders, Baghdad changed hands among the Turks eight times in two and a half years.

No wonder the Iraqi poet al-Abiwardi cried out in protest, putting despairing words in the mouth of the Prophet:

> I see my people slow to raise the lance against the enemy. I see the Faith resting on feeble pillars.
> Fear of death makes the Muslims evade the fire of battle. Though they believe it not, death will surely strike them.

For the time being at least, the crusaders were safe from Muslim attack in Jerusalem.

SYMBOLIC CAPTURE OF JERUSALEM

Safe or not, the crusaders were adamant that the city now belonged to them and they would keep it. Whatever the desire of Islam for Jerusalem, the Christians wanted it more, now that they had become fully aware of the holy mystery of the place, and had suffered for it. Chronicler Fulcher of

Chartres, who had followed every weary step of the long campaign, expressed very well the overwhelming feeling of awe and gratitude shown by the Christian army at the conquest of the Holy City:

> O, time so longed for! O, time remembered above all others! O, greatest of all deeds! So truly longed for, since it had always been desired with an inward yearning of soul by all believers of the Catholic faith. This was the place where God, the Creator of all creatures, made man, and in His manifold mercy for the human race brought the gift of spiritual rebirth. Here He was born, died and rose again. This holy place, cleansed from the contagion of the heathen, who contaminated it by their superstition for so long, was restored to its former glory by those believing and trusting in Him.

Fulcher was a priest, the possessor of an excitable religious temperament. Perhaps he was prone to an excess of veneration, but his feeling for Jerusalem was by no means unusual. Other more simple pilgrims – soldiers or laymen – experienced a similar wonder of the place, the feeling of intimate dread so close to the holiest of events, not just those of the New Testament but of the Old Testament also. The short 'Description of the Holy Places' appended to certain manuscripts of the *Gesta*, and written by the same hand in the same terse, commonplace Latin style, gave a picture of the ordinary Christian walking, as it were, through the pages of the Bible:

> In Jerusalem is a little cell, roofed with a single stone, where Solomon wrote the Book of Wisdom. And there, between the temple and the altar, on the marble pavement before the holy place, the blood of Zechariah was shed . . .
> There is the house of Hezekiah, king of Judah, to whose span of life God added fifteen years. Next to it is the house of Caiaphas, and the pillar where Christ was scourged. At the Nablus gate is Pilate's judgment-seat. Not far off is Golgotha, that Place of Skulls . . .
> From Mount Calvary, the navel of the world lies fifteen feet to the west . . .
> Two bowshots away, going eastwards, is the Temple of the Lord built by Solomon . . .

The tomb of Isaiah the prophet is quite near. A thousand paces away is Bethany, where Lazarus was restored to life. In the same direction, nineteen miles on the Jericho road, is the sycamore that Zachaeus climbed to see Christ. A thousand paces from Jericho is Elisha's spring, which he blessed by throwing in salt.

And so on . . .

The most haunting memories, the most affecting calls to the pilgrim spirit that tied Christians to Jerusalem, came from the proximity to the life of Jesus. The account of a German pilgrim, written some time soon after the fall of the city, was full of holy amazement:

Here is the Mount called Sion. Here the Lord had supper with His disciples. There He washed their feet. There was the place where the Apostles took refuge for fear of the Jews. There the Holy Spirit descended in fire on the disciples. There they composed the Creed. There also Blessed Mary died to the world . . .

Now let us go into the city itself. There is the Tomb of Him who was crucified for us, over which a temple has been built . . .

To the east is the Prison in which the Lord was placed. Next to this are the steps by which people come up to the temple. Next to these steps a stone cross stands, of the same size as the Cross that was carried by the Lord. Next to this cross is a small chapel where His clothes were divided, and where they cast lots over His garment . . .

Near this is the place of Calvary, where the Lord was crucified and where once Abraham sacrificed Isaac. At the foot of the hill there is an altar. It is in the same place where Adam was buried.

Once a Christian had seen all this, and savoured the air, and felt the weight of holy history, none would willingly let Jerusalem go.

'On the eighth day after the city was taken,' wrote the author of the *Gesta*, 'they chose Duke Godfrey as its ruler, so that he might fight the pagans and protect the Christians. Likewise a most experienced and distinguished man called Arnulf was chosen as patriarch, on the feast of St Peter Ad Vincula [1 August 1099].'

The *Gesta* made the establishment of crusader rule sound clear and straightforward, but that was far from the case. Raymond of Aguilers, who belonged to the Provençal contingent, gave another and more illuminating account:

> After six or seven days the princes solemnly began to consider the choice of a ruler, who would collect the tributes of the region, succour the peasants of the land, and save the country from further devastation. But some of the clergy assembled and said to the princes, 'If you are to proceed rightly and properly, you will first choose a spiritual vicar, as eternal matters come before temporal. After this, a ruler may deal with secular matters. If you do otherwise, we shall hold what you do invalid.' The princes were very angry at this, and went ahead with their election as quickly as possible. The clergy were weakened by the loss of Adhemar, the bishop of Le Puy, who in his life had held our army together with holy deeds and words, like a second Moses.
>
> The princes, disregarding admonition and opposition, urged Count Raymond of St Gilles to accept the kingdom. But he said he abhorred the name of king in that city, though he would consent if others accepted it. For this reason they came together and chose Duke Godfrey and placed him in charge of the Sepulchre of the Lord.

The election, as so often in the affairs of the crusaders, was soured by controversy, dislikes and frustrated ambitions. No provision had been made for the course of events after the conquest of the city. The fight alone had been preoccupation enough for feudal knights. No doubt most had expected that the legate Adhemar, had he lived, would have governed Jerusalem as the pope's representative. The spiritual, in the Holy City, would indeed have taken precedence over the temporal, but the good bishop had died, and the other senior clergy on the crusade had died also. Nor did Simeon, the Greek patriarch, survive to greet the crusaders' triumph.

A patriarch was urgently needed, though there was no

outstanding candidate. The only certain qualification was that the new man would have to be a priest of the Latin rite. The most active of the remaining clergy was the bishop of Martirano, from the Norman lands in southern Italy, and though he did not want the patriarchy for himself he argued strongly for his friend Arnulf, the chaplain of Robert of Normandy. This choice was immediately controversial, for it looked like a Norman plot, and Arnulf had antagonized many, in particular the Provençals, when he led the opposition to the Holy Lance and harried Peter Bartholomew to his death. The outraged opposition claimed that Arnulf was a man of loose life, the butt of many ribald camp songs, and was moreover the illegitimate son of a priest. Reluctantly, the clergy chose Arnulf, at least for the time being, until the pope should make his own preference known. In fact, though the crusaders did not know it, Pope Urban had already chosen a successor to Adhemar, a bishop called Daimbert of Pisa, who was even then on his way to the Holy Land. Arnulf, whatever his supposed faults, was a competent man and a vivacious preacher, and he sensibly confined himself to ecclesiastical affairs, leaving all other business in the hands of the princes.

The prize for the princes was the first place in the first city of Christendom. The foremost candidates were Count Raymond of St Gilles and Duke Godfrey of Bouillon. Of the other leaders, the well-liked Robert of Normandy and the dashing soldier Robert of Flanders both wished to return home. Tancred the Norman, a brave and daring general, was not considered. He was too hungry to trust, a poorer copy of his devious uncle Bohemond. Raymond of St Gilles seemed the most logical choice – the richest, most experienced, most powerful and most devout of the leaders – but his haughtiness, his thin rectitude, and his touchy dignity had made him deeply unpopular. Also, since he had taken charge of the army at Maarat an-Numan he had shown himself to be a poor general, though his own courage was not in doubt. His dogged, foolish obstinacy in allowing the siege at Arqa to drag on so disastrously still rankled with soldiers from all the factions. Even his chaplain, Raymond of Aguilers, had to admit that his own Provençals would be glad to see the back of their leader:

'And so the disputes were multiplied. The counts of Flanders and Normandy favoured the duke. Almost all from Count Raymond's own lands did likewise in the belief that if he failed he would return home. These Provençals opposed their own lord, and made up many vile stories about him so that he would not be chosen king.'

Duke Godfrey, on the other hand, was a man with far fewer enemies. Popular enough in the camp, gallant enough in battle, prominent enough in council, he had as his chief recommendation the fact that he was not Count Raymond. Otherwise little was known about him. When the electors took secret soundings within the army, to assess the character of the candidates, Godfrey's own household, according to William of Tyre, could only find one fault in their master:

> Once he had entered a church he could not be made to leave, even at the end of the celebration of the divine office. He continued to question priests and clergy as to the meaning of each image and picture until his companions, who had no interest in these things, were exceedingly bored. Moreover, because of this habit, the meats prepared for a fixed hour were overdone and tasteless when finally eaten, as a result of the long delay.

At first, with a sound sense of the realities of power, the electors offered the rule in Jerusalem to Count Raymond. To the astonishment of history, he refused. His chaplain claimed that the count could not bear to think of himself as king in the city that belonged to Christ the King. Since Count Raymond was a truly pious man, perhaps there was some truth in that. Perhaps also he knew that the gulf between himself and the people, between his own narrow nature and their unquantifiable hopes for glory and plunder, would make him unable to govern. So the count refused, and the choice fell, almost by default, on Godfrey of Bouillon. After a show of reluctance, Duke Godfrey accepted, but in deference to the place in which he was, and to the realm of the spiritual, he would not call himself king. He took the title of *Advocatus Sancti Sepulchri*, 'guardian and defender of the Holy Sepulchre'.

The new Christian era in Jerusalem began with a continuation of familiar old quarrels. Count Raymond still held the Tower of David, which had been surrendered to him, and he would not let it go even though Godfrey make it known most forcibly that he needed this strong and dominating tower to assert his full authority in the city. After many angry words the tower was delivered to Godfrey by a trick, and Count Raymond stormed out of the city in great displeasure. 'The count blazed forth,' wrote his chaplain, 'in great anger, saying he could not remain disgraced in that place.' Godfrey's high-handed behaviour had also annoyed Robert of Flanders and Robert of Normandy. Tancred and Count Eustace had gone to Nablus. The clergy and their various supporters were still in ferment over the choice of Arnulf as patriarch.

In early August, the danger from al-Afdal and the Egyptian army had caused the crusaders to set aside their quarrels. At Ascalon they closed ranks and delivered the kind of crushing military blow on which their fame as soldiers rested. Then the leaders fell apart again. Mutual suspicion between Raymond and Godfrey prevented the Christian army from gaining the full military fruits of the Ascalon victory. Disgusted by this bickering, the two Count Roberts were confirmed in their decision to leave Palestine and return to their homelands. Their crusader vows were completed, their duty to the Church in this respect was finished, and they wished to resume the ordinary life of a western prince. Count Raymond, still angry with Godfrey and in a great sulk, decided to go with them, though he later changed his mind and was tempted back to try to make for himself a principality in Syria, as Baldwin had done in Edessa and Bohemond in Antioch. In early September the three princes departed with all their followers, marching north to Latakieh.

This sudden, large departure drained much-needed soldiers from the Jerusalem garrison and left the new ruler with many worries. Despite the bad feeling among the leaders, Godfrey begged the outgoing princes to speak well for Jerusalem when they returned to the West and to urge western knights and pilgrims to come and help maintain the Christian grip on Palestine and the Holy City, for the Christians were still in danger. The Muslim population was unlikely to mount a concerted, well-organized campaign against the crusaders, but local chieftains were quite capable of guerrilla warfare, making life hard and death probable for the thinly-spread Christian communities of the land. Lines of communication between the little enclaves of fellow-believers were difficult and easily disrupted. Despite the opening of certain Mediterranean ports to western ships, Christians were very dependent on the surrounding countryside for their supplies. The serious problems, and the poor resources of the crusaders, were shown in November when Baldwin and Bohemond came south to complete their crusader vows in the Holy City. Fulcher of Chartres complained of the miserable journey:

> When we had entered these lands of the Saracens, we could get nothing edible from the hostile inhabitants. No one would give or sell to us, so we soon consumed our supplies and were distressed by hunger. And our horses and animals, for lack of grain, were in a double pain – having to move but unable to eat. Then we found certain crops in the fields, almost like reeds, which the people called *honey-cane*. From this crop a sort of wood-honey was ingeniously gathered. We hungry folk chewed these stalks all day, but with little satisfaction.
>
> So for love of God we suffered these things and many others, such as cold and exposure and excessive rain. Between the cold and the frequent rainstorms, the sun was not even warm enough to dry our soaked, pitiful clothes. Sometimes the rain would last for four or five days. I saw many, without tents, die from the wet and the cold, both men and women, and many beasts. I, Fulcher of Chartres, was present with them and saw their grief and pain.
>
> And often our people were killed by Saracens lying in ambush around the narrow paths, or were abducted by them as we searched for supplies. We were in a poor state. You could see knights of noble birth reduced to foot-soldiers for want of a horse. Only twice on the way did we get grain, from Tripoli and Caesarea, and that at a very high price. What great relief it was to come to Jerusalem!

This arrival of Bohemond and Baldwin was yet another conundrum for Godfrey. What were the intentions of these notoriously independent and self-seeking lords? Baldwin was Godfrey's brother but blood was no bar to ambition. Travelling with them was the new papal legate Daimbert of Pisa, another unknown quantity, a man who had made his mark as an energetic champion of the Church, but he was already tainted with rumours of corruption. The journey of the Pisan fleet carrying the legate to the Holy Land was a matter of scandal. The piratical instincts of the aggressive Italian city-state led to several raids on Byzantine towns in the eastern Mediterranean. What should have been a stately religious progress became a running battle with the Byzantine navy.

Godfrey recognized that all these men had lawful and religious reasons to be in Jerusalem, but he suspected bad faith and double-dealing. He had heard some shameful stories about Bohemond and Daimbert, who had met by chance at Latakieh in early September. Bohemond, who was always fearful that Emperor Alexius might try to reclaim Antioch from him, had gone to lay siege to the important Greek-held port of Latakieh. Though the Greeks controlled the western land-route to Antioch, Bohemond was hoping to break their grip on the main Mediterranean sea-route to his principality. When Bohemond and his army arrived at the coast they discovered a Pisan fleet sitting offshore, preparing to blockade, with the full approbation of the papal legate, a town of fellow-Christians in the midst of a hostile Muslim land.

At once, Bohemond saw the chance to join forces with Pisa against Latakieh, and he took steps to become an ally and confidant of Daimbert. They were somewhat alike, two powerful, intelligent egotists, and here their interests coincided. Then, at that very moment their plan was spoilt by the arrival of the three crusader princes who were travelling home from Jerusalem. When Count Raymond and the two Roberts learnt of the legate's conduct and his latest scheme, they were genuinely shocked. Had the crusade come to this, that Christian should fight Christian? They summoned Daimbert to Jabala and told him in the plainest language that his plan was an offence against Christendom, and that they would not allow it. Daimbert was forced to call off the Pisan blockade, and Bohemond, faced by the outrage (and the soldiers) of his old enemy Count Raymond, backed by the considerable following of Normandy and Flanders, abandoned the siege. In Latakieh, Raymond celebrated a final triumph over his old antagonist. Bohemond, however, was not one to brood on failure. He cemented his friendship with Daimbert and waited to see what the future had to offer. Joining Baldwin's party from Edessa, when they all met on the road, Bohemond and Daimbert set out for Jerusalem.

What was the mood of these awkward guests? Godfrey's first instinct was to be welcoming and conciliatory, for the newcomers arrived with a large following, perhaps as many as 25,000 pilgrims and soldiers, while Godfrey had, according to William of Tyre, no more than three hundred knights and two thousand foot-soldiers. In his present state of insecurity Godfrey needed as many reinforcements as he could find, and he hoped to persuade many of the men from Antioch and Edessa to stay in Jerusalem.

Soon it became clear that neither Baldwin nor Bohemond had ambitions in the Holy City, at least for the moment. They wished to confirm the rights that they had won for themselves in northern Syria. Then they intended to complete their crusading vows, spend Christmas among the Holy Places, and return quickly to their own principalities.

The two princes were chafing to leave, but Daimbert would remain. What was to be done with him? He was, after all, Pope Urban's own choice as successor to the much-lamented Adhemar. It seemed right that the Pisan bishop should become what Adhemar would have been, had he lived. The election of Arnulf as patriarch had been both controversial and provisional. Arnulf, a thorough realist, was willing to step down to a subordinate role. It was said that some money changed hands. Daimbert already had strong support from Bohemond, who was known to be a bad man to oppose, and soon after Christmas, he was installed as patriarch of Jerusalem:

As soon as Daimbert, the man of God, had been installed as patriarch, both Duke Godfrey and Lord Bohemond humbly received from his hand the investiture of their territories, for the one the kingdom of Jerusalem and for the other the principality of Antioch, and in this the two princes showed honour to Him whose viceregent on earth they believed the patriarch to be.

When this ceremony was over, revenues were assigned to the lord patriarch, so that he might be honourably supported, as was his due. After these matters were attended to, Bohemond and Baldwin took leave of the duke to return to their own lands.

This account by William of Tyre implied that the troublesome visit ended in relief for everyone. Daimbert was elevated to a great and holy responsibility. In return, he had given the princes what they most urgently needed – confirmation by the Church of their titles and possessions within the lands of the Lord. The principle that the Holy Land was the patrimony of the Church had been established, but at some cost for the future. For the moment, Godfrey was able to sigh with satisfaction and turn his attention to the state of his kingdom.

The defeat at Ascalon had left the Muslims with a precarious hold on the Palestinian coastal towns, except for Jaffa, but with no authority in the hills of Judaea and Samaria. The long-settled inhabitants of these parts were mainly Christian, small farmers with a history of modest exploitation by Muslim overlords. Naturally, the Christians welcomed the crusaders. With local sympathy, and a sparing use of men, Godfrey was able to extend his rule cautiously towards Hebron in the south and Nablus in the north. Tancred took a small band of adventurers, in which there were no more than twenty-four knights, and waged a brilliant little campaign north into Galilee. This land, disputed between the Fatimids and Amir Duqaq of Damascus, was a kind of Muslim limbo, unsure after Ascalon who was master. When Tancred approached the chief town of Tiberias, the Muslims fled, leaving the town to the Christian minority and to Tancred. From Tiberias, Tancred set out on a number of dashing raids, full of speedy movement, surprise and imagination, which gained him Nazareth and Scythopolis, and provided a large amount of plunder and riches. Tancred now had in his hands a compact little state that protected the kingdom of Jerusalem from the north. In gratitude Godfrey granted him the principality of Galilee, to hold as a fief of Jerusalem.

The gains, however, were only made by extreme effort amid constant danger and hardship. The Christian soldiers were so few, and there was so much to be done. Daily, on the campaign trail, in the fields, on the market road, in the shadow of the town walls, even on the city streets, the Christians of the kingdom lived on the edge of catastrophe. Death seemed a fellow-traveller on all their paths. William of Tyre, writing soon after this time, was struck by the insecurity of their lives in comparison with his own age:

> By this time there remained only the duke, to whom the kingdom had been committed, and Tancred. The resources and military strength of the Christians were very small. When all had been most diligently called together, barely three hundred knights and two thousand foot-soldiers could be found.
>
> Only a few cities were under our power, and these so placed in the midst of enemies that Christians could not go from one to another without great danger. The entire surrounding country was full of infidel Saracens, who were the cruellest enemies of our people. And these were all the more dangerous because they were so close at hand, for the pest who does the most harm is the one at the very door. Any Christian walking the highway without due caution and careful watch was likely to be killed by the Saracens, or seized and made a slave. Moreover, these infidels on our lands refused to cultivate the fields, so that our people might suffer from hunger. In fact, they were so obstinate they preferred famine themselves rather than feed the Christians.
>
> Nor was the danger only on the highways. Even within the city walls, in the very houses, there was scarcely any secure place. For the inhabitants were few and scattered, and the ruinous walls left chinks open for the enemy. Thieves stealthily made inroads by night, and overpowered many in their own houses. As a result many of our people quite openly abandoned the holdings they had won and began to return to their own lands. They could not help but fear that sooner or later their protectors would fail, or be overwhelmed by the enemy, and then who would save

them from massacre? So an edict was issued for an annual general accounting which would favour those who had kept going in the midst of troubles, and had held their tenure peacefully and without question for a year and a day. This law was introduced, as we have said, in resentment against those cowards who had left their possessions, that they should not be able to return and renew their claim.

In response to these calamities, soldiers such as Godfrey and his few knights went on in the only way they knew. When they had taken up the cross, answering the call from Pope Urban, they had offered to Christ their chief and distinguishing talent, which was strength and experience in war. 'Godfrey, beloved of God,' wrote William of Tyre, 'despite the poverty of his kingdom, worked under divine guidance to extend the domains of his realm. He assembled his militia and laid siege to a coastal town near Jaffa, formerly Antipatris but now known as Arsuf.'

A small, intermittent war went on, waged with customary brutality and ruthlessness. Arsuf held out at first. In order to give the crusaders pause, the garrison suspended from the wall a Christian hostage, the knight Gerard of Avesnes, who pleaded with his former comrades not to shoot. Godfrey refused to be deflected from the attack. He ordered the archers to shoot again and Gerard was severely wounded, though the town still did not fall. The example of the hostage reminded the Muslims that their own end was likely to be sudden, so the soldiers of the garrison redoubled their defence. However, French and Italian ships were beginning to gather in the eastern Mediterranean, attracted by the hope of trade now that the grip of the Egyptian navy was loosening, and when the ships started a blockade from the sea, and Godfrey's army cut off supplies from the land, one by one the coastal towns of Palestine capitulated.

In March 1100, the people of Arsuf handed their town keys to Jerusalem and agreed to pay tribute. In April, Ascalon, Acre and Caesarea followed, sending munificent gifts of horses and produce, and offering to pay a combined monthly tribute of 5,000 bezants in return for the right to cultivate their lands in peace. Godfrey willingly agreed. Other petty Muslim chieftains then saw that it was safer to negotiate than to fight. Soon a succession of Muslim embassies was descending from the Samarian hills, bearing gifts, eager to speak with the Christians but also curious to inspect these warlike devils on their own ground. The Muslims discovered Godfrey in surroundings of spartan simplicity, and according to William of Tyre they were impressed:

> Godfrey was sitting on a straw-filled sack on the ground, waiting for his men to return from foraging. When the Saracen chiefs saw him sitting thus, they were struck dumb with amazement. 'Why,' they wondered, 'did so great a prince and lord from the West, who had shaken the entire Orient and seized a mighty kingdom with his strong hand, sit in this inglorious manner? Where are the tapestries and silks, the throng of armed retainers, to put respect and fear in the hearts of those who approached him?'
>
> When these queries were translated for the duke, he replied that the ground would well suffice as a seat to mortal man, since after death it was destined to be his abode forever. Filled with admiration at this answer, those who had come to test him departed saying, 'Truly, this is a man capable of taking all lands by storm. Because of the merit of his life, rightly has he been given rule over peoples and nations.'
>
> And then the inhabitants of the neighbouring lands marvelled and at the same time were terrified by the courage and success of the crusaders. They learned these facts from the lips of their own friends, in whom they had confidence, and then they wondered the more. Consequently, this marvellous report was passed into all parts of the East.

Godfrey was a great hero to William of Tyre, and there is some myth-making here, but as with most myth it rested on a core of truth. In most of the Muslim lands within reach of Jerusalem an accommodation was developing between Christian and Muslim. Amir Duqaq in Damascus was angry enough to snap at the crusaders' heels whenever he could find them at a disadvantage, but he did not dare to meet them head on. Lesser Muslim lords preferred to pay tribute and live more peacefully. Godfrey accepted their tribute, for the moment. In time he intended to conquer their lands and towns. Until then the money and the breathing space were most welcome.

As the Muslims became less of a problem, Godfrey faced more and more difficulties with his own people in his own city. Godfrey had little notion of government beyond the scant wisdom provided by the practices of military feudalism. He had no council other than his own household, no properly constituted law-giving body, no adminsitration accountable to him. So long as he was on the move, at the head of an army with a sword in his hand, that seemed to him the limit of his role. His very title was anomalous. *Advocatus Sancti Sepulchri*, what exactly did that mean? When he had accepted investiture from the hand of Daimbert, very unwisely he had forfeited authority by making himself a suzerain of the Church, and soon Patriarch Daimbert began to demand more and more power for himself and more and more possessions for the Church. By June 1100, the patriarch was demanding control over Jaffa and over the whole of Jerusalem.

In the middle of June, Godfrey heard that a strong Venetian fleet had put in to Jaffa, and he hurried to greet the ships. He hoped, among other things, that the Venetians would effectively balance the Pisans who supported Daimbert. At Caesarea, Godfrey was feasted by the anxious amir, and he arrived at Jaffa feeling ill. The immediate suspicion was that he had been poisoned, but it is likely that he had typhus. He tried to do business but collapsed and was carried back to the better climate of Jerusalem. For a month Godfrey struggled against sickness, growing ever weaker, while Daimbert and Tancred set out to attack Acre with the help of the Venetian fleet. On Wednesday, 18 July, Godfrey died. He lay in state for five days and was buried in the Church of the Holy Sepulchre.

William of Tyre called his hero Godfrey 'the illustrious ruler of the kingdom of Jerusalem', but that description was much too fulsome. Godfrey of Bouillon was merely an archetype of the crusader. A brave, competent, tenacious soldier, he was caught between Christian idealism and self-interest, and he failed in the end to do justice to either of these sides of a simple, guileless character.

–10–
A NEW LIFE

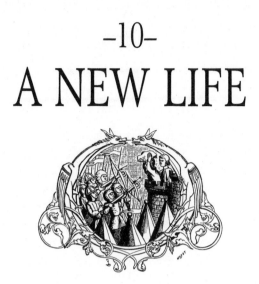

The task was done. Or so it seemed, for no one in the West had calculated beyond the capture of Jerusalem and the freeing of the Holy Places. The architect of the great enterprise, Pope Urban II, died on 29 July 1099, two weeks after the conquest of the city. The men who had given form to the pope's dream – Adhemar, Godfrey, Raymond of St Gilles, Hugh the Great, Stephen of Blois, the two Count Roberts, Bohemond – were all dead or dispersed. A year after the conquest, when a successor was needed on the sudden death of Godfrey, who was there to choose? The great lords, marked by the effort and weariness of the campaign, were gone. Bohemond was captured by the Turkish general Danishmand at Malatya in mid-August 1100. Tancred, the young hound, was still busy on his own account and more obliquely in the cause of Christendom, but he was too poor, junior and unreliably Norman to be taken into consideration. Only Baldwin, Godfrey's brother, was waiting in the wings, having watched with an easy conscience from the relative security of Edessa the painful crawl of the crusader march from Antioch to Jerusalem.

The crusaders had been given one clear aim, and they went forward guided by that light. The aim was fully expressed by the admonition that the historian-monk Baldric placed in the mouth of a preacher as the Christian army stood below the forbidding walls of Jerusalem in that parched summer of 1099:

> Rouse yourselves, O you of Christ's household! Knights and foot-soldiers, rouse yourselves and take hold of that city, which is our commonwealth! Give heed to Christ, now banished from the city and crucified. Forcefully take Christ away from these impious crucifiers. For all who deride and enslave your brothers crucify Christ. Every time they torment and kill your brothers, they also lance the side of Christ. What are you doing about these things? Can you know these things, and not lament them? I speak to you all, fathers and sons, brothers and nephews. If a stranger were to strike any of your kin, would you not avenge people of your blood? How much more ought you to avenge your God, your Father, your Brother, whom you see insulted, driven from His estates, crucified. You hear Him calling, desolate, and begging for help.

The question posed by the preacher was given a resounding answer on 15 July 1099, when Jerusalem fell. That triumph was taken as the culmination of the crusade and greeted with rapture by the Church and throughout the West. 'We owe boundless gratitude,' wrote Pope Paschal II, the successor to Urban, 'to the compassion of Almighty God, since in our time He has designed to wrest the Church in Asia from the hands of the Turks and to open to Christian soldiers the very city of the Lord's suffering and death and burial.' Later, the pope expanded on this feeling of joy, seeing in the fall of the city the realization of the prophecies of scripture: 'We see fulfilled in you what the Lord promised his people through the prophet: "I will live with them and I will walk with them." He has lived through the faith in your hearts and He has walked with you in your works, which is clearly to be seen in your defeat of His enemies. The Lord has renewed His miracles of old.'

The event was so extraordinary in the western mind that the monks who wrote history – only the Church had the learning, the resources and the time to piece together the elaborate record of the past – immediately set to and gave the crusade a moral and religious justification to raise the conquest of Jerusalem among the greatest events of world history. 'If we consider the battles of the gentiles,' wrote Abbot Guibert of Nogent, 'and think of great campaigns and invasions and kingdoms gained, we will find no army and absolutely no exploit comparable to ours.' To those who objected that the Israelites of old had been as divinely inspired and as successful in their wars, Guibert replied firmly that 'We have said not once but many times, and it is worth repeating again, that such a deed has never been done in this world.'

The reason for the transcendent importance of the crusade was easily apparent to the historians. Not only did God inspire the campaign but He led it too, as Guibert put it in his elegant and forceful propaganda:

> God himself, who makes miracles and does not allow another to assume the honour due to His name, was their only leader. He in person directed what had been begun to its conclusion. He personally extended the bounds of the Christian rule. He gathered the lambs, which he had fashioned from wolves, in His arms, not theirs. He embraced them in His protective care. He transported His brood of young, joyful in devout hope, to guide them towards their desire.

It was this intimate divine leadership, wrote Robert the Monk in the most outrageous claim of all, that made the successful conclusion of the crusade the most important human act after the creation, only equalled in world history by the redemptive suffering of Christ on the cross: 'Apart from the mystery of the healing cross, what more marvellous deed has there ever been since the creation of the world than that which was done in our own times in this journey of our men to Jerusalem?'

However, the praise of monks and the justification from theology did nothing to address the stark reality of the present. If the capture of the Holy City is the triumph and culmination of the crusade, what follows? No one had planned which of many possible lives should rise, phoenix-like, out of the ashes of the raped and shattered city, surrounded as it was by the green sea of Islam. The only certain thoughts in the minds of the few crusaders who remained – those, according to the historians, who were so favoured by God – were the desperation of the present and the fear of the future. For more than three years the crusaders had suffered almost to the limit of their capacity. Their army was reduced from the 60,000 or so who had set out from Constantinople to the three hundred knights and two thousand foot-soldiers who kept a lonely vigil with Godfrey in Jerusalem. Palestine might have been re-invigorated by Christian footsteps, but those steps were still infinitely dangerous, as a pilgrim called Saewulf from northern Europe complained when he made his journey about 1101:

> So we climbed up from Jaffa into the city of Jerusalem. This journey lasted two days, by a very hard mountain road. It was very dangerous too, because the Saracens were always plotting an ambush against Christians, hiding in caves and hills and rocky caverns. They were ready day and night, always on the lookout for stragglers, or for signs of fatigue or weakness.
>
> Anyone who has taken that road can see the human bodies by the wayside, and the countless corpses torn up by wild beasts. And it is no surprise why so many Christian corpses lie there unburied. There is little soil and the rocks are not easy to move. Even if there were enough soil, who would be so stupid as to leave his companions and stay to dig a grave! That would be like digging a grave, not for his fellow, but for himself! So in that road not only the poor and the weak have dangers to face, but also the rich and strong. Many are killed by the Saracens, and many by heat and thirst – some through lack of drink and some from drinking too much.

Belatedly, the West began to see that Christian Palestine needed manpower and aid to survive. Pope Paschal wrote to all the great churchmen of the West, urging them to persuade 'all the soldiers of your region to strive for remission and forgiveness of their sins by hastening to our Mother Church of the East'. In particular, he wished to compel, by threat of excommunication, all those shirkers who had taken the sign

CRUSADER MAN

of the cross but had failed to complete their vow, and also those disgraceful cowards who had deserted at Antioch and elsewhere, to redeem themselves by going to help the infant Christian community in the Holy Land.

Considerable pressure was put on the notable backsliders such as Stephen of Blois. Ordericus Vitalis wrote with some amusement of the subtle campaign waged by his wife, Adele, against the errant lord:

> Stephen was compelled both by fear and shame to undertake a fresh crusade. Among others, his wife Adele often urged him to it, reminding him even amid the endearments of conjugal caresses. 'Far be it from me, my lord,' she said, 'to submit any longer to the jibes you receive from all quarters. Pluck up the courage for which you were renowned in your youth, and take arms in a noble cause for the salvation of

thousands, so that Christians may have good reason to exult in all parts of the world, to the terror of the pagans and the public humiliation of their detestable religion.'

In 1101 Stephen returned on a new wave of French enthusiasm. With him were not ony former deserters, such as Hugh of Lusignan, half-brother to Raymond of St Gilles, but also famous men such as William of Aquitaine, the first of the French troubadours. There were three bishops and a large host of knights from northern France, Burgundy and southern Germany. The crusade was ill-starred. The army intended to drive the Abbasid caliphate from Baghdad but was cut off and routed in Roum long before it reached Syria. The soldiers were massacred and scattered, and the women taken into captivity. It was rumoured that Ida of Austria was taken into a harem where she gave birth to the great Turkish general Zangi. Only a few reached Jerusalem, among whom was Stephen of Blois, but his former sins did not go unpunished. He was killed in a sudden skirmish outside Jaffa as he was waiting for a ship to take him home.

Slowly it was dawning on the West that the crusade (however it was defined) was not yet finished. The fall of Jerusalem was not an end in itself. It was but a moment in a long history that would demand people, wealth and imagination from the West for as many years as Christian and Muslim fought out their mutual hostility in the hot, dry hills of the Holy Land.

If the praise of theologians was no guarantee of a Christian future, neither could theology give substance to a kingdom. Godfrey, a man of little political skill or insight, had intended to leave Jerusalem to Patriarch Daimbert, as he had promised, but in July 1100, when Godfrey died, Daimbert was away with Tancred attacking Haifa, and the crusaders of Godfrey's household, mainly knights from his duchy of Lorraine, did not mean the new kingdom of Jerusalem to fall under the theocratic rule of this newcomer, this bishop-adventurer from Italy. They quickly sent the bishop of Ramleh to summon Godfrey's brother Baldwin from Edessa, saying that they would only serve the kingdom under a kinsman of their late lord. Then they shut themselves in the Tower of David, refused to give it up, and awaited developments.

Opposition from Daimbert and Tancred was certain – the patriarch knew that he was being deprived of his inheritance, and Tancred had hated Baldwin from the early days of the crusader campaign when Baldwin had forced Tancred to hand over Tarsus in Cilicia – but the men of Lorraine and the other supporters of Godfrey's kin were able to hang on to the Tower of David while Baldwin began his preparation to come and claim Jerusalem. On 2 October 1100 Baldwin left Edessa in the hands of his cousin Baldwin of Le Bourg and started for the Holy City with an escort of two hundred knights and seven hundred foot-soldiers. His wife and his household possessions were sent by sea to Jaffa.

Daimbert had hoped that his friend and ally Bohemond would block Baldwin's way, but since August the Turks had had Bohemond in prison, and there was only a little hindrance for Baldwin from Muslims. Duqaq, the amir of Damascus, tried to force a battle at the Dog River, but the seasoned warrior Baldwin swept that aside and went on unopposed to Jerusalem, arriving on 9 November. Daimbert, who for more than three months had been unable to take the Tower of David, knew that he was defeated and retired to a monastery on Mount Sion. Tancred wisely withdrew to his lands in Galilee. On Sunday, 11 November, Baldwin was acclaimed by the city as king of Jerusalem.

The way was not yet quite clear for him, but Baldwin intended to go on with the same energy and sense of purpose that he had shown in Edessa. He was, said William of Tyre, 'a man who loved work and disdained idleness':

> The country was infested by bandits and robbers. These scourges of the highway had made the road between Ramleh and Jerusalem very dangerous. When Count Baldwin heard of this, he vigorously set out after these rogues. He had all sorts of burning material heaped at the entrances of their caves and set on fire, to force them to surrender or else the dense smoke would suffocate them. And this is what happened, for unable to endure the heat and the all-pervading

smoke the robbers came out choking and gave themselves up. Without mercy, the count at once ordered that a hundred should have their heads struck off, a summary punishment that their guilt seemed to deserve. From the stores of robbery discovered, Baldwin found food for his men and animals, then going on through the land of the tribe of Simeon, he climbed boldly into the hill country.

This was no man to trifle with, and acts like this no doubt persuaded Daimbert to be reconciled to the new king and the new state. Within a month both Baldwin and the patriarch had forgotten the past and joined together in a meeting of mutual interest. William of Tyre phrased the matter most tactfully: 'In the year of the Lord 1100, Patriarch Daimbert and Count Baldwin became reconciled through the laudable efforts of certain discreet mediators. On the holy day of the Lord's Nativity, in the presence of clergy and people, prelates and princes, Baldwin was consecrated and anointed king in the church at Bethlehem by the hand of Daimbert, and was solemnly crowned with the royal diadem.'

From the first moment of his reign, King Baldwin I stamped his authority on the new kingdom, and in the remaining eighteen years of his active, restless life he gave his lands in Palestine and Syria a characteristic Latin form that was largely retained so long as westerners came and struggled and lived and died in country that became a second home beyond the bounds of Europe.

What was that form? In theory at least, the patriarch, as the representative of Christ, held the highest position in the land, and in practice his voice was always important and sometimes decisive in political matters. The real power, however, was vested in the crown, and the early kings worked hard to avoid a theocratic state, with spiritual and political power exercised by the same person. The kingdom of Jerusalem became a typical feudal monarchy, with the one distinction that the kings were elected, though later the monarchy became hereditary. The Latin kingdom was organized and governed in much the same manner as the Christian lords had known in their homelands. These feudal arrangements, at first adopted out of expediency and familiarity, were in the mid-century codified by the Assizes of Jerusalem. How should it be otherwise? The feudal system grew up as a means to protect just such a state as the new kingdom of Jerusalem. Feudalism was based on a hierarchical pyramid of interlocking rights and duties, mainly of a military nature, devised to safeguard a weak and extended state surrounded, interpenetrated and endangered by many enemies.

The Latin kingdom quickly developed into four semi-independent principalities: Jerusalem, Antioch, Edessa and Tripoli, the last of these having been won by Raymond of St Gilles after he returned from Constantinople. These principalities were further divided into fiefs held by lesser lords under the ordinary conditions of feudalism. The coastal towns, so vital for the supply of the kingdom and for the transport of pilgrims, were usually administered by those powers which had the greatest interests in them, that is to say the Italian trading cities of Venice, Pisa and Genoa. Though the feudal nobles, fortified in their monstrous castles, gave stout resistance to Islam, in this loose organization of semi-autonomous military chieftains there were seeds for future trouble, and the many divisions of the temporal realm were mirrored in the Latin Church. There was a patriarch in Jerusalem and another in Antioch. There were eight metropolitan ecclesiastical provinces and sixteen bishoprics. There were many monasteries and, after a time, there were the religious military orders of the Knights Templar and the Hospitallers who later introduced a confusion of values into the life of the land: no one knew whether they were soldiers, or power-brokers, or a sort of clergy; whether they were men of God or men of wealth and influence.

All this was evidence of political and social development, in some ways peculiar because of local circumstances, but in general familiar enough to most people from the West. A holy invasion – a crusade – had been superseded by the formation of the enduring entity of the state. The temporary and unusual disturbance known as a crusade would have to be set in motion again and again, as often as the Christian kingdom lost ground to the Muslims, or when the Holy Places were endangered once more. The people from the West who arrived as members of a crusade stayed on, if they chose to stay, as settlers. For a few hundred years after the conquest of Jerusalem crusades were continually beginning and continually ending, in temporary success and in final failure. For most of this time, the Latin kingdom, though it too finally failed, went on with its distinctive life, giving sustenance, support and a means of living to generations of Christians who had once been people of the West but now were no longer quite that.

Just before Pope Urban preached the crusade in 1095, the Italian Bishop Bonizo of Sutri wrote a book on the Christian life that included the latest exposition on the nature and duties of knighthood. Both the crusade itself and the safety of the new-found Latin kingdom rested heavily on the great military institution of knighthood. The conquest of Jerusalem and the establishment of the kingdom might have been expected to rebound in glory on the knights, to give a large boost to their practice and prestige – but even contemporaries doubted that. Chroniclers and critics, in particular the querulous but influential Jacques de Vitry, who was bishop of Acre from 1217 to 1229, almost universally lamented a falling off from the knightly ideal and the miserable misbehaviour of the feudal knights in the kingdom. Much of this was nostalgia for the time of victories in a later age of disappointment, but the consequences of the crusade on the habits and institutions of western life were not predicted, and no doubt would have been a surprise to Bishop Bonizo himself.

Bonizo and his fellow-theorists saw knighthood as a deeply Christian institution in which the first duty of the knight was to save his soul by placing his military prowess in the service of Christ and the Church. In so far as a knight was virtuous, and accepted Christ as his leader, he would be successful. From this there followed the Christian doctrine of 'just war' and 'holy war'.

At first, Bonizo's ideal of Christian duty was enthusiastically accepted by the crusaders. They *were* embarked upon a holy war. When they shouted their battle-cry *Deus hoc vult*, they meant exactly that: 'God wills it.' In amazement at their success against the very numerous and dangerous enemy, they

could only conclude that God was truly with them and that
Christ was, in some real sense, their general. 'Truly God fights
for us,' Bishop Adhemar exulted, and his fellow clergy boasted
of the certainty that divine providence was working for the
benefit of the army: 'Why not one against a thousand? Where
we have a minor lord, the enemy has forty kings. Where we
have a company, the enemy has a legion. Where we have a
knight, they have a duke. Where we have a foot-soldier, they
have a lord. Where we have a castle, they have a kingdom. We
put no trust in the weight of numbers, nor in power nor in
presumption, but in the shield of Christ and in justice.'

The chronicles of the participants, not only those of the
priests Fulcher and Raymond but also that of the bluff
soldier who wrote the *Gesta Francorum*, were full of acknowl-
edgments of divine favour. Why did Kerbuqa fail at Antioch,
wrote Fulcher, when he had so many men and such an
excellent advantage? The answer was obvious: 'Since he tried
to make war on God, the Lord saw his pride from afar and
He shattered it and his power altogether.' Hundreds of such
statements, made with honest conviction, were sprinkled
throughout the records of the crusade.

Unselfconsciously they called themselves 'the army of
God'. The thought that the Lord actively intervened on their
behalf carried them through more or less to the triumph at
Jerusalem and helped to persuade knights (the knights, not
foot-soldiers, were the engine of destruction and the chief
military terror to the enemy) of the vital importance, the
honour, even the blessedness of their kind in the ranks
of society. To carry such a conviction towards a victory in
Jerusalem was one thing, however; to maintain it in the teeth
of adversity in the long attrition of the kingdom's struggle
against Islam was another matter.

Very soon the feeling of divine favour began to fade. King
Baldwin attempted the old stirring rhetoric at Ramleh in
the autumn of 1101: 'Soldiers of Christ, be strong and fear
nothing! Fight, I beg you, for the salvation of your souls.
Exalt the name of Christ, whom these degenerate pagans
despise and reproach, believing neither in His Nativity nor
His Resurrection. If you should be killed here, you will

certainly be blessed. Already the gates of heaven open for you.'

However, the words did not ring as they had done only a little time before. It was hard to think that a miserable scuffle at Ramleh, part of the customary warfare in a hostile land, bore the same holy weight as the mighty advance on Jerusalem. More and more, as time went on, it was seen that the Lord in fact gave no special favours to the Christians in battle. Sometimes the knights did well, at other times badly, and over a long period, as the Muslims gained strength and cohesion, the Christian kingdom whose safety rested in the hands of knights lost ground. What were the defenders of Christ to make of this? They had been assured that God was on their side, that they were engaged in a holy war. Perhaps it was not so, but just a species of man's age-old aggression. That doubt became a cause for cynicism and dejection. The defence of the Latin kingdom, which should have powerfully reinforced the ideals of knighthood, instead diminished them. Perhaps the knight was not the anointed soldier of God, but merely a suffering human engaged in the squalid mayhem of war.

Another fruitful consequence, which Bonizo hoped would flow from the ideal of Christian knighthood, was the taming and humane education of the knight, a figure who was in many respects little more than an armed brute and murderous bully. Pope Urban had this very much in mind when he preached at Clermont. In the crusade, under the softening influence of religion, a knight would become a dedicated and chivalrous warrior, not a brigand. He would follow the prescription of Bonizo, avoiding plunder, protecting the weak and poor, doing no violence to women or children, being prepared to fight to the death for the community of the Church and the commonwealth.

Alas, the crusade and its military aftermath in the Latin kingdom saw another kind of reality. The events of the time were not a humane education but a cause of further barbarism. The battles were no less brutal for being against Islam; indeed in the popular mind a Muslim could be killed with an easier conscience. The dreadful shambles after the capture of each

important town – Nicaea, Antioch, Maarat an-Numan,
Jerusalem – showed the undimmed capacity of the crusaders
to revel in blood. Perhaps these massacres were mainly the
work of the peasant rabble, the *tafurs* and the hungry foot-
soldiers, but the knights and the nobility showed no inclina-
tion to stand aside or to prevent the slaughter. They were at
one with their followers, brothers in blood. Neither did the
higher ranks do anything to prevent the gross scandal of can-
nibalism that Raymond of Aguilers reported after the siege of
Maarat. Very often the actions of the lords were an incitement
to indiscriminate killing. Again, at Antioch, Maarat and
Jerusalem the most important of the leaders – Bohemond,
Raymond of St Gilles, Godfrey – sanctioned abominable acts
of self-interested cruelty. Often it seemed that the higher the
lord, the more certain was his execution of Muslims. The very
piety of Raymond of St Gilles guaranteed a death warrant for
devout Muslims, as Robert the Monk reported at al-Bara: 'The
count ordered that all those captured should be chained, and
those who would not believe in Christ our Saviour should be
beheaded. Not one from such a great number was saved unless
he willingly confessed Christ and was baptized. So that city
was cleansed and called to true worship.'

In truth, the conditions of the campaign produced such
stress within the army that humanitarian and unselfish conduct became a great rarity. Wounds, disease, fatigue, hunger
and thirst, heat and cold, fear and hatred stripped men of their
good intentions and left them at the mercy of naked passions.
In an army so insecurely and capriciously financed that
the purchase of each day's supplies was a minor miracle, it
was not possible to expect soldiers to refrain from loot and
plunder. Had not the greatest lords shown the way? What
larger piece of booty could there be than the principality won
by Baldwin from the Armenians at Edessa, or the city of
Antioch stolen from the Greek emperor by Bohemond? Nor
were women likely to discover the tenderness and delicacy of
ideal chivalry from soldiers deprived of home and a conjugal
bed for year after weary year. The men that the Latin kingdom
inherited from the crusade as the new guardians of the Holy
Land were not reformed examples of Christian chivalry. In

the main they were tough ruffians, with an eye to their own advantage, and a sound sense of self-preservation – and the adventurers who followed them out from Europe, without even the excuse of holy warfare, were likely to be no better.

Among other qualities of knighthood, which Bonizo hoped to see strengthened, was respect for hierarchical order. Feudalism was based on hierarchy, and a knight who took his proper place in the scheme of things was expected to show deference and devotion to his lord and a willingness to defend him even to death. It was hoped that villeins and other lesser folk would have a similar upward-looking respect for knights, but since the lower orders, illiterate and poverty-stricken, were often regarded as little more than vile, low-bred cattle, nothing much was expected from them.

Once again, the conditions of the crusade produced not the ideal but the unexpected. Deprivation and the whip of suffering broke up the normal social bonds within the camp, even the strong military bonds of feudalism, and introduced a kind of democracy of misery. One of the strangest manifestations of the crusade was the appearance of the *tafurs*, a dangerous rabble whose mysterious history (even the derivation of their name is unknown) was celebrated in the *Chanson d'Antioche* written by a crusader who called himself Richard the Pilgrim.

The *tafurs* emerged out of the *pauperes homines pedites*, the poor foot-sloggers, or as the *Chanson* called them the *menu peuple*, the lesser folk. The King of Tafur was said to be a Norman knight reduced to fighting on foot by poverty and the lack of a horse, which was the unhappy fate of many knights. His followers became a barefoot band of filthy, ragged cut-throats, a lice-covered, scabby offence to discipline and good order. Too poor to have proper arms, they wielded rustic weapons, not only knives, axes and hay-forks but also bird-catapults, sharpened sticks, clubs, chains and spades. Their grim looks, wild violence, and indifference to pain and death terrorized all they met, both friends and foes. The Muslims called them 'devils not Franks', and the leaders of the crusade found them a danger and an extreme embarrassment.

Was it the *tafurs* who (according to Anna Comnena) 'cut in

pieces some of the babes, impaled others on spits and roasted them over a fire' at Nicaea? Was it the *tafurs* also who dug up the graves at Maarat and ate the corpses? If not the *tafurs* alone, they would have been in the van of the horror. When there was an opportunity for rape and looting, the *tafurs* led the way. 'Where are the *menu peuple* who have nothing?' cried the King of Tafur in the *Chanson d'Antioche* just before the assault on Jerusalem. 'Let them follow me, for today I'll win enough to fill many a mule-load.' Later, seeing a display of Muslim riches beyond the walls, the King rallied his ragged band. 'Are we in prison,' he shouted with scorn, 'that we dare not go out and grab that treasure? What matter if I die? I do whatever I want.'

The *tafurs* were people to be taken seriously, not just for their wilful violence, but also for a deeper reason. The *Chanson d'Antioche*, an epic of fanciful imagination but firmly based on observation and true history, had a scene in which Godfrey received the crown of Jerusalem from the King of Tafur himself, who also swore that he at least would stay to defend the Holy City with his army of the poor, however many great lords found it expedient to run back to their homelands. The scene was imaginary but there was much truth in the implication that the army of the poor was an arbiter of events in Jerusalem. The lords and the knights might never have reached the Holy City at all, so keen were they on self-inter-est and personal rivalries, had not the *plebs pauperum* driven them to it by a revolt first at Antioch and then, with greater effect, at Maarat an-Numan. 'My lords,' cried the King of Tafur to the nobles before the walls of Jerusalem, 'what are we doing? Why are we holding back for so long when we should be attacking the city and this evil race? If it rested with me and the poor alone, the pagans would find us the worst neighbours they ever had!'

Raymond of Aguilers, the chronicler who had the most sympathy for the plight of the poor and the down-trodden, certainly seemed to accept this reading of history. Throughout his book he insisted on the worth and proper dignity of those humble folk on whom the suffering of the campaign bore most heavily. In one passage where Raymond was relating the appearance of St Andrew to Peter Bartholomew in a vision at Antioch, he had the Apostle say to the Provençal peasant: 'The Lord has chosen you poor folk from among all other people, as ears of wheat are separated out in a field of oats. In merit and grace you surpass all who have been before you and all who shall come after you, even as gold surpasses silver.'

God had given a stamp of approval to the aspirations and achievements of the poor. The upsurge of popular resentment in the pauperized army and among the peasant pilgrims, breaking out most spectacularly in the savagery of the *tafurs*, was an authentic people's rebellion. The higher ranks of the army had to take account of it, not just because the reckless passion of the *tafurs* swept all before it and induced fear even among the most powerful leaders, but because the frustrated aim of the poor, to reach and take Jerusalem as soon as possible despite the obstruction and selfishness of the greater folk, *was* the true aim of the crusade. This potent democratic intervention was an ironic comment on the praise that the monk Baldric of Bourgueil gave to the worthy conduct of the crusade: 'In the campaign dukes themselves fought and took turns to man the watch, so that one could not tell duke from knight or knight from duke. Beyond this, so many things were held for the common good that hardly anyone could say exactly what was his own. But just as in the primitive Church, nearly all things were shared in common.'

Far from being such paragons of Christian virtue, the 'dukes and knights' had been found wanting, and it was the poor people who kept them up to the mark. Again, it was the people who expected to defend the Latin kingdom after the nobles had gone home. The people were subjects of a feudal monarchy, no doubt, but the flow of power and authority went not just from top to bottom. If the lords did not speak, the *menu peuple* were prepared to shout out loud.

The ideas of the crusaders originated in their homelands, but nothing shaped the Latin kingdom, or constrained and influenced its inhabitants, so much as the presence of Islam. The fall of Jerusalem and the setting up of a Christian kingdom in lands that had been theirs for so long left the Muslims

SARACENS APPROACH THE CRUSADERS IN THEIR CAMP
From Chroniques of St Denis

wretched and disorganized, and they remained in this frame
of mind for several years. When, in 1110, a Hashimite sharif,
one of the privileged who claimed descent from the Prophet,
travelled from Aleppo to the sultan in Baghdad to bewail the
state of Syria, he had at first scarcely more effect than the
qadi from Jerusalem in 1099. A group of sufis, merchants and
lawyers, Ibn al-Qalanisi wrote, made such a commotion in the
mosque, 'groaning for the disaster that had befallen Islam',
that the peace of the caliph was disturbed:

> Not long after this, the sultan's sister, who was the wife of
> the caliph, arrived in Baghdad from Isfahan, bringing a train
> of endless and indescribable splendour – jewels, furnish-
> ings, horses and equipage, clothes and ornaments, slaves,
> handmaidens and servants. The sharif's cries for help upset
> the joy and gaiety of the occasion. Caliph al-Mustazhir,
> Prince of the Faithful, was much annoyed. He wanted
> to arrest the offenders and punish them severely. But the
> sultan intervened. He ordered the amirs and the army
> commanders to return to their posts and prepare to advance
> in the Holy War against the infidel enemies of Allah.

The mention of Holy War – the *jihad* – was ominous for
the West. Until this time, though the crusaders had marched
under the banner of Christ in a 'holy war', the response of

Islam had not been given the dignity of *jihad*. The concept, which had come from the Prophet himself, had not been invoked in Islam for a century or so. The great expansion of Islam was more or less over, and the wars of Muslims were in general with one another.

Then the obdurate presence of the Franks in Palestine, and the aggressive expansion of the Latin kingdom, caused a Muslim reassessment. At last the Turks, whose military power made them the natural defenders of Islam, began to take on that responsibility. After 1118, when Baldwin I died, Tughtikin, atabeg of Damascus, and then Zangi and Nur ad-Din, both atabegs of Mosul, began the work of Islamic recovery. The historian Ibn al-Athir was well-aware that the drift of history altered with the coming of his hero Zangi:

> If Allah in His mercy had not granted that the atabeg Zangi should conquer Syria, the Franks would have overrun it completely. They had attacked this town and that, but at the first whisper of news Tughtikin had mustered his men and marched out to meet the Franks. He besieged them and raided them, and in this way he forced the Franks to leave off their Syrian campaign. Now in this year [1128], by the decree of Allah, Tughtikin died, and Syria would have been left utterly defenceless had not Allah in His mercy to Muslims been pleased to raise to power Imad ad-Din [Zangi], whose deeds in the battle with the Franks we happily record here.

The feeble drama of Muslim division and rivalry was gradually cleared away, and a firm road laid down that led unerringly to the catastrophic defeat of the westerners by Saladin at Hittin in 1187. Then for nearly fifty years Jerusalem was once again in Muslim hands. The Latin kingdom recovered briefly, retook Jerusalem, and limped on for a while, but the logic of the *jihad* permitted the West no long breathing-space. The Mamluk sultans, implacable and brutally effective military adventurers descended from slaves, swept away the westerners with almost contemptuous ease.

Most of the Christian inhabitants of the Latin kingdom were not crusaders, though they may have started as such. They were colonial settlers, doing the hundreds of useful tasks necessary to any state, conducting the ordinary business of life together with their wives and families. A colony takes a character and a form as much from its environment as from the direction of the state. To live day by day among the Muslims of Palestine and Syria, even to fight them again and again, inevitably meant an accommodation to their ways, and this intermingling was helped by the military strategy of the kingdom.

With too few troops to cover the whole land, Baldwin I began to build a number of strong castles to dominate the routes of trade and communication. In particular, he tried to control the traffic on the traditional caravan routes of the Middle East. This was not so much a studied policy as an answer to the call of the moment, but it was successful and led to a distinctive kind of colonial life. In time, many large, forbidding fortresses rode like grey stone battleships in the dry seas of the landscape. These vast structures or 'kraks' – the most famous of them were the Krak de Montréal, the Krak des Chevaliers, and Reynald of Châtillon's Kerak in the Moab desert – were more than mere castles. They were mighty citadels, almost small towns, cut off from the crown in Jerusalem and independently governed by feudal nobles, not by the king. They became centres of local life, surrounded by a huddle of Christian farmers and settlers, whose fields often abutted on to Muslim fields. The settlers looked to the castle for protection, yet in the long years of relative peace both the castle and the settlers needed the goodwill and the productivity of the Muslim countryside to make life bearable. To many in these Christian communities, isolated and following their own rules, what the Muslim neighbours were doing was of more importance than the acts of the king in Jerusalem.

In the Latin kingdom, considering the weak and over-stretched resources of the state, some accommodation with the Muslims was not only desirable but also essential for the safety of the Christians. Baldwin I, who gave the keynote for so much future development, encouraged trade with Muslims and welcomed the Italian houses of commerce in the Mediterranean ports, which traded with everyone. To make trade with Muslims easier, Baldwin struck his own coins with inscriptions in Arabic.

The people took heart from these acts of their king and were encouraged to continue in the direction they were already following. To the disgust of conservative observers, to whom the contest between Christendom and Islam meant unrelenting struggle, Christians were becoming puzzling creatures, marrying native women, dressing in the comfortable eastern style, eating strange foods, listening to new music and, worst of all, losing the hardness of warriors. William of Tyre lamented the old crusader days when 'venerable men, full of holy zeal and the ardour of faith, first descended on the East'. These were the men for war, austere, disciplined, trained and brave, but look now at these new *pullani*, these Christians tainted by the seductive ease of the East! Jacques de Vitry excoriated their habits:

> These children of noble ancestors are called *pullani*, soft and effeminate people reared in luxury, more used to baths than battles. They dress like women in soft robes. How idle, faint-hearted and timid they show themselves to be against the enemies of Christ. A handful of their fathers would rout a multitude of Muslims, but these descendants are feared no more than women.

However, the Christians of the Latin kingdom did not seem so effeminate to Usama ibn Munqidh, the cultured amir of Shaizar, whose vivacious autobiography covered most of the first century of colonization. 'Among the Franks', he wrote, 'no quality is more highly esteemed in a man than military prowess. The knights have a monopoly of the positions of honour and importance, and no one else has any prestige in their eyes.' Usama did acknowledge though, in many vivid glimpses of contemporary life, that some westerners had grown towards an eastern manner of living. 'There are some Franks,' he noted, 'who have settled in our land and taken to living like Muslims. These are better than those who have just arrived from their homelands, though they are the exception,' He gave a little story as an example:

> A Frankish friend had invited me to come and see how his people lived. I went with him to the house of one of the

old knights who had come with the first Christian expedition. This man had retired from the army and was living
on a property that he owned in Antioch. He had a fine table
brought out, spread with wonderful appetizing food. He
saw that I was not eating and said, 'Please don't worry.
Eat what you like. I don't eat Frankish food, but I take
whatever my Egyptian cooks serve me. You'll find no pig's
flesh in my house.'

People of the West were a curious enigma to Usama, and
he approached them, not with hatred or anathemas, but with
interest and exasperation. He related another story, told by a
Muslim bath attendant, of a knight in a Muslim bath-house:

> One day a Frankish knight came in. They do not follow our
> custom of wearing a cloth around the waist at the baths,
> and this fellow snatched off my loin-cloth and saw that I
> had just shaved my pubic hair. 'Salim,' he cried, 'it's mag-
> nificent! You shall certainly do the same for me.' He lay
> down and I shaved his hair there, which was as long as a
> beard, and when he felt the place so agreeably smooth he
> said, 'Salim, you shall do the same for my *Dama*.' Then his
> valet fetched his wife, and she lay down on her back and
> the knight said, 'Now do to her as you did to me.' So I
> shaved her pubic hair, and all the time her husband was
> watching. Then he thanked me and paid me.

To this instructive tale, Usama added a little commentary.
'You will observe a strange contradiction,' he wrote, 'in the
character of the Franks. They are without jealousy or a sense
of honour, and yet at the same time they have the courage
that as a rule springs only from the sense of honour and a
readiness to take offence.'

What was one to do with such people? To claim the right
to ancient lands, and for the dignity of religion and history,
one might fight them inch by inch. In the last resort Usama
was not against that, but where property was secured one way
or the other, and lives were going on and converging together,
it was better to come to friendly agreements and to treat all
humans as God's creatures. Usama himself became so close
and intimate with one high-ranking Frankish knight that this

KNEELING KNIGHT

friend offered to take Usama's 14-year-old son to Europe, to learn 'the arts of politics and chivalry'. If only the amir of Shaizar had had the confidence to allow this – the young man, marrying East and West, might well have returned home, as the Frankish knight expected, 'a truly cultivated man'.

For already in the Latin kingdom East and West were coming together to some degree in society and culture, if not in politics and religion, and the kingdom was prospering for it. Fulcher of Chartres was no friend to Islam nor an apologist for an intermingling of peoples, but he had followed the crusade from beginning to end, and he knew what had happened in the kingdom afterwards. He was honest enough to point the contrast between a niggardly and fear-stricken start and the plenitude, even resplendence of a quarter century later:

> At the start of his reign Baldwin had few towns and people. Yet through that same winter he protected his kingdom from enemies on all sides, and because he was a most courageous fighter they hardly dared to attack him. The land route was still completely blocked to our pilgrims who had to come timidly to Jaffa in a few ships – English, French, Italian or Venetian – the Lord alone leading them as they risked pirates and the hostile navy of the Saracens. Then we hurried joyfully to Jaffa, to meet our fellow-countrymen as if they were saints. Each of us enquired anxiously concerning home and family. At good news we were gladdened, at bad news we were cast down. Then they came to Jerusalem to visit the Holy of Holies, for which purpose they had come. A few remained in the Holy Land, but most returned to their native homes. For this reason Jerusalem was without citizens, and there were not enough people to defend the city from the Saracens.

Yet in one generation another picture had unfolded, which Fulcher could not help but approve:

> Consider and reflect, I pray you, how in our time God has transferred the West into the East. For we who were Occidentals now have been made Orientals. He who was a Roman or a Frank is now a man of Galilee or a Palestinian. Those from Rheims or Chartres are now citizens of Tyre or Antioch. We have already forgotten the places of our birth.

Already sons have received homes and servants from their fathers. Some have taken Syrians, or Armenians, or even Saracens to wife, who have received the grace of baptism. Some have with them in-laws of all kinds, and here too are grandchildren and great-grand-children. One cultivates vines, another the fields. Our languages run together and become familiar to both peoples. Faith unites those whose forefathers were strangers. As it is written, 'The lion and the ox shall eat straw together.'

Those who were strangers are now natives, and he who was a visitor has become a resident. Those who were poor in their own country, God here makes rich. They had a few coins, now they have almost countless bezants. Roofless when they arrived, now by the gift of God they possess cities. So why should they return to Europe, those who have found such favour in the East? A great miracle has happened, one that must truly astonish the whole world. Who has heard anything like it?

Jacques de Vitry, writing about a century after Fulcher, though he condemned the falling off from old military virtues, also admitted that 'the Holy Land flourished like a garden of delight':

Although for a time the Lord had somewhat left it desolate, yet of His great loving kindness He gathered together its children and made all the land so full of people of different races of men, and of various tongues and nations, that the prophecy seemed to be fulfilled: 'Thy sons shall come from far, and thy daughters shall be nursed by thy side.' The land saw it and was full, and its heart was glad when the multitude flowed there from the sea.

Furthermore, in the Holy Land there are many other nations, with different customs, that is to say Syrians, Greeks, Jacobites, Maronites, Nestorians, Armenians and Georgians, who for trade, farming and other useful arts are very necessary to the Holy Land, that they may sow the land and plant vineyards to yield them fruits of increase. Seeing, then, that the clouds dropped fatness at the Lord's bidding, and the Holy Land yielded her fruits, men ran there with joy and rejoiced as men do when they divide the spoil.

Both Fulcher and Jacques de Vitry, Christian priests and propagandists, were careful to leave the Muslims out of the account of the good times, but, like ghosts at the feast, though they were not mentioned the Muslims could not be forgotten. Both the Christian writers knew, from long residence in the Holy Land, that the prosperity they described could not have been achieved in such a land and at such a time without a very real accommodation with the people of Islam who lived with them and among them day by day.

The experiment in living did not last. It could not do so as long as the main driving force, on both sides, derived not from the hope of a viable, healthy society, but from the exclusivity of religion expressed in 'holy war' and *jihad*. Yet the experience of the Latin kingdom made some wonder what might have happened, outside the realm of religion, if only this little world had not begun with a presumptuous religious invasion and continued in a war of faiths. It is fitting that the last word should be given to Usama ibn Munqidh, a man of open curiosity and genial intelligence who knew more than most, and regretted, what might have been:

I paid a visit to the tomb of John, called the Baptist, the son of Zechariah – the blessing of Allah on both of them! – in the village of Sebastea in the province of Nablus. After I had said my prayers, I came out into the square bounded on one side by the Holy Precinct. I found a half-closed door, pushed through and entered a church. Inside were about ten old men with bare heads as white as combed cotton. They were facing the east and wore on their breasts staves ending in crossbars turned up like the back of a saddle. They took their oath on this sign and gave hospitality to those who needed it. The sight of their piety touched my heart, but at the same time it displeased and saddened me, for I had never seen such zeal and devotion among the Muslims.

For some time I brooded on this experience. Then one day, as Muin ad-Din and I were passing the monastery of *Dar at-Tawawis* [the Peacock House], he said to me, 'I want to dismount here and visit the ascetics, the Old Men.'

I willingly agreed, so we dismounted and went into a long building set at an angle to the road. For a moment I thought there was no one there. Then I saw about a hundred prayer-mats, and on each was a sufi, his face expressing peaceful serenity, and his body humble devotion. This was a reassuring sight, and I gave thanks to Allah the Great that there should be among the Muslims men of even more zealous devotion than those Christian priests.

There is an equivalence, a community, in true piety. God – Allah – is not best served, if at all, by fighting.

INDEX